Interviewing for Journalists

Third edition

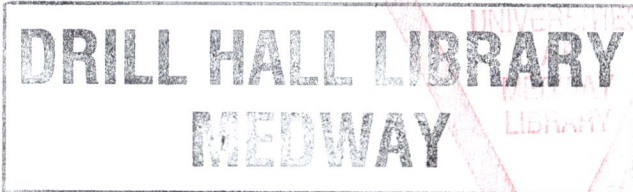

Interviewing for Journalists focuses on the central journalistic skill of how to ask the right questions in the right way. It is a practical and concise guide for all print and online journalists – professionals, students and trainees – who write news stories and features for newspapers, magazines and online publications. In the age of digital journalism, where computer-based research is easily available, this new edition seeks to emphasise the value of getting out there, engaging with people directly and building relationships to create original and meaningful media content.

Interviewing for Journalists highlights the many different approaches to interviewing, from vox pops and press conferences to news interviews and in-depth profiles. This third edition features brand new interviews with some of the most successful journalists in the industry, including Camilla Long of *The Sunday Times*, Heidi Blake of BuzzFeed UK, Brian Viner of the *Daily Mail* and award-winning freelance writers Cole Moreton and Stephanie Rafanelli. It covers every stage of interviewing, such as research, fixing interviews, structuring questions, body language, how to get vivid quotes and how to handle challenging interviews.

The third edition of *Interviewing for Journalists* includes:

- advice on how to carry out face-to-face, telephone and online interviews;
- tips on taking notes, shorthand and recording interviews;
- guidance on dealing with different interviewees, such as celebrities, politicians and vulnerable people;
- interviewing tasks to put your journalistic skills into practice;
- a discussion of ethical and legal issues by Professor Tim Crook of Goldsmiths, University of London.

Emma Lee-Potter is a freelance journalist and editor, as well as a visiting lecturer at the University of Winchester. She trained with Mirror Group Newspapers and later worked as a staff news reporter and feature writer for the *Evening Standard,*

Sunday Express and *Today*. She has written for the *Guardian*, *The Times*, *New Statesman*, *Daily Mail*, *Daily Express* and *The Week* and was a contributor to the second edition of *Interviewing for Journalists*. She is the author of four novels.

Tim Crook is Professor of Media and Communication, Head of Media Law and Ethics and Radio at Goldsmiths, University of London. He is also Visiting Professor of Broadcast Journalism at Birmingham City University. He has worked professionally in radio, theatre, television and film as a journalist, producer, playwright, director and sound designer for more than 40 years. Throughout this period he has taught media law and ethics to professional journalists and students at all levels.

Media Skills

EDITED BY RICHARD KEEBLE, LINCOLN UNIVERSITY

The *Media Skills* series provides a concise and thorough introduction to a rapidly changing media landscape. Each book is written by media and journalism lecturers or experienced professionals and is a key resource for a particular industry. Offering helpful advice and information and using practical examples from print, broadcast and digital media, as well as discussing ethical and regulatory issues, *Media Skills* books are essential guides for students and media professionals.

Designing for Newspapers and Magazines
2nd edition
Chris Frost

English for Journalists
Twentieth Anniversary Edition
Wynford Hicks

Ethics for Journalists
2nd edition
Richard Keeble

Feature Writing for Journalists
Sharon Wheeler

Freelancing for Television and Radio
Leslie Mitchell

Interviewing for Journalists
3rd edition
Emma Lee-Potter

Interviewing for Radio
2nd edition
Jim Beaman

Magazine Production
2nd edition
Jason Whittaker

Production Management for Television
Leslie Mitchell

Programme Making for Radio
Jim Beaman

Reporting for Journalists
2nd edition
Chris Frost

Researching for the Media
2nd edition
Adèle Emm

Subediting and Production for Journalists
2nd edition
Tim Holmes

Writing for Broadcast Journalists
2nd edition
Rick Thompson

Writing for Journalists
3rd edition
Wynford Hicks with Sally Adams, Harriett Gilbert, Tim Holmes and Jane Bentley

Interviewing for Journalists

THIRD EDITION

Emma Lee-Potter

Routledge
Taylor & Francis Group

LONDON AND NEW YORK

Third edition published 2017
by Routledge
2 Park Square, Milton Park, Abingdon, Oxon, OX14 4RN

and by Routledge
711 Third Avenue, New York, NY 10017

Routledge is an imprint of the Taylor & Francis Group, an informa business

First edition published by Routledge 2001
Second edition published by Routledge 2009

British Library Cataloguing in Publication Data
A catalogue record for this book is available from the British Library

Library of Congress Cataloging in Publication Data
Names: Lee-Potter, Emma author.
Title: Interviewing for journalists / Emma Lee-Potter.
Description: Third edition. | London ; New York : Routledge, 2017. |
Series: Media skills | Previous editions have authors: Sally Adams with Wynford
Hicks. | Includes bibliographical references and index.
Identifiers: LCCN 2016049338 | ISBN 9781138650220 (hardback : alk. paper) |
ISBN 9781138650237 (pbk. : alk. paper) | ISBN 9781315625485 (ebook)
Subjects: LCSH: Interviewing in journalism.
Classification: LCC PN4784.I6 A33 2017 | DDC 070.4/3—dc23
LC record available at https://lccn.loc.gov/2016049338

ISBN: 978-1-138-65022-0 (hbk)
ISBN: 978-1-138-65023-7 (pbk)
ISBN: 978-1-315-62548-5 (ebk)

Typeset in Goudy and Scala Sans
by Keystroke, Neville Lodge, Tettenhall, Wolverhampton

MIX
Paper from
responsible sources
FSC
www.fsc.org   FSC® C013056

Printed and bound in Great Britain by
TJ International Ltd, Padstow, Cornwall

For Lottie, Ned and Adam.
And in memory of my mother, Lynda Lee-Potter.

Contents

Acknowledgements

I would like to thank the hugely talented journalists who contributed their insight, enthusiasm and expertise to this book, especially: Heidi Blake, Sheron Boyle, Emma Brockes, Constance Craig Smith, Tim Crook, Justin Davenport, Caroline Davies, Susan Grossman, Wendy Holden, Dorothy Lepkowska, Paul Lewis, Camilla Long, Cole Moreton, Stephanie Rafanelli, Brian Viner and Melanie Whitehouse.

Thank you, too, to my friends in the *Evening Standard* news room, who were the most inspiring colleagues you could ever wish for. They include Colin Adamson, Shekhar Bhatia, Diane Chanteau, Paul Cheston, Neil Darbyshire, Colin Davey, Steve Doughty, Philip Evans, Jim Gallagher, Charles Garside, Peter Gruner, Peter Kingston, John Lamb, Mike Lawn, Valentine Low, Paul Massey, David Meilton, John Minihan, Mike Moore, Stuart Nicol, Aldo Nicolotti, Lizzie Peck, Lois Rogers, Jeremy Selwyn, Ken Towner, Gervase Webb, Peter Wilson, the late Patrick McGowan and the late Mike Peck.

My particular thanks go to Niall Kennedy and Kitty Imbert at Routledge for their expert guidance, to Charlie Lee-Potter and Jeremy Lee-Potter for their unwavering support and to the staff at the British Library in London.

Most of all, I'd like to pay tribute to my great friend Sally Adams, who wrote the first two editions of *Interviewing for Journalists*. As an editor and lecturer she inspired generations of young journalists with her knowledge, flair, wisdom and *joie de vivre*. She had a major influence on my own career and like so many of her friends, students and fellow journalists, I owe a huge debt of gratitude to her.

Extracts from the *Editors' Code of Practice* are reproduced by kind permission of The Regulatory Funding Company and are © 2016 The Regulatory Funding Company.

Extract from 'My son the ISIS executioner' by Jane Bradley is reproduced by kind permission of BuzzFeed UK.

Extract from 'The day I tried to butter up the Duke of Edinburgh' by Brian Viner is reproduced by kind permission of the *Independent*.

1
Introduction

'The star interview is dead.' So declared Martin Amis in a collection of journalistic essays entitled *Visiting Mrs Nabokov and Other Excursions*. To put his words into context, this was the early 1990s and Madonna had initially agreed to do an interview with him, then changed her mind and decided that she didn't want to do it after all.

'Sent to New York to interview Madonna, I felt no significant disruption in my plans when Madonna refused to see me,' wrote Amis. 'The great post-modern celebrities are a part of their publicity machines, and that is all you are ever going to get to write about: their publicity machines. You review the publicity machine. Even the humble literary interview is dying, or growing old: "It was with dread/detachment/high hopes that I approached X's townhouse/office/potting shed. The door opened. He is fatter/smaller/taller/balder than I expected. Pityingly/perfunctorily/politely he offered me instant coffee/a cigarette/dinner. Everyone told me how modest/craven/suave/vain/charming I would find him, so I was naturally unsurprised/taken aback by his obvious charm/vanity, etc., etc."'[1]

More than two decades on, it's clear that Amis's prediction (originally published in the *Observer*) was wide of the mark. In the twenty-first-century interviews with rock stars, actors, politicians, sports personalities and anyone else for that matter are very much alive and kicking. Whether an interview is conducted face to face, on the telephone or via Skype, FaceTime, email or text, it is still the principal way in which reporters and feature writers gather their material.

In my view it always will be. Virtually all news stories and features depend on an interview of some kind. It could be an interview with a police officer appealing for witnesses to a crime, an interview with a minister seeking to explain a new government policy or an interview with an author on a mission to promote their latest book – whatever the rationale, interviews give journalists the opportunity to assemble the facts, details and quotes that will inform, inspire and entertain their readers.

Cedric Pulford, one of my tutors on the Mirror Group Newspapers training scheme in the 1980s, described the interview as 'the chief tool of active journalism' and he was right. After all, he argued, 'without talking to people who can give us information or opinions, by phone or face to face, we can only print what others send us or recycle what has appeared somewhere else'.[2] Interviews with experts and prominent people add credibility and authority to copy, while interviews with those involved in a news event – an eyewitness to an accident, for example – take a story beyond the bare facts and enable readers to understand what it was like to be there.

At a time of huge turbulence in the media industry, journalists with the ability to conduct fair, accurate and illuminating interviews are more important than ever. In this brave new world of digital journalism we still need journalists, citizen journalists among them, to go out and talk to people, to uncover stories, to expose wrongdoing and to raise awareness of important issues. Roy Greenslade, the former *Daily Mirror* editor and professor of journalism at London's City University, expressed his own fears for journalism in a comment piece for the *Guardian* in 2016. 'I see journalism turning into "churnalism" on a daily basis,' he wrote. 'And that's what frightens me most about the future: how will democracy be served if journalism means no more than the publishing of PR-packaged content "mediated" by people who never leave their computer screens?'[3]

The third edition of *Interviewing for Journalists* seeks to highlight the importance of journalists leaving their desks and generating their own original content rather than repackaging other people's work. Despite the wealth of computer-based research and data now available to journalists, getting out and talking to people is crucial. As the award-winning *Sunday Times* Insight editor Jonathan Calvert (who was responsible for award-winning scoops like the original House of Commons cash-for-questions exposé and the FIFA corruption scandal) pointed out in 2015, talking to people and building up relationships are still the best ways to find great stories. 'There can be a temptation for modern journalists to just trawl the internet hoping that they are going to find a story,' Calvert told *Press Gazette*'s Dominic Ponsford. 'It's not impossible to do that, but you are rarely going to get something that's really great from that. The best stuff comes from your fellow human beings.'[4]

Jonathan Calvert was absolutely right. The best journalism does indeed come from talking to 'your fellow human beings'. With precisely that in mind, this edition features a host of new and exclusive interviews with some of the most successful journalists in the industry, including Camilla Long, Cole Moreton, Stephanie Rafanelli, Brian Viner and Heidi Blake. They all have their own distinctive interviewing styles but they were happy to share their advice, experience and techniques. Each chapter also includes a selection of their top tips for journalism students and trainees and interviewing tasks to put your journalistic skills into practice.

A verbal or online exchange

An interview can be defined as a verbal or online exchange between a journalist, who asks questions, and an interviewee, who answers them. As F. W. Hodgson explained so succinctly in *Modern Newspaper Practice*, his primer on the press: 'Meeting, talking to and dealing with people is a vital part of the reporter's work.'[5]

When conducted skilfully and professionally, interviews have the potential to set the news agenda and to lead news bulletins around the world. Take Richard Nixon's confessional interviews with David Frost in 1977, for example, or Princess Diana's revelatory interview about her marriage to Prince Charles ('there were three of us in this marriage, so it was a bit crowded') with Martin Bashir for BBC One's *Panorama* programme in 1995.

Even though this book focuses principally on interviewing for print and online publications there is still a lot that newspaper, magazine and online journalists can learn from the best TV and radio interviewers – everything from building up trust and formulating concise, open-ended questions to maintaining good eye contact, listening hard to an interviewee's answers and not letting a reply hang in the air with a glaringly obvious follow-up question left unasked. Martin Bashir's unrivalled ability to gain the trust of his interviewees was remarked on in 2003, after he managed to get a rare interview with singer Michael Jackson. In an interview with the *Guardian*, Steve Anderson, who was ITV's news and current affairs controller at the time, said of Bashir: 'I wonder in the end if his real skill is of someone who might otherwise have been a psychologist. He really seems to be someone who is able to get into people's heads, and get their trust.'[6]

History of the interview

According to the author and journalist Christopher Silvester the interview dates back to the mid-nineteenth century. The credit for inventing the form has been attributed to two men – Horace Greeley, the editor of the *New York Tribune*, and James Gordon Bennett Sr, the proprietor of the *New York Herald*. In *The Penguin Book of Interviews*, Silvester declares that Horace Greeley's 1859 interview with Brigham Young, the leader of the Mormon Church, 'can lay claim to being the first fully fledged interview with a celebrity, much of it in the question-and-answer format familiar to modern readers'.[7] Although James Gordon Bennett had interviewed US president Martin Van Buren 20 years earlier, his subsequent newspaper report, wrote George Turnbull in 'Some notes on the history of the interview',[8] merely amounted to a description of the meeting and some observations about his subject's appearance. Unlike today's interviews, there was virtually no reported speech in the piece.

From this modest start the journalistic interview developed rapidly. As Wynford Hicks explained in the second edition of *Interviewing for Journalists*, journalism metamorphosed from 'a stuffy, pompous thing that could interest only a minority of the serious-minded' into 'a lively means of informing and entertaining millions of people'.[9]

Interviews have since become increasingly integral to journalism. It's true that journalists still spend much of their time observing and recording – particularly in parliaments, councils and courts – but the majority of news stories and features depend on first-hand accounts to bring them to life and, equally importantly, to give a human perspective. Readers want to know what eyewitnesses heard and saw, how bystanders felt and the ways in which participants reacted – and the only means to discover these things is by asking them. None of us will forget the graphic accounts of those who witnessed the 9/11 attacks and summed up the horror to interviewers in a few powerful words: 'Windows shattered, people were screaming and diving for cover.' 'People walked around like ghosts, covered in dirt, weeping and wandering dazed.' 'Everyone was screaming, crying, running, cops, people, firefighters, everyone. It's like a war zone.'[10]

Feelings of apprehension

Journalists, particularly those in the early stages of their careers, often mention feelings of apprehension at the thought of interviewing people who have lost loved ones or suffered huge trauma in their lives. If you find the idea of conducting an interview daunting, you are not alone. Rest assured, however, that interviewing is a skill that can be learned. It becomes less intimidating the more often you do it and the more confident you become.

Even the most experienced journalists admit to nervousness at some point during their careers. A news reporter who has covered conflicts all over the world says he always feels a twinge of anxiety when picking up the phone to interview someone – 'but as soon as the interview starts the nerves disappear and the adrenalin kicks in'. More than one person I interviewed for this book confessed to feeling sick to the stomach before interviews. Freelance writer and former *Harper's Bazaar* features director Stephanie Rafanelli says she gets 'performance anxiety beforehand, although it never lasts', while award-winning interviewer Cole Moreton told me: 'I often get very nervous. I think it's just like stage fright. If you don't get it you're in trouble.' A veteran feature writer recalls stumbling out of an awkward interview with an uncooperative celebrity and telling the press officer that the star had clearly loathed her. 'What do you mean?' retorted the press officer. 'It was the best interview of the day by far.'

The TV presenter and former BBC political editor Andrew Marr wrote of 'natural shyness' during his days as a trainee journalist on the *Scotsman*, where he learned to type, do shorthand, understand libel law and report court cases. Marr did part of his training at Thomson Regional Newspapers' training centre in Newcastle upon Tyne and in his history of British journalism, *My Trade*, he recalls how he learned to find stories.

'We were sent off to local villages and outlying suburbs of Newcastle and told not to come back until we had half a dozen publishable stories for the evening paper, the *Chronicle*. That meant slowly scrubbing away any natural shyness, banging on vicars' doors, stopping shopkeepers and pleading with councillors for anything – anything. Stray dog? Upset at the Guild? Oldest villager? Proud parents of footballer?'[11]

I've rarely, if ever, met anyone who emulates the swaggering, rude and insensitive approach of journalists portrayed in novels, films and TV dramas. Remember the ruthless Rita Skeeter and her 'Quick-Quotes Quill' of *Harry Potter* fame? Or the scheming tabloid reporter Karen White in the first series of ITV's *Broadchurch*? In real life journalists know full well that being boorish, bad-mannered or lacking in charm won't get them anywhere – and certainly won't get interviewees to open up to them. The journalist's job is to get people to talk, so you need to be polite, professional, charming and empathetic. Persistent perhaps, but churlish and discourteous, no.

My early interviewing days

My first experience of interviewing was as a Mirror Group Newspapers trainee in the 1980s. I started out as a reporter on the *Mid-Devon Advertiser*, a local newspaper that was owned at the time by the Mirror Group and sold the grand total of 16,000 copies a week.

I spent my days ringing round the police, fire and ambulance stations, inter-viewing councillors, teachers and company bosses, writing profiles of mid-wives, health visitors, head teachers and even zookeepers (the local zoo was a favourite source of stories) and covering flower shows, school speech days and summer fetes. Each of these events required at least one interview – in some cases several – and as I talked to octogenarians about their youthful romances or asked councillors about controversial planning decisions I figured out how to handle challenging interviews, how to ask difficult questions and how to read people's body language, all skills that I use to this day.

I learned one of the most useful lessons from veteran newspaper photographer Arthur Kay. Early on in my career he accompanied me on a story about an elderly couple in the quiet market town of Newton Abbot who were about to celebrate their golden wedding anniversary. As always, I had scribbled down a list of questions in advance and immediately started working my way through them, so eager to ask the next question that I barely listened to the previous answer. Half an hour later, as I left the house with Arthur, interview and pictures completed in double-quick time, he told me: 'Don't be afraid of silences. Once an interviewee has answered a question give them a bit of time to think. You often get the best quotes then.'

Arthur Kay was absolutely right. In the intervening years I've always made a point of pausing between questions, usually finding that interviewees fill the gaps in the conversation with interview gold. It's an interview technique that radio presenter Stephen Nolan uses to impressive effect on his phone-in programmes on BBC Radio 5 live and BBC Radio Ulster. Nolan is an assured interviewer who is prepared to wait for an interviewee to answer in their own time rather than rushing them on and it pays dividends. Freelance writer Stephanie Rafanelli takes a similar approach. 'It's amazing the amount of times when you keep silent after they have finished speaking,' she says. 'They pick up again – and you get the quote.'

Lessons from a professional

My mother, *Daily Mail* columnist Lynda Lee-Potter, taught me more than anyone about interviewing. She trained as an actress (which gave her an acute ear for dialogue) and switched to journalism in her late twenties. One of the most successful journalists of her generation, she interviewed everyone from politicians and actors to showbiz names and sporting heroes during her 40-year career. After her death in 2004 I found an after-dinner speech that she'd once written about interviewing. It has never been published before and reading it now, much of her advice still holds true.

'Everybody has a different technique, but I can only tell you what works for me,' she said. 'It doesn't always work because there is no interviewer in the world who hasn't failed on more than one occasion.'

She made a point of doing as much research as possible before interviews – ploughing through reams of cuttings (then stored in buff-coloured A4 folders in the *Daily Mail* library rather than online), reading interviewees' autobiographies and talking to friends and relations of the people she was scheduled to meet.

'This all sounds very obvious but certainly on television I've seen so many interviewers who clearly know very little about the subject,' she said.

'If a star in particular sees you haven't done your homework you will alienate him or her. It's very sloppy to ask the very famous where they come from, how many children they have or who they are married to because you can easily find all this out in advance. I once overheard a journalist saying to John Mortimer (the writer and creator of *Rumpole of the Bailey*): "Now, Mr Mortimer, tell me all about yourself."'

My mother used a hardback reporter's notebook as well as a tape recorder but always kept her eyes glued to the person she was interviewing, somehow managing to write without looking down at her notebook. She developed her own form of shorthand, writing only a few words on each page – which meant she needed a new notebook for every interview. If possible, she preferred to interview people at home – 'because if they are not mesmeric talkers I can get lots of copy from the way their house is furnished, the books they possess and the friendliness or otherwise of their dog. I may even get a quick quote from their daily, the au pair or when I interviewed Princess Anne, their bodyguard.'

She also warned journalists against the temptation to show off. Some interviewers, she pointed out, ask long, convoluted questions simply to demonstrate how clever they are but only succeed in confusing the people they are interviewing. 'I rather sympathise with Mel Brooks, who says that if he's ever asked a question with more than a dozen words in it he always answers "no",' she said.

The confrontational and the confessional

In my mother's opinion there were two main types of interview – the confrontational and the confessional. She preferred the confessional approach, talking little and listening intently. 'My own preference is to almost become the other person, to have no personality, to fade into the background, which is why I invariably wear black when I'm working,' she said. 'I'd describe my own technique as gently probing. Having said this, it's not a technique that works with everybody. In one case I learned the hard way that the only way to get any information was to be extremely aggressive. But in the majority of cases the person you are interviewing is the star. You are merely the listener.'

In her view a journalist's instinct was hugely important. She once arrived to interview a famous singer, having no idea beforehand that the star's marriage was in difficulty. 'But there was a slight evasiveness about one of her replies which gave me a clue and in fact when the right questions were asked she talked very touchingly about the difficulties she and her husband were experiencing at the time.'

She made it a rule not to answer questions about herself during an interview. 'As far as I'm concerned the less I talk the better,' she said. 'I'm a great believer in very direct, simple and very short questions. If the interviewee asks you about yourself then deflect it if you can, or answer very briefly.'

A stickler for accurate quoting

She was a stickler for accurate quoting and throughout her career took pains to quote interviewees exactly. 'If you quote people accurately you will on the whole find that the next time you approach them they will be delighted to see you,' she said. 'An approximation of what they said is not good enough. It has to be 100 per cent accurate. Sometimes I read interviews with people I've met and I know that what they are purported to have said is utterly false.'

Asked to sum up in one word the most valuable quality for a good interviewer she reckoned it was 'concentration'. 'When you're interviewing somebody, nobody else should exist for you. I once interviewed Norman Tebbit (the Conservative politician) at the Savoy Grill. When he'd left I looked up and saw that the editor of the *Daily Mail* was sitting at the table to my left, the editor of *The Times* was at the table on my right – and I'd never even noticed. In the normal course of events I'd have spotted them at 90 paces.'

Another piece of advice she gave was to read as many interviews as you can. Work out for yourself the interviewers who are at the top of their game – and, more importantly, try to understand what makes them so good. A writer turned senior national newspaper executive admitted that when he started out he used to conduct a forensic examination of interviews he admired, noting the style of the intros, where quotes were introduced and even the length and sequence of sentences and paragraphs. He then incorporated the best techniques into his own writing.

Many writers post their best interviews on their websites so it's worth studying these carefully. Cole Moreton, who won the interviewer of the year (popular press) title at the 2015 Press Awards in the UK, was described as an 'insightful and a master craftsman, producing entertaining and memorable pieces'. His website (www.colemoreton.com) includes his interviews with everyone from the Archbishop of Canterbury to Sir Richard Branson and from David Cameron to Jeffrey Archer. Stephanie Rafanelli, who specialises in in-depth, long form interviews for publications like the *Guardian*, the *Telegraph* magazine, *The Times* magazine and the *Sunday Telegraph*, features interviews with Cate Blanchett, Penélope Cruz, Arianna Huffington, David Walliams and many more on her website (www.stephanierafanelli.com).

The difference between written and broadcast interviews

Lynn Barber is second to none as an interviewer. She worked for *Penthouse* magazine for seven years, interviewing the likes of Salvador Dali and Gore Vidal, and later moved to the *Sunday Express*, the *Independent on Sunday*, *Vanity Fair*, the *Observer* and *The Sunday Times*. She has won a raft of awards and her two collections of interviews, *Mostly Men* and *Demon Barber*, and her memoir, *A Curious Career*, are essential reading for all journalism students. As well as being riotously entertaining, they are full of useful guidance and advice for fellow interviewers. In *A Curious Career*, she explained how press interviews differ so fundamentally from broadcast interviews.

'Broadcast interviews have to include lots of information in the questions, because there is no other place to put it, therefore the questions have to be to some extent pre-planned,' she wrote. 'But press interviews aren't like that because the questions don't need to carry any information. They just have to be as effective as possible at getting the subject to talk. Hopefully, the questions will always be much shorter than the answer – my absolutely favourite question is always: Why? If an interviewee says that he decided to move away from London a couple of years ago, this is not of any great interest until you interject "Why?" and it comes tumbling out – "Oh you know, because I was spending too much time getting pissed in the Groucho and ending up in bed with people whose names I couldn't remember in the morning." So that's a cue to ask: What was the worst occasion? And then, with any luck, the interview has moved from mildly interesting into riveting.'[12]

A few seconds to ask a question

While the majority of Lynn Barber's interviews are with the famous and infamous, this edition of *Interviewing for Journalists* covers all manner of interviews, including vox pops (and where and when you can do them), press conferences, where you will be one of a huge crowd of journalists vying to ask a question, and doorstep interviews, when you may only have a few seconds to get the information you need.

I remember standing outside Michael Heseltine's house in London as a young *Evening Standard* reporter in 1986. It was the height of the Westland affair (a struggle in government over whether a US or Europe-led consortium should take over Britain's last remaining helicopter company) and he was the defence secretary at the time. The pavement was filled with reporters, photographers and TV crews, all trying to elbow each other out of the way. I knew there would be barely any time between Heseltine leaving his house and getting into the ministerial car parked in the road so I hastily shouted, 'Are you looking forward to seeing the Prime Minister today?' 'I always look forward to seeing the Prime Minister,' he replied smoothly as he stepped into his chauffeur-driven car and was driven away.

I learned from my mistake that day, realising how important it is to work out a concise, open-ended question in advance – in other words, a question that will elicit a full and meaningful response instead of asking something that can be batted away with ease, especially by an experienced and polished interviewee. I should, of course, have asked something along the lines of 'What are you going to say to Mrs Thatcher today?' As the journalism trainer Susan Grossman points out, if you are up against a tight deadline on a news story, 'there isn't time to ask this, that and the other. You need to think "what does the audience want to know about the situation at this very minute?" and ask *that* question.'

Clickbait

In our celebrity-obsessed age, most journalists will be sent to interview well-known showbiz and sporting names at some point in their career. Don't assume that because you want to be a sports reporter you won't be doing interviews. Whatever the sport, there will always be a post-match interview with the manager and players, plus a host of conversations about tactics, form and future plans, all of which require interviews. Not only that, many columns by sports personalities – and showbiz celebrities too – are based on prior interviews with a journalist, who then ghosts the column on their behalf.

Celebrities are regarded as 'clickbait' these days, attracting readers to newspaper websites in their millions. If you get an enthralling interview with a celebrity it will almost certainly be viewed and commented on by people all over the world – so with this in mind *Interviewing for Journalists* includes a chapter on interviewing the famous. The breakfast TV broadcaster Susanna Reid offered a useful insight into the way her fellow presenter, former *News of the World* and *Daily Mirror* editor Piers Morgan, interviews people. Asked by *You* magazine in 2016 whether she had learned anything from Morgan's interviewing style she replied, 'He always gives his interviews a bit of an edge. He takes them by the collar and shakes them until nuggets of headline fall out. We could all learn from that.'[13] Reid was right. Every time you do an interview listen hard for the stories that might make the front page as well as the inside pages of your publication.

Persuading famous people to do interviews, as Martin Amis found to his cost, requires a huge amount of tenacity. The award-winning *Sunday Times* journalist Camilla Long spent months and months chasing an interview with Imelda Marcos, the former first lady of the Philippines – before finally getting the go-ahead. When Long answered her phone early on Boxing Day it was Marcos, who instructed her to fly out there and then.

'I thought, "My God, is this a wind-up? Is she telling the truth?" because it's a 14-hour flight to Manila,' said Long, who was working for *Tatler* magazine at the time. 'Anyway I took a punt and went and it was fabulous. She did a five-hour interview one day, a five-hour interview the next day. One smiling, happy and laughing. The next in tears . . .'

The renowned *Daily Express* columnist and feature writer Jean Rook was equally persistent. In her autobiography, *The Cowardly Lioness*, Rook recalled her repeated attempts to get an exclusive interview with movie star Elizabeth Taylor. 'An exclusive, no-holds-barred, two-hour interview with Taylor is as rare as her Krupp diamond, and trickier than a house of cards to set up,' Rook wrote in her typically forthright style. 'It takes months on the phone and paper to build up her agents' and entourage's confidence. It takes La Liz a mere whim to change her mind and everyone else's overnight, and tear up the deal with one tiny, imperious hand.

'*The Express* had paid £100,000 for Taylor's sensationally revealing book on her battle with booze, drugs and obesity, *Elizabeth Takes Off*, on condition that she gave us a one-to-one interview. I was asked to write what had to be a newspaper bestseller.'

'Pinning Taylor down was like trying to drink tea out of the Holy Grail. Through the autumn and winter of '87, she gave me the slip from day to day, and country to country, in which she would/wouldn't/might be filming. My calendar was as black with cancelled dates as I was with frustrated fury at the wayward woman.'[14]

Even if you've managed to secure an interview, getting celebrities to talk can be a challenge, especially when a PR is sitting in on the conversation, the star's entourage insists you can only ask about his or her new film and nothing else and you're just one of a multitude of journalists waiting in a long line to see them. Interestingly, Oscar-winning actress Cate Blanchett hinted in a *Telegraph* magazine interview with Sheryl Garratt in 2016 that film stars find promotional interviews every bit as testing as journalists. Here is what Blanchett said: 'You feel like you're saying the same thing over and over again, and by the time you're done you really do want to take a bath, put some gaffer tape over your mouth and take a vow of silence. You get so sick of the sound of your own voice.'[15]

Similarly, when journalist Rosamund Dean interviewed the actress Renée Zellweger for *Red* magazine in 2016 she said of her: 'One of the most interesting women in Hollywood, she rarely gives interviews, because "if you're going to talk about yourself for an hour then you're bound to say something stupid, you just are".'[16]

Skills and confidence

As well as aiming to give you the skills and the confidence to fix up interviews, research them in advance and ask the right questions in the right way, this book sets out to guide you through the basics of interviewing everyone from monosyllabic teenagers to high-profile politicians, many of whom will have a tendency to answer their own questions rather than yours. As Sally Adams wisely put it: you will need to 'calm the excitable, reassure the uncertain and steer the confident and knowledgeable'.[17]

This edition also features checklists of crucial points to remember when you are interviewing, new material on the technology and apps available to journalists and advice on online interviewing. The last of these is particularly important. A report published in 2016 by the Reuters Institute for the Study of Journalism at the University of Oxford found that more than half the journalists it surveyed worked online. It reported that the proportion of journalists in the UK working in print versions of newspapers had fallen from 56 per cent to 44 per cent since 2012 while the proportion working online had risen from 26 per cent to 52 per cent in that time.[18]

In the twenty-first century reporters and feature writers need to be multi-skilled, so even though you might have a brilliant interview in your notebook or on your voice recorder that might not be enough. Your news desk might want you to tweet a few details, upload a podcast or even produce a short video. How do you achieve all that from a single interview – and keep to your deadline too?

Shorthand or voice recorder?

Another powerful influence on the evolution of the print interview has been the development of easy-to-use voice recorders and this book will look at the pros and cons of phones, audio and video recorders as opposed to shorthand. My trusty 100 words per minute Teeline (learned in a scruffy Plymouth

Portakabin alongside Alastair Campbell, who later became Tony Blair's chief spokesman and strategist and passed his shorthand exams months before anyone else) has stood me in good stead over the years.

Not everyone uses shorthand though; many journalists never learn it at all. Lynn Barber says she is completely reliant on voice recorders and takes two to every interview, just in case one breaks down. Every big-name feature writer I interviewed for this book said the same. They all use a minimum of two voice recorders or a voice recorder and an iPhone. When I placed a solitary voice recorder on the table ahead of one interview for this book the writer's eyes widened with astonishment. 'Only one recorder?' he asked.

'The . . . great virtue of recorders is that they allow you to quote someone's words *exactly* and not just the gist,' Barber wrote in A *Curious Career*. 'In fact this seems to me the whole joy of interviews – to capture people's way of speaking. Do they speak disjointedly, or do they form complete sentences? Do they repeat themselves? Do they have favourite words they use far too much? (Basically is a big offender here.) Do they use those giveaway phrases "to be perfectly frank" or "I must be honest with you" which always suggest they've been lying the rest of the time? Or, worst of all, do they say "know what I mean" because if they say it at all, they will tend to say it in every sentence.'[19]

The downside of taping an interview, of course, is the time it takes to transcribe the recording, time that you may not have, especially if you need to file your story to a tight deadline. Some journalists now use transcription services or computer programs that convert speech into writing but I remain sceptical about these. I've always found that playing an interview back makes writing a piece far easier in the long run. If possible, all trainee journalists should learn shorthand – as an invaluable back-up for the times when you can't use a voice recorder or for the heart-stopping moments when your recording equipment fails.

When interviews don't go according to plan

Other chapters cover how to handle challenging interviews and what to do when interviews don't go according to plan. Award-winning feature writer Emma Brockes had to contend with Oscar-winning actor Robert De Niro walking out of an interview she did for the *Radio Times*, the UK TV and radio listings magazine. De Niro was there to promote his latest film but objected to a question about how he avoided falling into 'autopilot' mode on set. 'You try to be respectful and polite, which I was,' Brockes said afterwards. 'It wasn't a hostile interview.'[20]

As Emma Brockes showed during her De Niro interview, the best journalists think on their feet when they are interviewing. Her experience shows that no matter how well you have prepared in advance, it's impossible to predict exactly how an interview will go. Oscar Wilde summed it up beautifully in his 1895 stage play, *An Ideal Husband* – 'to expect the unexpected shows a thoroughly modern intellect'.

Legal and ethical issues

This edition of *Interviewing for Journalists* includes a new chapter by Professor Tim Crook of Goldsmiths, University of London on the legal and ethical aspects of interviewing. In the light of the Leveson Inquiry into the culture, practice and ethics of the press, these issues have never been more important. Journalists must familiarise themselves with the laws of libel, slander, justification, trespass and copyright, as well as the codes of conduct of their own publications. You need a working knowledge of everything from how to deal with 'off-the-record' information to the importance of seeking legal advice if you think your story may be libellous.

Journalists have a fundamental duty to tell the truth, or as Tony Harcup described it in the excellent *Journalism: Principles and Practice*, 'something that can be backed up with evidence, verified and demonstrated to be the case'.[21] Brian Winston emphasised the point in *Lies, Damn Lies and Documentaries*, writing that 'truth telling is a necessary and essential limitation on journalism, and is accepted as such by the profession: facts are sacred.'[22]

It is important, too, to heed the case of the writer Johann Hari, who was suspended from the *Independent* in 2011 after being accused of using other writers' material without acknowledging it. As the *Guardian*'s Decca Aitkenhead wrote in a 2015 interview with him, Hari was once 'the *Independent*'s star columnist, a prolific polemicist and darling of the left, until his career imploded in disgrace when it emerged in 2011 that many of his articles contained quotes apparently said to him but in fact lifted from his interviewees' books, or from previous interviews by other journalists.'[23] The lesson to be learned from this, obviously, is: do your own interviews. What's more, if you decide to mention additional quotes from interviews by other journalists, attribute them accordingly. In other words, make it clear where they came from.

Standing out from the crowd

As you read the work of different interviewers and scrutinise their very varied styles, take a moment or two to evaluate exactly what it is that makes them stand out from the crowd.

Look at the work of *Sunday Times* writer Bryan Appleyard, for example. He won the 2014 Interviewer of the Year Award and has been named feature writer of the year three times at the UK's Press Awards. Appleyard grabbed readers' attention in a flash in his 2016 interview with Dame Helen Mirren by recalling his interview with her 15 years earlier.

'We got drunk in a French restaurant near Victoria station, discovering, among other possibilities, the use of nuns as drug smugglers,' he wrote. 'Waiters dropped plates at the sight of her. She was very rude about the treatment of Hollywood stars and she said f*** a lot.'[24]

In a few short lines Appleyard managed to convey more about Mirren's character than other interviewers might get across in 2,000 words.

Develop your own interviewing style

Bryan Appleyard's words illustrate a fundamental point about interviewing. While it's crucial to learn the essentials and to observe your editor's brief it's important to develop your own interviewing and writing style.

This book will help you along the way but as you gain experience during the course of your career remember to stop and reflect on what worked and what didn't. Interviews vary in every way so journalists need to adapt their interviewing techniques to suit the occasion. The skills needed for a quick phone call to a local contact to check facts or ascertain details on a breaking news story will be quite different to those required for an in-depth interview that takes place over several days and in several locations (politicians on election trails are particularly keen on these).

When I asked freelance writer Sheron Boyle about her interviewing technique she said: 'It's all about instinct for me – I just do it.' Boyle specialises in crime and health stories and has conducted hundreds of highly sensitive interviews for newspapers like the *Sunday Mirror*, the *Sun* and the *Daily Mail* during her career. She believes the most important thing to remember as an interviewer is to engage the person you are interviewing. 'Just be straight with them,' she says. 'Most people are really nervous so put them at their ease.'

Whatever an interview's length, setting, tone or purpose, this book will give you the tools to conduct the best news and features interviews you can. As Stephanie Rafanelli says: 'You've got to find out what your interviewing style is, what your own voice is and what your strengths are. You need to be yourself – because people can smell bullshit a mile off, and then you are in trouble.'

Use your initiative

It's vital, too, for journalists to use their initiative and spot valuable interviewing opportunities when they arise. An anecdote about the *Daily Mail* feature writer and critic Peter Lewis, who died in April 2016, illustrates this point perfectly. His obituary in *The Times* recalled that he started his journalistic career as a sub on the *Daily Express*, where one night he had to caption a photograph of T. S. Eliot that didn't have any copy with it. 'So he plucked up courage to ring Eliot himself. During their short interview, Eliot confessed that he often could not recall lines from his own poems. This launched Lewis's career as a feature writer, and he shortly after moved to the *Daily Mail*.'[25]

The *Daily Mail* film critic Brian Viner, who reckons that interviewing is 'one of the most enjoyable aspects of journalism', showed his journalistic initiative before he even got his first staff job. *Who's Who*, the directory of more than 30,000 'noteworthy and influential' people in the UK and worldwide, used to publish people's home addresses. As an enterprising student 30 years ago Viner worked his way through the directory and wrote letters to 50 famous people, asking if he could interview them. Four said yes, including the writer and broadcaster Melvyn Bragg and the theatre and opera director Jonathan Miller, and Viner interviewed them all.

During the course of my research for this book I've interviewed scores of journalists. Some were happy to be named, others preferred to remain anonymous, but all were very generous with their time and expertise and I owe a huge debt of gratitude to each of them. I've been interviewing for many years but thanks to them I've learned that everyone loathes transcribing with a passion, everyone lives in terror of their voice recorders seizing up and almost everyone gets nervous before a big interview.

On the other hand every journalist was passionate about the art of interviewing and could hardly believe their good fortune at being paid to talk to some of the most fascinating characters of our age. I feel much the same. During my career I've interviewed Sir Richard Branson 40,000 feet above the Atlantic on Virgin Atlantic's first flight to Miami, sat in a Bedouin tent in the middle of the Saudi desert with Prince Charles and Princess Diana, driven a Land Rover across the equator in search of a missing doctor and met a host of extraordinary people. There have been plenty of days when I've been stuck on doorsteps in the rain or had to plough through interminable planning reports in search of a news-line but interviewing is fascinating, revealing – and very rarely dull.

Notes

1 M. Amis, *Visiting Mrs Nabokov and Other Excursions*, Jonathan Cape, 1993, p. viii.

2 C. Pulford, *JournoLISTS: 201 Ways to Improve Your Journalism*, Ituri Publications, 2001, p. 17.

3 R. Greenslade, 'Mass media is over, but where does journalism go from here?', *Guardian*. Available from: www.theguardian.com/media/greenslade/2016/may/31/mass-media-is-over-but-where-does-journalism-go-from-here (accessed 1 June 2016).

4 D. Ponsford, 'Insight editor Jonathan Calvert: 99% journalism "not about trawling through databases, it's talking to people"', *Press Gazette*, December 2015. Available from: www.pressgazette.co.uk/insight-editor-jonathan-calvert-journalism-not-about-trawling-through-databases-its-talking-people (accessed 28 July 2016).

5 F. W. Hodgson, *Modern Newspaper Practice* (2nd edn), Heinemann Professional Publishing, 1989, p. 15.

6 M. Wells, 'Talk to me', *Guardian*. Available from: www.theguardian.com/media/2003/jan/22/broadcasting.g2 (accessed 12 May 2016).

7 C. Silvester, *The Penguin Book of Interviews: An Anthology from 1859 to the Present Day*, Penguin Books, 1994, p. 4.

8 G. Turnbull, 'Some notes on the history of the interview', *Journalism Quarterly*, September 1936.

9 S. Adams, *Interviewing for Journalists* (2nd edn), Routledge, 2009, p. 1.

10 J. Borger, D. Campbell, C. Porter and S. Millar, 'Everyone was screaming, crying, running. It's like a war zone', *Guardian*. Available from: www.theguardian.com/world/2001/sep/12/expertopinions.charlieporteronmensfashion (accessed 11 October 2016).

11 A. Marr, *My Trade: A Short History of British Journalism*, Macmillan, 2004, p. xxi.

12 L. Barber, *A Curious Career*, Bloomsbury Publishing, 2014, pp. 40–1.

13 *You* magazine, 'Susanna Reid on staying top of the morning', 10 April 2016.

14 J. Rook, *The Cowardly Lioness*, Sidgwick & Jackson, 1989, p. 102.

15 S. Garratt, 'Truth and beauty', *Telegraph* magazine, 2 February 2016.

16 R. Dean, 'The real Renée', *Red* magazine, October 2016.

17 S. Adams, *Interviewing for Journalists* (2nd edn), Routledge, 2009, p. 39.

18 N. Thurman, A. Cornia and J. Kunert, *Journalists in the UK*, Reuters Institute for the Study of Journalism, 2016. Available from: http://reutersinstitute.politics.ox.ac.uk/sites/default/files/Journalists%20in%20the%20UK.pdf (accessed 12 May 2016).

19 L. Barber, *A Curious Career*, Bloomsbury Publishing, 2014, p. 44.

20 B. Lee and E. Addley, 'Robert De Niro walks out of *Radio Times* interview', *Guardian*. Available from: www.theguardian.com/film/2015/sep/22/robert-de-niro-walks-out-radio-times-interview (accessed 9 August 2016).

21 T. Harcup, *Journalism: Principles and Practice* (3rd edn), Sage Publications, 2015, p. 77.

22 B. Winston, *Lies, Damn Lies and Documentaries*, British Film Institute, 2000, p. 119.

23 D. Aitkenhead, 'Johann Hari: "I failed badly. When you harm people, you should shut up, go away and reflect on what happened"', *Guardian*. Available from: www.theguardian.com/media/2015/jan/02/johann-hari-interview-drugs-book-independent (accessed 24 May 2016).

24 B. Appleyard, 'Not always in command', *The Sunday Times*. Available from: www.thesundaytimes.co.uk/sto/culture/film_and_tv/article1681098.ece (accessed 4 September 2016).

25 *The Times*, 'Peter Lewis: versatile theatre and book critic', 13 April 2016.

2
Communicating and interviewing: the basics

The best interviewers make interviewing look easy. All interviewers have to do, say the cynics, is roll up to the designated place at the designated time, ask a list of questions, note down the answers and then write the interview up for their readers. Simple. Except, of course, it isn't simple at all. The best interviewers have learned, through a combination of trial and error, what works and what doesn't. They phrase questions that produce informative, insightful replies, listen intently to what their interviewee says, write it down (even if they are using a voice recorder most will make notes of the interviewee's key points, expressions, tone, house, furniture and clothes), think of follow-up questions and keep the conversation running smoothly.

All of these things must be done simultaneously – while at the same time remaining calm, unflustered and supremely professional, or at least giving the impression of being so.

'There is a huge amount to think about when you are in a position of an interviewer,' says journalism lecturer Susan Grossman. 'It's not just about what the person you are interviewing says, it's also about the effect that it will have on your readers.'

In the second edition of *Interviewing for Journalists* Sally Adams compared interviewing to driving a car. 'There are a lot of unrelated skills to master and like learning to drive a car, interviewing is daunting and difficult at first. But with practice, setting off smoothly, signalling, changing gear, steering and watching the instruments become second nature. So it is with interviewing.'[1]

Personality and temperament

If that isn't enough to think about, journalists must also factor in the personality and temperament of the person they are talking to. Many interviewees are a delight, with great stories to tell and the ability (and willingness) to talk fluently and informatively. They prove beyond any shadow of a doubt Cole Moreton's view that 'good conversation is one of the joys of life'.

There's no denying, however, that a handful of interviewees will turn out to be ill-tempered, obstreperous and unforthcoming. Some will barely utter a word (take a look on YouTube at presenter Eamonn Holmes's TV interview with David Blaine, when the magician remained silent and refused to answer questions) and others will be long-winded, verbose or prone to wild exaggeration. Some will be nervous and inexperienced, so you'll need to do your utmost to put them at their ease, and some will be hazy and unclear in their recollections. Whatever your interviewees' idiosyncrasies or foibles, it is your job to get them to relax, trust you and talk.

The most important character trait you need as an interviewer, therefore, is to be likeable – the sort of person who gets on with people and is interested in everybody and everything. If you are the type of person who asks a question and takes little interest in the answer then journalism probably isn't the job for you.

Writing in *Modern Newspaper Practice*, F. W. Hodgson reckoned that interviewing requires 'tact, patience, psychology and courtesy'[2] – attributes that were mentioned time and time again by the journalists featured in this book. To these qualities I would add what TV presenter and former BBC political editor Andrew Marr has called 'a certain native nosiness, an urgent, itchy curiosity, or more than that, the ability to spot a "story" in a mass of apparently random facts'.[3] Curiosity, inquisitiveness, a keen interest in people and the ability to listen and empathise are all key components of interviewing.

Sally Adams, who inspired legions of journalism students during her long career, was interested in everyone she met – and as a result was a natural interviewer who could get almost anyone to talk to her. 'Everyone has got something fascinating to say,' she once told me. 'It's just a matter of finding it.' Freelance writer Sheron Boyle agrees. She believes that every journalist should be able to find great stories. 'You need to have an ear for a story,' she says. 'It doesn't have to be rocket science but you should be picking up stuff. Listen to what people tell you, read the local paper, keep an eye on court cases and think "Is there something in there I could follow up?"'

Other key attributes for journalists include charm, empathy, astuteness, tenacity, flexibility and fairness. You should also add the ability to think on your feet, good general knowledge and a healthy dose of scepticism.

Questions are part of everyday life

If you feel overwhelmed at the thought of interviewing someone remember that talking to people and asking questions are part of everyday life. The difference in a journalistic context is that you'll be asking your questions in a more structured way, recording the answers you get and crafting the interview into a readable article. Take heart, too, from the advice given in David Randall's guide to good journalistic practice, *The Universal Journalist*.[4] Most interviewing, he declared, is 'straightforward'. There are only two exceptions: interviewing someone who is 'uneasy and reluctant to talk' and interviewing a character who is 'positively evasive or even hostile'.

Having said that, few journalists master every type of interview. Subject knowledge is important, so a city correspondent accustomed to grilling economists, politicians and financiers about the state of the world's economy might struggle to conduct a post-match discussion with a football manager or a sensitive interview with a parent who has lost a child. An arts writer accustomed to asking actors, painters and writers about their creative work might lack the in-depth knowledge to be able to quiz a chief executive about their annual results. Having said that, some publications make a point of rotating their specialist writers so they learn new knowledge and skills, make new contacts and don't get stuck in a rut.

Each type of interview requires a different approach. An interview with the boss of a struggling business will require you to be hot on detail and able to get to grips with a company balance sheet. An interview with someone who's survived a terrorist attack or been badly injured in an accident will require compassion, empathy, understanding and patience.

Bear in mind, too, that no interview is 100 per cent – or indeed 50 per cent – predictable. Despite the best efforts of increasingly sophisticated public relations teams to direct and control them, interviews can't be scripted in advance and don't necessarily turn out the way you might expect. There is always an outside chance, for example, that an interviewee might take umbrage at a question (even one that is seemingly uncontroversial) and storm out. Actor Robert Downey Jr walked out of an interview in 2015 when *Channel 4 News* presenter Krishnan Guru-Murthy asked him about his personal life and defence secretary John Nott did the same in 1982 when interviewer Sir Robin Day called him a 'here-today, gone-tomorrow' politician. Sir John (he was knighted in 1983) explained his actions in an interview with the *Daily Telegraph* ten years later. 'I received about 850 letters after the walk-out, with only about 20 or 30 saying I had behaved petulantly and should have had the professional skill to sit it out,' he said. 'The overwhelming view was that it was high time that Robin Day and all those other interviewers were given their comeuppance.'[5]

It's helpful to remember that for the most part people aren't forced to give interviews (although some contracts stipulate that film actors, for instance, must do their bit to publicise their films). As Lynn Barber explained in *Demon Barber*, her collection of celebrity interviews: 'I don't doorstep anyone or pester them; I put in a request and accept the answer, yes or no. Moreover, the people I interview are not novices. They know the game and have usually benefited from it for most of their careers. They don't give interviews out of the kindness of their hearts – they are usually trying to plug whatever new film or book or record they are launching.'[6]

Different types of interview

Virtually all journalists conduct interviews at some point during their careers. Subs, critics, columnists and editors rarely do interviews, admittedly, but many started out as news reporters or feature writers, where interviewing is a fundamental part of the job.

Interviews take myriad different forms, however, so from the outset it's important to be clear about the kind of story you are covering and the type of interview required. The key question is: is your interview for a news story or a feature? If it's for a news story your aim will be to summarise a recent or breaking news item, interview the people who can explain the story and write it up in a clear and succinct way (often using the traditional inverted pyramid structure, with the most important news points at the top). If it's for a feature you are likely to have more time and more flexibility but you will be expected to cover the subject you are writing about in greater depth.

Chris Frost, Professor of Journalism at Liverpool John Moores University in the UK and chair of the National Union of Journalists' (NUJ) Ethics Council, believes there are four kinds of interview: informational, emotional, interpretive and adversarial or accountable.

The purpose of the informational interview, he says in *Reporting for Journalists*, 'is to provide information about a news event, often a breaking story', whereas the emotional interview 'allows us to share someone's personal experience'.[7] The interpretive interview tends to follow on from the informational interview, getting experts or campaigners to 'analyse and explain' events. The adversarial or accountable interview follows on from this, often asking someone in authority 'to explain previous policy, justify why it failed in this instance, and explain how they intend to change things'. In this world of round-the-clock news coverage, emotional, interpretive and accountable interviews often follow hard on the heels of the informational interview. Daily and Sunday newspapers, however, may choose to run an emotional interview with the survivor of a tragedy on their front pages and use the informational interview on an inside page.

Breaking news stories

These will be dealt with more fully in Chapter 3 but if you are covering a breaking news story you will need to conduct a series of interviews, either on the phone or in person, to ascertain the facts. Interviews like this involve talking to individuals who can give you the preliminary details of an incident that has either just happened or is still happening. Your interviewees could be police officers, emergency services, eyewitnesses, victims of accidents or crime – or, in major news stories, all of these. It's very likely that you won't have much time to prepare for these interviews so always remember to ask the basic factual questions of 'Who? What? When? Where? Why? How?' in order to garner the essential information.

Eyewitness interviews

These can vary from the traumatic to the happy, from people who have witnessed a terror attack, crime or accident to those who have met a member of the royal family, seen an eclipse or watched a rock star play an impromptu concert in the local pub. It is very important to give eyewitnesses time to tell their story in detail. If you hurry them along or interrupt too much they may skip the key points and information. It's essential to put them at their ease, encourage them and empathise with what they have experienced.

Doorstepping

Doorstep interviews are among the most challenging parts of a journalist's job. Usually assigned to news reporters, they involve knocking on someone's door or waiting outside their place of work in the hope of securing an impromptu interview. They range from waiting outside a politician's house to get their reaction to a particular issue to knocking on the door of a person caught up in a breaking or ongoing news story.

Interestingly, individuals at the eye of a media storm react in a host of different ways when a pack of reporters and photographers gathers outside their house. I remember an occasion where the furious family of a well-known singer who had been charged with drugs offences tipped a bucket of water over the press from an upstairs window (rather than being appalled at being drenched, the reporters were delighted to have something to write about on a slow news day). On the other hand there were plenty of others who happily served tea and biscuits when the press pack turned up on their doorsteps, even when they didn't want to comment on the story in question.

When you knock on the door remember that in many cases the occupants won't be expecting you and may be surprised to find you there. When the door opens give your name and the publication you work for, explain why you would like to talk to them – and as always, be polite and professional. Take a leaf out of Sheron Boyle's book and remember that it can be daunting for people to find the press on their doorstep all of a sudden, particularly at a traumatic time. It's important to reassure them and get them to see they can trust you.

When it comes to high-profile stories there may be scores of other journalists on the doorstep too. Don't give up if other reporters have already been turned away when they knocked on the door. The occupants may change their mind, prefer to talk to your publication instead or perhaps like your approach better. Even if they refuse your request, give them your card and ask them to get in touch if they change their minds at any point. Don't under any circumstances argue with them or harass them.

In her bestselling novel, *The Widow*, former *Mail on Sunday* chief reporter turned crime writer Fiona Barton gives a vivid insight into the world of the news reporter and into doorstepping techniques too. Barton's book features the fictional character of Kate Waters, an experienced reporter with a fascinating, if cynical, view of how news reporters persuade people to talk on the doorstep.

'Reporters had different techniques on the doorstep; one friend she'd trained with called it his "last puppy in the basket" look to get sympathy, another always blamed her news editor for making her knock on the door again, and one had once stuffed a pillow up her jumper to pretend she was pregnant and asked to use the loo to get in.'[8]

On a more serious note, it is important to be familiar with your publication's policy on approaching people at home or work. The *Editors' Code of Practice* (regulated by the Independent Press Standards Organisation (IPSO)) does not specifically mention doorstepping but the clause on harassment states: 'Journalists must not engage in intimidation, harassment or persistent pursuit. They must not persist in questioning, telephoning, pursuing or photographing individuals once asked to desist; nor remain on property when asked to leave and must not follow them. If requested, they must identify themselves and whom they represent.'[9]

Remember too, that while most roads and pavements in the UK are deemed to be public spaces, it's wise to check this. Shopping centres, for example, are often privately owned, so you can't conduct an interview there without permission (this is particularly pertinent when it comes to conducting vox pops). Similarly, journalists can't doorstep individuals on property where there is a long, private drive.

The best approach for a doorstep interview

BuzzFeed UK investigations editor Heidi Blake says that being sympathetic and straightforward is the best means of persuading someone to talk to you when you arrive on their doorstep out of the blue, especially if you're covering a difficult and/or sensitive story. She cites the example of Jane Bradley, a member of BuzzFeed UK's investigations team, who managed to get an extraordinary 90-minute interview with Maha Elgizouli, the mother of one of four ISIS guards who beheaded 27 hostages.

Below is the introduction to Bradley's remarkable piece, which looked at 'what makes studious, unassuming young men susceptible to an ideology that so swiftly turns them into killers' and was published on the BuzzFeed site in May 2016.

'When El Shafee Elsheikh was a little boy, after his father had left, his mother would find him at the workbench by the summerhouse at the bottom of the garden in White City, west London, tinkering endlessly with engine motors, bicycle parts, and old computers. Elsheikh was slight and elfin-featured, with wide almond eyes and pointed ears under a cloud of dark curls. He cut a sombre figure, intently turning the parts over in his small hands, finding out what made things work, how to fix them when they got broken. On warm nights, his mother says, he liked to sleep alone down here, in the makeshift old wooden summerhouse with a sheet drawn over the door.

'Years later, in 2011, when Elsheikh had grown into a striking young man in his early twenties, his mother found him here skulking with his CD player, listening to a torrent of hate. The words streaming out of his headphones, when she snatched them from him, were those of the notorious al-Qaeda-affiliated west London preacher Hani al-Sibai. By now Elsheikh had qualified as a mechanical engineer and was earning his living fixing cars and fairground rides. He was quiet, studious, and devoted to his family, and he made his mother proud. But on that day in the garden, she says, she feared for the first time that she was losing him to an ideology she did not understand.

'Now, five years on, Maha Elgizouli stands down here by the summerhouse, struggling to conceive of how the son she still calls her "little one" turned into one of the world's most wanted terrorists. Elsheikh has just been identified by BuzzFeed News and the *Washington Post* as a member of the notorious ISIS execution cell of four British guards known as the "Beatles" and responsible for beheading 27 hostages and torturing captives with electric shocks, waterboarding, and mock executions.'[10]

Heidi Blake says that Jane Bradley secured this interview by turning up on Maha Elgizouli's doorstep and asking for an interview – in other words, by simple, old-fashioned journalistic enterprise.

'We had done a series of stories unmasking the four guards and trying to paint a picture of how they had been radicalised,' says Blake. 'We went to the families to warn them that we might be going to publish this story. We obviously thought it would be great to get an interview with them – but we weren't particularly expecting any of the families to want to talk to us.

'Jane is absolutely superb on the doorstep, instantly developing a rapport with people and getting them to talk to her. She did it beautifully with the mother of this young man – by being incredibly authentic, a very real, warm person. She knocked on the door and asked if she could to talk to her about her son and his radicalisation. She said: "I'm not going to pretend that this is not going to be a very hard thing for you to talk about but we want you to have an opportunity to tell your side of the story and that's why I'm here." She didn't try and pretend it wasn't hard and the woman immediately responded to that.'

Blake says that turning up in person when covering news stories like this is far more effective than messaging or phoning. 'Always go to them in person first – because it's so much harder to shut someone off if they are right there in front of you and they are a real human being, a living, breathing person who has knocked on your door. It's so much harder to close the door on someone than it is to ignore a message.'

Death knocks

All journalists find death knocks difficult. Knocking on the door of a family who has recently endured the death of a loved one, usually in tragic circumstances, is one of the hardest things you will be required to do as a journalist. Increasingly, when the police are involved, police press officers will release a statement from the bereaved family and request that the media leaves them alone. In my experience news desks always heed requests like this; it would be very unethical, not to say callous and disrespectful, to disregard such a request.

In other cases, you may find that the family wants to talk, particularly if they are keen to raise awareness about a particular issue. As a young reporter, I was asked to go and knock on the door of a couple whose young son had recently died. I was nervous about approaching them but to my surprise the father opened the door, invited me inside and gave me a heart-rending interview about his son, followed by an appeal to people to donate their organs after death. The interview was gentle, respectful and sombre – and the family wrote to thank me afterwards.

Your news desk may also ask you to talk to friends, relations and neighbours of the person at the centre of the story. As with other types of doorstep interviews, you should state who you are, the publication you work for, why you are there and, as always, be courteous and professional. People's reactions at times like these are hard to predict. Some will be willing to talk about the person who has died and pay tribute to them, but others may be hostile and even downright aggressive. Try not to get upset if this happens. Leave immediately if you are asked to do so and remember that at the end of the day you are only doing your job.

Sue White, a former *Birmingham Evening Mail* reporter, described her approach to death knocks in the second edition of *Interviewing for Journalists*. 'If the death had happened overnight, say a 17-year-old boy on a motorbike, I'd write the story for the first edition and then set off, not knowing what I would find. Normally it would be quiet and I'd knock on the door. It would open a crack and someone would answer … I'd say: "Hello, I'm Sue White from the *Birmingham Evening Mail*. We've heard from the police about the dreadful accident last night. Could I come in and have a word with you about it?" Almost everyone would say "All right" … It's important to be very courteous and understanding. I'd repeat where I was from and that we wanted to check we had all the details correct. I'd be taken in and sat in the lounge. It would be very quiet, they'd be stunned. I felt if I talked openly, in as friendly and sympathetic a way as possible – one person to another, making it clear I just wanted to confirm some facts – people would give me that information. I was usually right.'[11]

Heidi Blake agrees that in circumstances like these it is important to be completely straightforward about why you are there. She warns against being disingenuous. If, for instance, a person has died in 'grisly circumstances', telling the relative who answers the door that you're seeking to write a tribute to the deceased isn't appropriate. 'I'd rather say something along the lines of "look, we know what happened and it was really awful and we wanted to ask you about the circumstances of the death,"' says Blake. 'Be honest.'

Interviews with experts

Once you have ascertained the basic details of a news story and interviewed the people directly involved (from police officers to eyewitnesses) you will need to dig a little deeper and talk to experts in the field. If the story is about an earthquake, for example, your news editor will probably want you to talk to experts who can explain the science behind it or talk about how the community infrastructure can be rebuilt and at what cost. If the story is about a motorway pile-up during a torrential storm, you may need to find experts who can tell you about speed limits, stopping distances and advice for motorists on driving in adverse weather conditions. Make sure you cover both sides of an argument. If you're writing about a controversial planning decision, talk to the developers who believe it will bring much needed investment, infrastructure and jobs to the area *and* to the protesters who say it will cause more traffic congestion, ruin the countryside and disrupt wildlife.

An additional point to mention is that TV and radio journalists often conduct what they call 'research interviews' in preparation for doing a more focused interview later on. How many times have you heard a caller on a radio phone-in mention that they've already had a conversation with a researcher prior to going live on air? Research interviews are rare in print and online journalism, however, so make the most of any interviewing opportunity you get. It's the real thing – not a rehearsal – and you may not have a second chance.

Case study interviews

Magazines frequently use case studies to illustrate stories – and newspapers are increasingly making use of them too.

If you are writing a story about the increase in hospital waiting times, a case study interview with a patient who has been waiting for an operation for months will reinforce the effect that this is having on individuals and will bring the subject to life. Similarly, if you are covering a story about thousands of children missing out on their first choice of secondary school you will need to talk to a disgruntled parent or two. Remember that case studies tend to be written in the first person, so you will need strong quotes.

If you find it difficult to find suitable case studies ask colleagues and friends for suggestions, contact relevant charities (most of whom keep lists of potential interviewees) and even post on social media. You will often see appeals on Twitter with the hashtag #journorequest.

Features interviews

These tend to be longer (both in terms of the time they take and the word count), less prescriptive in style and more extensive than news interviews. They might range from a hard-hitting feature on global water shortages, featuring interviews with politicians, environmentalists and business leaders, to a lifestyle piece on current fashion trends, including interviews with designers, stylists and bloggers.

Celebrity interviews

These will be covered more extensively in Chapter 10 but suffice it to say they are often the most difficult interviews of all. Why? Because celebrity interviews are so tightly controlled and orchestrated these days and famous people are interviewed so often that it's hard to get original lines out of them. Celebrity interviewers need to be at the top of their game to extract something new, especially if publicists ask for questions to be submitted and approved in advance. Read the wise advice of journalists like Camilla Long, Stephanie Rafanelli and Cole Moreton later in this book.

Interviews with politicians

Politicians are generally astute, informed and motivated. They are often more interested, however, in telling you what *they* want you to know and less enthusiastic about telling you what they'd rather you didn't know. Many of them have received media training, learning how to speak in soundbites (which don't necessarily make good copy) and how to avoid answering difficult questions without seeming discourteous or evasive. Media training, which is sometimes done by former journalists, is a double-edged sword and varies hugely in quality and content. When done well, media training can give interviewees the confidence to answer difficult questions but when done less successfully it can result in interviewees appearing defensive and stilted.

The best way to get a fascinating interview out of a politician is to do your research, prepare your questions thoroughly and take a robust approach. A former government press officer who sat in on ministerial interviews for years advised: 'Know your stuff. Politicians, whatever party, don't want to be interviewed by fools who haven't done their homework. They can tell from the first few questions what the journalist's agenda is and how clued up they are.'

Former Mayor of London Boris Johnson is a past master at being interviewed, and always good value, as he showed in 2016 during a revealing pre-referendum interview with Tim Shipman, the political editor of *The Sunday Times*. When Shipman asked Johnson about the most important thing he had learned from his father, this is how the politician reacted. "'Swerverama!" he blurts. "The most important thing I learnt from him was not answering tricky questions about one's family. It was a brilliant lesson."'[12]

Interviews over lunch

These often work well, largely because interviewees tend to relax and talk more freely over lunch. Don't forget, however, to choose somewhere quiet and check whether your interviewee has any dietary requirements – or indeed a favourite restaurant – before you book a table. Booking is always advisable. It's more professional and will maximise your interviewing time.

The *Financial Times* has turned the concept of interviews over lunch into a much-admired regular feature. 'Lunch with the FT' is a weekly interview with leading cultural, business and political figures. In recent years this series has featured everyone from Angela Merkel to Twiggy and has proved so successful that it has now been adopted by other publications. Written by a variety of *Financial Times* journalists, 'Lunch with the FT' shows that even the most reticent of interviewees reveal far more about themselves than you might expect over an excellent lunch. The interviews always feature a description of the restaurant chosen by the interviewee and a breakdown of the bill. The details of what the interviewee and interviewer ate and drank and how much it cost are often as fascinating as the interview itself.

A collection of 52 'Lunch with the FT' interviews was published in 2013 and is well worth reading. As *Financial Times* editor Lionel Barber, who edited the collection, explains in the introduction: 'The original idea behind *Lunch with the FT* was to rediscover the art of conversation in a convivial setting. Good food was essential, preferably washed down with a decent bottle of wine to elicit insights and the occasional indiscretion. The combination led to some memorable encounters, notably a liquid lunch of biblical proportions at the Café Royal between Nigel Spivey, a Cambridge don and freelance *Financial Times* writer, and Gavin Ewart, the 79-year-old poet. The next day, Spivey received a call from Mrs Ewart, saying that her husband had returned home happier than she had seen him in a long time. The second [thing] – and you are not to feel bad about this – is that he died this morning.'[13]

Other notable 'Lunch with the FT' interviewees include former UKIP leader Nigel Farage, who talked to *Financial Times* political correspondent Henry

Mance over six pints, a bottle of wine and two large glasses of port[14] and comedian turned activist Russell Brand, who chatted to *Financial Times* columnist Lucy Kellaway over a bowl of leek and potato soup at an East End cooperative that helps the homeless find work.[15]

Starting out as an interviewer

There's no doubt that interviewing gets less intimidating the more you do it and the more experienced you become. But in the early stages of your career you will benefit hugely from spending time on the basics – from dressing appropriately to learning to spot what Cole Morton calls 'a killer quote' when you hear it.

First of all, it's crucial to understand what the relationship between the interviewee and the interviewer entails.

At its most simplistic, the interviewee has the information at their fingertips and it's the interviewer's role to extract it. The process may not be straightforward, however. As journalism tutor Sally Adams explained: 'You will use people, and you will be used. You will find some people who divulge little, others who tell you more than you wish to know. You will be trusted with secrets, you will be lied to. You will be bombarded with what seem like irrelevancies and only later realise what a key piece one of them is in the information jigsaw. You will be rebuffed, you will be courted.'[16]

Lynn Barber described interviews as 'just two people alone in a room, with a tape recorder'[17] but it's much more complicated than that. Sometimes interviewees want to cooperate, sometimes they don't, although experience will teach you how to handle each of these scenarios.

The power of interviews

It's important to remember that interviews can have a powerful and lasting effect on people's lives. Former *Mail on Sunday* chief reporter Fiona Barton caught the essence of it in *The Widow*, her crime novel. 'When you're talking to real people – people without an ego or something to sell – it can be complete exposure of one person to another, an intense intimacy that excludes everyone and everything else.'[18]

As a result of what journalists write, people risk losing their jobs, companies close and relationships fall apart. On the other hand, many interviews have happy consequences. They enable people to progress in their careers, sell their books, win awards and raise money for charity. In some instances they lead to lifelong friendships and, occasionally, marriage. The journalist Keely Shaye Smith interviewed former Bond star Pierce Brosnan in 1994 and they married seven years later.

In a few cases journalists' interviews lead to book deals. If an interviewee likes your work they may well ask you to 'ghost' their autobiography or write a book about their life and experience.

Sensitive subjects

There's no doubt that striking a balance between asking questions that interviewees are happy to answer and covering areas that are sensitive and difficult to talk about is tricky. This will be discussed at greater length in Chapter 11 but the challenge faced by interviewee and interviewer alike was illustrated in Krissi Murison's interview with Thomas Cohen, the widower of Peaches Geldof, for The Sunday Times magazine in 2016.

Cohen did the interview to promote his first solo album but Murison commented that she was 'surprised he's speaking to me at all', given that any interview with him was bound to mention his late wife and her tragic death from an accidental heroin overdose at the tender age of 25. Seeking to explain why he'd agreed to do the interview, Murison added: 'In doing so, he has chosen to replay his most personal experiences in the public eye and put himself up for scrutiny and difficult questions. I wonder if he understands the bargain he has made.'[19]

Murison was right to highlight this conundrum. Some people undoubtedly give interviews because they like talking about themselves and enjoy being the centre of attention but they are probably in the minority. Most interviewees have specific reasons for talking to the press. They perhaps want to highlight a particular issue, explain the background to a story or publicise their work, be it a new book they have written or a building they have designed. It's important, therefore, to give people time to talk about their projects but remember that you're a journalist, not a PR or advertising executive. You need to probe further and ask other questions too.

A controversial view

The American journalist Janet Malcolm took a far more controversial view of the ethical dilemma faced by interviewers. In The Journalist and the Murderer she depicted the interviewer as someone who befriends the interviewee and then betrays them. 'The catastrophe suffered by the subject is no simple matter of an unflattering likeness or a misrepresentation of his views; what pains him, what rankles and sometimes drives him to extremes of vengefulness is the deception that has been practiced on him,' she wrote. 'On reading the article or book in question, he has to face the fact that the journalist – who seemed so friendly and sympathetic, so keen to understand him fully, so remarkably attuned to his vision of things – never had the slightest intention of collaborating with him on his story but always intended to write a story of his own.'[20] A cynical view perhaps, but a perceptive observation all the same.

Some journalists swear by the 'flirtation, seduction and betrayal' approach to interviewing but this is a high-risk strategy. The role of the interviewer, after all, is to bring their interviewee to life in their copy, no more, no less. The journalist and author Nigel Farndale wrote a highly entertaining book entitled *Flirtation, Seduction, Betrayal: Interviews with Heroes and Villains*, attributing the 'flirtation, seduction and betrayal' line to Andrew Billen of the *Evening Standard* and, more recently, *The Times*. Farndale declared that Billen 'compares the exercise to a mutual seduction. "The three stages of a successful interview," he believes, "are flirtation, seduction and betrayal. The fundamental problem is the elapse of time between encounter and composition. Just as you don't know your subject until you teach it, as an interviewer you do not know your subject until you recreate him in print."'[21]

Journalist Elizabeth Day questioned the role of the interviewer in her third novel, *Paradise City*, and came to the conclusion that the aim is to bring the interviewee's emotion to the surface. One of the book's four protagonists is a young journalist called Esme Reade, who manages to get an exclusive interview with Howard Pink, a self-made millionaire whose daughter is missing. Here, she relates her feelings about the encounter.

'It is a false conversation, this circular question and answer. A carefully scripted play masquerading as spontaneity, with neither of the main actors willing to acknowledge the fakery of it.

'The art of the interviewer, Esme knows, is to coax the emotion of the interviewee to the surface, casting off with a wriggling question and letting the bait glitter and skim on the water until they have taken it and been hooked. And part of Howard has been grateful to be hooked, she knows that. Everyone wants to talk, deep down.'[22]

Editorial policy

Most publications have an editorial policy and journalists should make sure that they read it. As well as highlighting the importance of maintaining the highest professional standards, this document will in all likelihood cover areas such as not using intimidation, harassment or persistent pursuit and approaching people who have suffered bereavement or shock with sympathy and discretion.

You should also take the time to understand the publication you work for – and its audience. Who reads it? What is their demographic profile? What interests them? The more you know about your readers the clearer your job as an interviewer will be. Why? Because during an interview it's useful to try and put yourself in the position of a typical reader. What would they want to know if they were in your place? What would be their most pressing concerns? What questions would they ask?

Publishing deadlines have a huge impact on interviews too. If you write for a monthly magazine you may have all the time in the world to conduct an interview and write it up. Most journalists don't have this luxury. Today's 24-hour news cycle means that the emphasis in most media offices is on productivity and speed. If you work for an online news service you may be required to cover six or seven stories a day, constantly updating them as you go. Nick Davies, author of *Flat Earth News*, described journalists who have to write vast numbers of stories as being 'chained to a keyboard on a production line in a news factory, churning out trivia and cliché to fill space in the paper'.[23] A bit harsh perhaps, but the intensity of meeting deadlines means that interviews are increasingly conducted on the telephone, via Skype or by email rather than in person. If you have plenty of time though, interviewing someone face to face is preferable – and will always produce a better story in the end.

Interviewing task

Choose a topic or campaign in the news and list the people you would interview in order to be able to write a fair, accurate and contemporaneous story. Make sure you cover all sides and perspectives of the story.

HOW I INTERVIEW: CAMILLA LONG

Camilla Long began her career as an editorial assistant at *Vogue* in London – 'I sent about 60 letters to newspapers and magazines asking for jobs and I got 59 letters back saying "no, we can't offer you a job or work experience". But *Vogue* asked me to come in and they gave me a job.' After a year she moved to *Tatler*, where the then editor Geordie Greig (more recently editor of the *Mail on Sunday*) sent her to do her first interviews. She later joined *The Sunday Times*'s *Style* magazine – 'and that's where my style developed'. She is now a columnist, interviewer and film critic for *The Sunday Times*.

Long was named broadsheet interviewer of the year at the 2015 Press Awards for her interviews with George Galloway, Viscount Weymouth (the Marquess of Bath's son) and Labour MP Simon Danczuk and his then wife Karen. 'From being a columnist she has branched out to being an exceptionally good interviewer who continues to be fresh, exciting, brave, revealing and unpredictable,' said the judges.

In Long's view the first and foremost responsibility of an interviewer is to give 'a sense of what it's like to be in the company of the person you're interviewing'. She chooses to do this with a lot of physical description and some scene setting. 'Remember to keep yourself in the action as little as you reasonably can,' she advises.

'The temptation when you are nervous about an interview is to insert yourself a lot but I think that keeping it to a clever minimum is the key – so you don't hinder the reader. So lots of stuff about tape failings, your internal monologue before you meet the person or too much gush about how excited you are to meet them – I would definitely keep that to a minimum.'

Fixing interviews

When it comes to arranging interviews, Long fixes some herself and others are fixed for her. 'It's about 50–50 for me – 50 per cent chasing myself, 50 per cent brilliant fixers being super-tenacious in getting me the best interviews. I wouldn't say there are any hard and fast rules but you have to be on the ball yourself, not just have someone else putting in for interviews. The most hilarious interview that I fixed myself was Imelda Marcos and that involved months and months of persuading her to let me come and visit her in Manila. I remember the final day when she decided that she was going to say yes. I woke up on Boxing Day morning and my phone was going and it was Imelda Marcos on the phone saying "hello – you come?"'

When Long emails potential interviewees she keeps the wording succinct, simple and straightforward.

'Find the email that will get to them directly, so either their personal email if you can manage that or their PA's email,' she says. 'Failing that, go to their PR but really you want to get past the PR because the PR will try and make the interview happen in their own particular way.'

Her advice is to explain who you are at the top of the email, then write a couple of lines giving specific reasons about why you want to interview them and why they might want to be interviewed – 'which is the hardest sentence'. She ends by saying: 'If you'd like to discuss this further, here is my mobile number.' She occasionally sends a handwritten letter to an interviewee's home address. 'I'm thinking particularly of politicians, who are quite difficult to pin down. Most of them monitor their emails but if you're trying to get somebody who doesn't or who has a massive team around them, just write to their home address.'

She always asks for at least an hour for interviews although she has a theory that it takes 75 minutes for people to relax. 'I think it's because they think the end is nigh so they relax ever so slightly. They start being honest about themselves and you get a better sense of who they are.' Having said that, she was only granted 11 minutes with Jennifer Lopez, although she made a virtue of it by writing the following: 'We all have 15 minutes, "or maybe less", says the publicist, a chlorine blonde with David Bowie fangs. If the interview starts to "lose heat", J.Lo will give a signal to her American publicist, Mark, to wrap things up.'[24]

Given the choice Long prefers to interview people at home although she says that interviewees are increasingly reluctant to agree to this. 'The next best thing,' she says, 'is to let them choose where they'd like to meet. Then it's a sliding scale all the way down to the anonymous hotel suite, at which point you need to make sure you have really good questions.' If she's interviewing someone over lunch she offers her interviewees alcohol, but adds the caveat: 'Don't get wasted yourself.'

Take the first interview slot you're offered

Long spends as much time as possible preparing for interviews. 'When I was doing news interviews I'd often have to do an interview at an hour's notice. It was quite stressful but by the time the interview had been confirmed it was my responsibility to have boned up on the whys and wherefores and the fors and againsts. A lot of people will come to you with an interview and there will be something that they specifically want to say. I'm fine with them saying whatever they like but you need to work out what *you* would like from the interview and what you think your readers would like to hear. Usually, unfortunately, it's the most difficult subject to approach. It's "why did you have gastric band surgery?" or "why did you do this, that and the other?"'

Long always takes the first interview slot she's offered – to avoid the interviewee changing their mind. 'The temptation is to say "oh, can we do it a bit later?" so you have more time to prepare – but don't mess about. If they say "come and see me in an hour and a half" you have to go.'

'If it's a celebrity you've been following all your life you'll probably know all the details already but if you're doing a deep news interview on the intricacies of the education system, race relations or DEFRA (Department for Environment,

Food and Rural Affairs), talk to an expert beforehand if you can. If you have a mate on the news desk whose expertise it is, talk to them. Read the cuts for the last three months so you have an idea of the news angle that you need to go in on. Then, at the end of the interview ask, "Is there any way I could have a ten-minute top-up on the phone? Do you have a number? Who do I call?" Always ask for contact details at the end of an interview. It means that you will be able to check facts, clarify things you are concerned about and top up any aspects you are confused about or you need more information about.'

Two voice recorders

At the start of her career Long used tapes, so she has stacks of tapes at home. These days she always uses two voice recorders – 'although anything that can go wrong has gone wrong. I remember doing one interview with Martin Amis and it came out so soft and quiet on the tape that I had to get it professionally enhanced in order for me to hear his voice. It was all really stressful but fine in the end.'

She reckons that taking notes distracts interviewees. 'You kind of need to make them forget the tape recorder is there, so I try not to check it too much, although once you've had one collapse of the tape recorder you do think "my goodness, please can it not happen again."'

Long writes a page of 'the most open, most precise' questions she can think of. She doesn't consult her list during the interview but at the end she'll check that she's covered everything. 'Sometimes I will be quite precise and I'll have thought of questions that I hope will crack open the subject in a particular way but mostly I feel more comfortable if the interview resembles a real conversation. I'm naturally quite conversational and quite nosy. There will always be one or two things I know I shouldn't be asking but I'm just desperate to ask. You have to make sure you ask those questions, because otherwise you're not serving your readers – and you have to remember that you are there for your readers. Your readers are the most important thing – and I can absolutely guarantee that they will be the most important thing to the interviewee.'

While she is interviewing Long focuses 100 per cent on the conversation. She doesn't take more than a page of notes 'of visual things, partly because if they question the interview later you have a record of what you've seen. So if I'm looking around and see books on the shelves I note down the titles. It eliminates wrangles later. You need to make sure that everything you write is perfectly clean and truthful.'

Tricky questions

Long doesn't pull her punches – and she doesn't baulk at asking tricky questions either. In recent years she has inquired of Michael Fassbender 'Are you a very sexual person?' and 'Weren't you worried about getting an erection during filming?'[25] and once asked Hugh Hefner what kind of pornography he watches.[26] She usually asks challenging questions four-fifths of the way through, 'unless it's sort of amusing to ask it at the beginning'. After all, she says, 'if you are interviewing a celebrity on the morning that he's been caught in a swimming pool of olive oil I think it would be dishonest to then say "so tell me about your new album". Judge the situation – and for God's sake don't leave without asking the difficult question.'

The only person to walk out of one of her interviews was the radical preacher Anjem Choudary, who arrived with five followers in tow, called her 'Audrey' throughout and left after 45 minutes. She had plenty of material to write up the interview though, as her feisty first paragraph shows.

'Obviously I was never going to see eye to eye with the benefitchogging [sic] Muslim hate cleric Anjem Choudary, but I didn't realise how many of his own community think he's dreadful, too.'[27]

A jolly conversation

In person Long is charming, self-deprecating and funny and insists that she is 'not very abrasive' during interviews. 'I suppose I like the interview to be a jolly conversation and that's mostly what they resemble – unless I really can't bear them and we have an obvious disagreement, which does happen. If someone throws a tantrum or is rude to you or is dismissive you can be pretty much guaranteed that behind closed doors they will be completely ghastly – because if they are unable to keep themselves together in an interview what must they be like at home?

'It's your job to see past niceties and not to be too impressed by people being courteous, getting the door or offering you drinks. If they don't do that you must write it in your article. But don't let your powers of critical analysis drop because they are being nice to you.'

She doesn't mind 'a bit of chit-chat' with interviewees but agrees with Lynn Barber that interviews aren't about the interviewer. Where she differs from Barber though is that she doesn't mind if PRs sit in on her interviews (although she'd prefer them not to). 'I ask them not to but if they insist and they interrupt then they can probably expect to turn up in the piece. It's bad PR to control your client in that manner because it says you think they are a moron – and it's disrespectful to the interviewer because it says you think they are going to do something dodgy.'

During her interviews Long observes people's body language keenly. 'The body will be telling you 50 per cent of what is going on,' she says. 'Body scrunched up, arms folded – you'll know that the topic you're talking about is awkward for them. Similarly, if they are too open and touchy that's another sign of strangeness and should probably be noted.'

Interviewing Dave Lee Travis

One of Long's most traumatic interviews was with former DJ Dave Lee Travis. The interview was published in *The Sunday Times* in 2012, two years before Travis was convicted of groping a researcher working on the Mrs Merton show in 1995. This was Long's intro: 'I spent 90 minutes with the former Radio 1 DJ Dave Lee Travis last Thursday and I don't think there is a part of my body that he didn't grope.'[28]

Looking back on the interview, Long says she wouldn't have been doing her duty if she hadn't written exactly what had happened. 'About eight minutes in I thought: "My God, this man can't keep his hands to himself." Part of your job is to relax the other person but it's unusual to find that they are so relaxed they are pawing you already. I never hesitated about writing it. I was very lucky to have *The Sunday Times* saying "we believe you, write it all down as it is" – and they ran it.'

The incident backs up Long's belief that interviewers have to be 'forensic' about their material. 'If someone has done something terrible, say what they did and why,' she says. 'Definitely limit your own feelings about it and let the facts speak for themselves.'

Playing interviews back

The moment the interview is over Long downloads the recordings to her laptop and then emails them to herself 'so even if my laptop is stolen and my handset is stolen and my dictaphone is stolen I still have the interview'.

She usually transcribes her own interviews – 'it gives a good sense of the interview again and it's a helpful primer for how you felt' – although if she is frantically busy she uses a transcription service.

Like other writers she loathes playing her interviews back, 'because you listen to yourself yapping on, distracting the interviewee and cutting them off when they are just about to tell you the most amazing nugget of their life story and dreams. I've now trained myself not to interrupt. First of all it's rude and secondly it's incredibly stupid because you break the train and then you have to pick up the ball again and it's never quite the same. You definitely want to say less rather than more in the interview. The more interviews I've done the more I've realised that less is best.'

Best interview

One of the interviews she is most proud was with Simon Cowell in 2010, when she flew out to Marbella as the *X Factor* team was filming the judges' houses segment of the show. 'I spoke to him for four and a half hours and he said nothing,' she recalls. 'But it was amazing access and it was fascinating meeting him – it was probably one of the last proper interviews he did. It was the year he found One Direction and they were all singing in the driveway. He said to me: "We've put them together and we think it might work."'

The resulting piece was Long at her best. 'He stands for a beat,' she wrote, 'like Versace on the steps of his mansion, and then the contestants swarm up, screaming and jumping and shouting, teaming through the villa, sweeping out to a pagoda where he talks to them in front of the cameras . . .'[29]

Long is undoubtedly a brave interviewer but she insists that 'it's taken me a while to get this brave'. She's reluctant to give advice to people who want to become interviewers but is keen to give advice to people who want to become interviewers' editors 'because as a writer you need an editor who is going to go "fabulous. This is great. Let's run it tomorrow." That's what I've got at *The Sunday Times* – and that's what you need. You need unwavering support and I've been very lucky in that.'

Camilla Long's top tip

Tell the truth.

Notes

1 S. Adams, *Interviewing for Journalists* (2nd edn), Routledge, 2009, p. 5.
2 F. W. Hodgson, *Modern Newspaper Practice* (2nd edn), Heinemann Professional Publishing, 1989, p. 15.
3 A. Marr, *My Trade: A Short History of British Journalism*, Macmillan, 2004, p. 5.
4 D. Randall, *The Universal Journalist*, Pluto Press, 1996, p. 42.
5 J. Nott, 'Why I walked out on Robin Day', *Daily Telegraph*. Available from: www.telegraph.co.uk/culture/4727494/Why-I-walked-out-on-Robin-Day.html (accessed 9 August 2016).
6 L. Barber, *Demon Barber*, Viking, 1998, p. ix.
7 C. Frost, *Reporting for Journalists* (2nd edn), Routledge, 2010, pp. 176–8.
8 F. Barton, *The Widow*, Transworld, 2016, p. 21.
9 Editors' Code of Practice Committee, *The Code in Full*. Available from: www.editorscode.org.uk/index.php (accessed 1 June 2016).

10 J. Bradley, 'My son the ISIS executioner', BuzzFeed. Available from: www.buzzfeed. com/janebradley/my-son-the-isis-executioner?utm_term=.waYGgZe7l#. ih8VDpx7o (accessed 28 July 2016).

11 S. Adams, *Interviewing for Journalists* (2nd edn), Routledge, 2009, p. 180.

12 T. Shipman, 'I didn't want to go against the prime minister. The desire for a quiet life was strong,' *The Sunday Times* magazine, 12 June 2016.

13 L. Barber (ed.), *Lunch with the FT: 52 Classic Interviews*, Portfolio Penguin, 2013, p. xi.

14 *Financial Times*, 'Lunch with the FT: Nigel Farage'. Available from: https://next. ft.com/content/864c3a96-fbf1-11e5-b5f5-070dca6d0a0d (accessed 21 May 2016).

15 *Financial Times*, 'Lunch with the FT: Russell Brand'. Available from: https://next. ft.com/content/64206eb2-583f-11e4-a31b-00144feab7de (accessed 21 May 2016).

16 S. Adams, *Interviewing for Journalists* (2nd edn), Routledge, 2009, p. 6.

17 L. Barber, *A Curious Career*, Bloomsbury Publishing, 2014, p. 44.

18 F. Barton, *The Widow*, Transworld, 2016, p. 60.

19 K. Murison, 'My life after Peaches', *The Sunday Times* magazine. Available from: www.thetimes.co.uk/article/tom-cohen-i-refused-to-lose-myself-and-become-a-traumatised-grief-stricken-single-father-2swd3lx69 (accessed 2 June 2016).

20 J. Malcolm, *The Journalist and the Murderer*, Bloomsbury Publishing, 1991, p. 3.

21 N. Farndale, *Flirtation, Seduction, Betrayal: Interviews with Heroes and Villains*, Constable, 2002, p. 3.

22 E. Day, *Paradise City*, Bloomsbury Publishing, 2015, p. 211.

23 N. Davies, *Flat Earth News*, Vintage, 2009, p. 56.

24 C. Long, 'What a performance', *The Sunday Times*. Available from: www.the sundaytimes.co.uk/sto/culture/music/pop_and_rock/article648966.ece#prev%20 (accessed 20 May 2016).

25 C. Long, 'Dirty pretty thing', *The Sunday Times*. Available from: www.thesunday times.co.uk/sto/Magazine/Interviews/article856056.ece (accessed 11 October 2016).

26 C. Long, 'Playboy meets girl', *The Sunday Times*. Available from: www.the sundaytimes.co.uk/sto/Magazine/Interviews/article551556.ece#next (accessed 16 May 2016).

27 C. Long, 'Anjem Choudary: I'm smiling because sharia is coming', *The Sunday Times*. Available from: www.thesundaytimes.co.uk/sto/news/uk_news/ article195085.ece#prev (accessed 11 October 2016).

28 C. Long, 'Dave Lee Travis: Look out, Suu Kyi – he's a bit touchy', *The Sunday Times*. Available from: www.thesundaytimes.co.uk/sto/newsreview/features/ article1061997.ece (accessed 11 October 2016).

29 C. Long, 'Simon Cowell: X-rated', *The Sunday Times*. Available from: www. thesundaytimes.co.uk/sto/Magazine/Interviews/article391569.ece#page-1 (accessed 11 October 2016).

3
News interviewing

Before you start to fix up and plan news interviews you need to learn how to recognise a good story. Or, as freelance journalist Sheron Boyle puts it: 'To be a good journalist you need to be able, first of all, to spot a story outside the blindingly obvious. Then after spotting the story you have to be able to *get* the story. You can be the cleverest writer going but it doesn't matter if you can't spot a story in the first place.'

If you think this is self-evident, it isn't. We've all heard the anecdote about the trainee journalist who was sent to interview a women's football team and came back disheartened. 'No luck,' he said. 'They're not playing. They're all pregnant.'

I had a similar experience as a young reporter when I turned up at a village hall in the wilds of Dartmoor to review the annual village pantomime for the local paper. Halfway through the performance some of the cast rushed off and their understudies rushed on. It turned out that the originals were volunteer firefighters and had been called out to tackle a blaze. It wasn't until the next day when I told my news editor what had happened that I realised that I'd very nearly missed a cracking news story.

Like Andrew Marr and Sheron Boyle, I spent my early years in journalism on a local newspaper, where as well as covering the local magistrates' court and council meetings reporters were expected to bring in their own stories. How did we do it? By keeping our ears close to the ground, frequenting the pub, keeping in touch with people we'd interviewed before and scouring rival media outlets for possible follow-ups to stories.

The more I talked to my contacts the easier it became to sniff out a decent news story. In fact my biggest coup came during a routine call, when a police officer mentioned in passing that he'd recently apprehended a couple for shoplifting from a city store. The detail that grabbed my attention immediately was that they'd taken their four-year-old son along with them and got him to stash the stolen goods down the sides of his wellington boots. The story duly made the front page of my paper, the *Sunday Independent* in Devon, and was splashed across the national papers the very next day.

Who? What? When? Where? Why? How?

Newspapers and magazines have changed out of all recognition during my 30 years in journalism. When it comes to covering a news story, however, the basic six questions are as essential as ever. Who? What? When? Where? Why? How? If you've asked these questions (known as the five Ws and one H) of your interviewees you won't go far wrong. Better still, if you keep them in mind when you're writing your copy you'll find it much easier to produce a well-rounded, informative story.

Cole Moreton, an award-winning interviewer who writes for the *Mail on Sunday*, always advises new and inexperienced journalists to keep 'the narrative strand' of a story in their head when they're working.

'For example if you're interviewing someone whose house has burned down the best way is to start by asking them what they were doing before they first smelled smoke and take them through the story chronologically,' he says. 'Ask them "what happened?" "What happened next?" "What happened next?"'

Another tip is to imagine you are relaying the incident to a friend. What are the salient details that you would tell them first? In Cole Moreton's scenario of a blazing house you would probably talk about the people who had tragically lost their lives or been injured in the fire, the individuals who raised the alarm, those who were rescued (and by whom), the extent of the damage and the possible cause of the fire. These are the 'top news lines' of your story – the details you need to include in the first few paragraphs when you come to write it.

The calls

Many journalists begin their careers as news reporters, learning interviewing skills they use throughout their working lives. As a news reporter, one of the first types of interview you are likely to do is what are known as 'the calls'.

When I started out in journalism the calls were an integral part of a news reporter's role. This meant calling the local police, fire, ambulance and coastguard services first thing every morning to check whether any stories were breaking on our patch (which included two coastal towns). It was a very effective way of making contacts and learning to get the relevant details of a story quickly and efficiently.

Reporters working for local and regional newspapers or for news agencies still do the calls, a task that requires you to be clear, confident and courteous to the people you are speaking to. Make sure, by the way, that you have the telephone numbers assigned for media calls and don't emulate the example of the Labour MP Owen Smith when he joined BBC Radio 4's *Today* programme in the 1990s. As the BBC website reported in 2016: 'Asked to call the police to check on a breaking story, the young producer stunned more experienced newsroom hands by dialling 999 to demand an interview with the chief constable.'[1]

In addition to phoning the police, fire and ambulance services, reporters also monitor social media channels, voicebanks (recorded messages featuring the latest news) and websites for news stories.

Twitter is a useful source of stories, so follow all the key agencies in your area – police, fire, ambulance, coastguard, local papers, local TV and radio – and check their Twitter feeds regularly. If you spot a tweet reporting a hit-and-run in your area, for instance, you can then check the details with the emergency services. You'll need to find out where the incident happened, whether people have been killed or injured (and if so, how many), which hospital they have been taken to and whether the road has been closed.

You are also likely to be asked to follow up tip-offs. News desks frequently receive tip-offs about stories – either by phone, email or in person. Tip-offs don't necessarily result in publishable stories but they still need to be checked out, just in case. Whether it's a tip-off about graffiti being scrawled across the front of the town hall or a tip-off about a fallen tree that's blocking a main road, you'll need to ask the six basic news questions. Who? What? When? Where? Why? How?

Getting people's names right

As well as learning to report and write stories journalists need to be fair, accurate and able to spell people's names correctly. Don't assume the subs will check spellings for you. Publications in the UK (unlike the US) don't use fact-checkers so you are responsible for ensuring that your work is correct. Indeed, if you're writing for an online publication your story may go live the moment you finish writing and upload it to the site. Save yourself the ignominy of hundreds of readers commenting on your mistake by checking and double-checking every detail before you file. Whatever the outlet, don't assume that Jane is spelled Jane or Ian is spelled Ian. Your interviewees could be Jayne and

Iain. Check their surnames with them, letter by letter. Is it Nixon, Nickson, Nicksen? Is it Mackenzie, MacKenzie, McKenzie, Mackensie?

If you get a name wrong, your readers will start to doubt the accuracy and authenticity of your work. Indeed, if you're working for a local paper, your readers might even call into the office to express their displeasure. I once covered a parish council meeting in Devon where the villagers were up in arms about double yellow lines being painted down the main street. I mistakenly reported that one councillor supported the idea and on the day the paper came out he marched into the office and shouted at me for getting his views wrong.

Phillip Knightley, who was a special correspondent for *The Sunday Times* for 20 years, recalled how he learned to be accurate as a reporter on the *Northern Star* in New South Wales, Australia. In *A Hack's Progress*, his book about his journalistic career, he explained that in those days reporters always interviewed people in person. 'The idea of interviewing someone on the telephone never occurred to us – we went out and met people face to face. We were part of the community. We knew everybody and everybody knew us. If I got someone's second initial wrong, they would stop me on the street to complain. If I got the whole story wrong, I would never hear the end of it. The *Northern Star* taught me to be accurate, that people had feelings, and that you could not use your privileged access as a journalist to come into their lives, suck them dry and then leave them. You had personal and civic responsibilities.'[2]

Accuracy also applies to the names of roads, streets, villages and towns. Unless you know for certain how they are spelled, check the spellings letter by letter. The English town of Middlesbrough, for instance, is frequently spelled wrong, as is Teesside, while the Scottish town of Penicuik is pronounced Pennycook and Bicester in Oxfordshire is pronounced Bister.

Geographical area

If you're working for a local publication make sure you are familiar with the geographical area it covers. Local newspapers, magazines and online media organisations tend to be strict about the geographical boundaries of their patch and won't feature stories a metre outside them.

National publications sometimes make a point of focusing on particular regions too, so always pay close attention to the brief given by your news editor or features editor. The legendary newspaper columnist and playwright Keith Waterhouse discovered this to his cost at the start of his journalistic career. Former *Daily Mirror* editor Mike Molloy recalled the story in his obituary of Waterhouse for the *Guardian* in 2009, describing how the features editor of the *Daily Mirror* offered

Waterhouse freelance shifts on the paper. One of Waterhouse's first assignments involved being sent out with instructions to find a talking dog.

Molloy wrote: 'Waterhouse called the office a few days later, announcing airily that he had fulfilled his brief. "Where's the dog?" snarled the features editor. "Cardiff," answered Waterhouse. "That's no bloody good," came the reply. "The circulation drive is in the north-west. Find me a talking dog in Liverpool!"'[3]

House style

At this juncture it's worth mentioning the house style of the publication you're writing for. Most publications have their own style guide, detailing everything from whether you should use single quotation marks or double quotation marks to words, clichés and phrases to avoid. When David Marsh retired from his job as production editor of the *Guardian* in 2016 he said that being responsible for the newspaper's style guide had been the role that had given him the most pleasure, although it had clearly been challenging.

His 20-year battle against clichés had ended in 'a score draw', he wrote. 'The problem is that, like the Hydra's heads, every time you think you've chopped one off, another sprouts up. You may feel you have "elephant in the room" and "fit for purpose" under control, then the writers suddenly discover "national treasure" and "game-changing".'[4]

The king of style guides, of course, was the aforementioned Keith Waterhouse, who as well as being a playwright and columnist was the author of *Waterhouse on Newspaper Style*,[5] a book he wrote in 1979 as a series of style notes for *Daily Mirror* journalists. If you can get hold of a copy (it was originally called *Daily Mirror Style: The Mirror's Way with Words*) it's an excellent guide to writing for newspapers and well worth reading.

Asking the right news questions

Learning to ask the right news questions is fairly straightforward. Below are two news scenarios, followed by the questions you would need to ask in order to write a competent news story.

Case study 1

The news desk of an evening newspaper receives a call saying there has been a gas explosion at a house in a residential area on your patch. The address is confirmed by calls to the police, fire and ambulance services. When you, the reporter, arrive at the scene, the immediate area has been cordoned off but you spot a neighbour standing in his front garden. What should you ask him?

After introducing yourself (give your name and the publication you work for) and saying a few sympathetic words, the most effective way to start is by asking: 'Please can you tell me what happened?' Take the neighbour through the events step by step and note down what he says (if you are working for an evening paper you won't have time to transcribe a recorded interview so taking notes is the best option).

Make sure you cover the following Who? What? When? Where? Why? How? questions, although not necessarily in that order.

- *Who* lives at the house where the explosion took place? If possible, check their names, ages and occupations. Were the householders in the house at the time of the explosion? Was anyone killed, injured or trapped? Did anyone try and rescue them – and if so, who? Don't forget to get the name of your interviewee, together with his age and occupation.
- *What* happened? Ask for a first-hand account of what the neighbour saw. Use simple and clear questions.
- *When* was the explosion? When did the neighbour notice that something was wrong? What did he see and hear?
- *Where* exactly was the explosion?
- *Why* did the explosion happen? You don't want to pre-empt any investigation, obviously, but eyewitnesses may have their own theories as to what caused it.
- *How* much damage has been caused? How are the owners of the property and the local community likely to be affected?

These questions will help you to build up a vivid and authentic story. The neighbour's account of what he saw will give you a good start but you will need to make additional calls to the police, fire and ambulance services to check/confirm whether anyone has been killed or injured and to get an official account of the incident. If possible, you should also speak to the owner of the house and, if the explosion could have been caused by a gas leak, for instance, to the relevant gas network.

The key to news interviewing is to have every angle covered. Get the contact details of everyone you talk to at the scene. The odds are that you will need to write a follow-up at a later date and the more contacts you have the easier your task will be.

Case study 2

The news desk of a weekly newspaper receives a call from a woman who wants to complain about traffic congestion in a small village in your area. More and more cars are using the village's narrow lanes as a cut-through to a dual carriageway and she's worried that the extra traffic could be dangerous for local residents. The news editor gives you the woman's details and asks you to check out the story.

The best way to follow up this story – time permitting – is to visit the village, see the problem for yourself and interview the woman and other villagers face to face. You will need to ask Who? What? When? Where? Why? and How?

- *Who* is unhappy about the traffic congestion? Get their basic details (name, age, occupation, address, how long they have lived in the village, whether they have any specific village responsibilities, such as sitting on the parish council, etc.).
- *What* is their complaint? Have the villagers surveyed the volume of traffic? Is the congestion worse at particular times of the day – and if so, when? Have there been any accidents?
- *When* did the congestion start?
- *Where* is the congestion? You will need to name and identify the roads involved.
- *Why* did the congestion start? Is there a particular reason for the additional traffic on the roads, such as the closure of another road or roadworks nearby?
- *How* do residents plan to show their concern? Have they contacted the council, started a petition and/or involved their local MP? Are they planning any meetings?

Once you have the answers to these questions (and some vivid quotes from the residents) it's important to get the views of other relevant parties, including the council. All councils have press or communications offices so contact them and they will put you in touch with the relevant council officers and councillors.

Practising the five Ws and one H

Here are two more examples of news stories, with the Who? What? When? Where? Why? How? questions you should ask.

News story 1

After laying flowers at her late husband's grave, a grieving widow finds that her bag containing cash and treasured family photographs has disappeared.

- *Who* is the widow? Find out as many details about her as you can – her age, address, details of her husband, when she was widowed. Who was the thief – or thieves? The police may have issued a description and/or photo-fit.
- *What* was stolen? You need details of the amount of cash, the photographs and anything else of sentimental value that have been taken.
- *When* did the theft take place? Find out the date and the time of day. Was the date significant in some way? It could, for example, have been the first anniversary of her husband's death or the date of their wedding anniversary. Specific details like these make the story more affecting and more memorable.
- *Where* did the theft take place? You need to know where the graveyard is. If you have time it might be useful to visit it yourself. You will then be able to describe whether it is busy, remote, well-kept or rundown.
- *Why* did the theft take place? Did the widow leave the items in her bag or in her car? Was she followed? Have there been thefts at the graveyard in the past?
- *How* did the theft take place? Was the graveyard deserted at the time of the theft? Was the widow distracted by the thief?

News story 2

A row is simmering over a planning application for a luxury block of flats in a busy high street.

- *Who* are the individuals, company or organisation seeking planning permission – and who are those protesting against it?
- *What* does the planning application entail? How many flats are planned? How many floors will the building have? What other amenities are planned (shops, parking, gym, swimming pool, etc.)?
- *When* are the key dates? When was the planning application submitted? When will a decision be made? If the application goes ahead, when will the flats be built?
- *Where* is the proposed development?
- *Why* are protesters so unhappy about it? Why do supporters think the flats should be built? It's crucial to get the views of both sides in order to write a balanced story.

- *How* are protesters planning to show their disapproval? How will supporters seek to convince the community that the flats will be beneficial for
  the area?

Interviewing task

Choose one of these news scenarios and think of six additional questions
to ask.

HOW I INTERVIEW: JUSTIN DAVENPORT

Justin Davenport has been the crime editor of the *Evening Standard* in London
for 20 years. He trained as a reporter on the *Marlborough Times*, a weekly
newspaper in Wiltshire, then moved to the *Swindon Evening Advertiser* and the
Western Daily Press in Bristol. He worked for the *Daily Mail* for seven years,
before switching to the *Evening Standard* to specialise in crime reporting. He is
one of a number of crime reporters featured in *We'll All be Murdered in Our
Beds! The Shocking History of Crime Reporting in Britain*, by former *Guardian*
crime reporter Duncan Campbell.

During his time at the *Evening Standard* Davenport has reported on the major
crime stories of the day, from the murder of TV presenter Jill Dando in 1999 to
the 7/7 terror attacks in London in 2005.

'There are two types of interview in news,' he says. 'The interviews I generally do
are simply talking to people about breaking news stories, interviewing people
who are involved in news events. But I also talk to people on a more formal
basis, interviewing police officers about their jobs, roles and current policing,
things like that. For example, I recently interviewed the commissioner of the
City of London Police about the scale of fraud in the UK.

'Crime is such a broad subject and you can't follow everything all the time so
the absolutely crucial thing for every interview is to prepare, prepare, prepare.
We have a very good online cuttings library at the *Evening Standard*, shared with
the *Daily Mail*, so I will research what the person I'm interviewing has done,
their areas of expertise and what they are responsible for. The cuttings library
covers everything in newspapers but these days there are so many online
stories so I will research online too. That can simply mean using Google but
obviously you have to be more cautious about the accuracy of the information.

'In a one-to-one interview I think it's important to try and make people feel at
ease, rather than just jumping in with confrontational questions. In my world
police are often suspicious of journalists so it is important to establish a
rapport.'

Keep an open mind

'I ask simple questions and really listen to what people are saying. You have got to be open and agile and keep an open mind. If someone says "It's all going well. Crime is down by such and such per cent but we have had a bit of an issue with phone snatches", I'll say "Hang on. What do you mean by that? What issue with phone snatches?" You want to try and get them to reveal something that they probably don't want to tell you and the best way to do that is to be sympathetic, open and ready to go where the interview takes you.'

For longer one-to-one interviews Davenport uses a voice recorder but the rest of the time he uses the 120 wpm Pitman's shorthand he learned as a trainee reporter. 'It's a very important skill, a great asset and much quicker – as long as you can write everything down and read it back.'

Davenport emphasises that it's vital to appear interested in what your interviewee is saying. 'You've got to look as though they are the most interesting person in the world. Also, if you don't understand something don't be afraid to ask for it to be explained and if you haven't got something down then say "I'm sorry, I didn't quite get that. Can you explain again?" It's totally fine to say that – remember that your interviewee wants to have what they're saying understood.'

Following the Leveson Inquiry, there is generally a press officer in the room when journalists interview police officers. 'It's the world we live in,' says Davenport. 'I went into an interview the other day with four police officers and two press officers and you just have to put up with press officers being there. You try and engage with the person you're interviewing and make sure they're talking to you rather than looking at the press officer.'

Sensitive or difficult questions

Davenport always makes a point of checking how much time his interviewee has got, then working out the most suitable moment to ask any sensitive or difficult questions. 'If you only have ten minutes then you've got to put in all the key questions very quickly. If you've got an hour you can spend time on general things and then put the more difficult questions in ten minutes before the end. You can't leave them till the very end though, because you risk the interviewee saying "Right, I'm out of time now. I'm off."'

Off-the-record police briefings are a thing of the past but Davenport advises that if an interviewee does say something 'off the record' it's important not to abuse it. 'As a specialist your reputation is the most crucial thing,' he says. 'If you have a reputation as someone who is not to be trusted, who breaks confidences in interviews, then people won't talk to you again. Word gets around, so you could destroy your own career by doing something like that.'

When it comes to breaking news stories a lot of his interviews are done on the phone – in an eye-wateringly tight timeframe.

'It's a matter of going back to the simple journalistic tenets of Who? What? When? Where? Why? How?,' says Davenport. 'One thing I learned when I started at the *Daily Mail* was that if you're talking to someone about an event the key questions are often the simple, obvious ones. "What happened?" "What was it like?" "How did it feel?" "What did you see?" They sound really banal but actually they produce the better quotes – things like "It was terrifying. I thought I was going to die."

'If I was reporting on a terrible accident I'd ring up, explain who I am and say that I'm sorry to trouble them. Then I'd say: "I understand there has been an accident. Did you see it?" If they say "yes," you ask what happened, what they saw and heard, what's happening now, what can they see now.

'It's important to be nice to people and to be compassionate but at the same time you've got to get the facts quickly. Sometimes you might only have 30 seconds if you're talking to someone at the scene. It's often just a snatched moment.'

Justin Davenport's top tip

In news reporting the key questions are often the simple, obvious ones. 'What happened?' 'What was it like?' 'How did it feel?' 'What did you see?'

Notes

1   B. Wheeler, 'Profile: the Owen Smith story', *BBC News*. Available from: www.bbc.co.uk/news/uk-politics-36834096 (accessed 26 August 2016).
2   P. Knightley, *A Hack's Progress*, Jonathan Cape, 1997, p. 13.
3   M. Molloy, 'Keith Waterhouse', *Guardian*. Available from: www.theguardian.com/media/2009/sep/04/keith-waterhouse-obituary (accessed 3 August 2016).
4   D. Marsh, 'Capital letters out, swearwords in: one journalist's legacy', *Guardian*. Available from: www.theguardian.com/media/mind-your-language/2016/aug/01/capital-letters-out-swearwords-in-one-journalists-legacy (accessed 26 February 2017).
5   K. Waterhouse, *Waterhouse on Newspaper Style*, Revel Barker, 2010.

4
Planning and preparation

You may have as little as five minutes to prepare for an interview or you may have a week. However much time you've got, you need to use it well. Read, research, plan and prepare as much as you can.

Before you start your research though, ask your news editor, commissioning editor or features editor for a brief. What exactly do they want from the interview they've asked you to do? The same applies if you're a freelance journalist and have been commissioned to write a piece by a newspaper, magazine or online publication. The last thing you want is to interview someone about one thing and discover at a later date that the editor was expecting something completely different. At the very least your brief should include the subject of the story, the angle, the interviews required, the word count and the deadline.

To give you an idea, below are excerpts from two recent features briefs from national newspapers – the first about apprenticeships and the second about private tutors.

> I'd like a 700-word piece on the accountancy sector and the higher-level apprenticeships on offer. It will mean talking to the big four accountancy firms and also the Institute of Chartered Accountants in England and Wales, then writing a news piece about the sense of momentum in the sector and a brief account of the different types of apprenticeships on offer. No jargon, please!

> Please write a feature about tutoring – why some parents opt for private tuition for their children and whether it makes any difference to the children's exam results. The piece is 1,000 words, aimed at parents and featuring the pros and cons of tutoring. I'd like you to interview parents, teachers and tutors and to include facts, figures and some recent research.

Both briefs tell the journalist exactly what is required – even down to the people to interview. The briefs are clear and to the point and, sure enough, the ensuing pieces were both published.

Fixing the interview

National newspapers tend to use dedicated 'fixers' to set up celebrity and high-profile interviews but most other journalists – and certainly those in the early stages of their careers – don't have that luxury. They still have to plan and fix their own interviews, from getting in touch with the interviewee in the first instance to persuading them to talk and arranging a time and place to meet.

If you're planning your first journalistic assignment it's important to remember that there are no set ways of fixing interviews. Sometimes a direct approach to the individual in question will work, while other people, particularly the rich and famous, will insist that you go via their agent, publicist, press officer or personal assistant (PA). Publicists will sometimes ask you to email all the details (and often a list of questions too) before the prospective interviewee makes up their mind whether to go ahead. Some writers baulk at the idea of sending questions in advance but it's up to you (and your editor) to make a judgement on this. After all, you could email your questions and get the interview or refuse to email your questions and risk losing the interview completely.

Another decision you must make is *how* to get in touch with the person you want to interview. Emails have made this far easier and feature writers almost always choose to email prospective interviewees. 'Email is a good approach, particularly for people who aren't celebrities, because it's a gentle way in,' says Cole Moreton. 'People are much more accessible online than they are by phone anyway and an email doesn't come as a shock like a phone call does.'

If you're working in news, however, you might not have time to wait for a reply to an email. You'll sometimes be required to ring the person – or to go and knock on their front door and do the interview there and then (see the section on doorstepping in Chapter 2).

If you decide to ring a prospective interviewee the secret is to be 100 per cent prepared. They may be happy to do an interview immediately, so you need to have a good set of questions at the ready. It's unlikely that you'll get straight through to a high-profile figure on the phone, but occasionally you might, so have a clear idea of what you want to ask them.

The same goes for 'off-the-cuff' interviews, where you manage to get a chat with an interviewee without fixing up an interview beforehand.

Newspaper diarists, for example, find many of their stories at book launches, film premieres and society parties and are past masters at impromptu interviews. As they sip champagne and nibble on canapés, they're on the *qui vive* at all times, ready to ask the type of questions that might result in a diary item.

Left-field questions – unconventional questions that produce intriguing or unexpected answers – often work on these occasions, as *The Times* writer Patrick Kidd reported in a diary column in 2016. Kidd's story was about the experience of veteran journalist John McEntee when he interviewed the Swedish film star Britt Ekland back in the 1980s. Kidd explained that diarists are often 'asked to put an idiotic question to a celebrity' and related how the *Evening Standard* diary editor once despatched McEntee to interview Ekland, who was appearing in panto at the time.

'"What shall I say?" McEntee asked his boss. "Ask her about Salman Rushdie's fatwa" was the facetious reply. It was 1989 and the tetchy Ayatollah Khomeini was in the papers.'

McEntee, who wrote about his years as a diarist in *I'm Not One to Gossip, But . . .*, duly put the question to the former Bond girl. After the journalist explained the controversy of *The Satanic Verses* to her she declared that if the Ayatollah was there, she'd punch him on the nose. McEntee wrote the story and next day got a call from Ekland. '"At last," she said. "Someone has taken me seriously."'[1]

Tracking people down

If you're finding it difficult to track down the individual you want to interview by phone or email try social media. Most people have a Twitter or Instagram account and these can be an efficient way of messaging them. I've frequently followed people I want to interview on Twitter, asked them to follow me back and then sent them a direct message outlining the details of the publication I'm working for and the interview I'd like to do. This is a better approach than tweeting an interview request that the whole world can see.

Former *News of the World* and *Daily Mirror* editor Piers Morgan enthused about the effectiveness of Twitter in fixing interviews for his CNN chat show, *Piers Morgan Live*, in his book, *Shooting Straight*.

'Someone tweeted that they'd love me to interview Jessica Alba for the show.
I retweeted, with the comment, "I agree, she'd be fantastic . . ."
And minutes later, Jessica tweeted back, "Thank u, I'd be honoured!"
As simple as that. No agents, managers, publicists, lawyers.
Just one quick Twitter exchange and the deal was done.
As a news source, Twitter's extraordinary.'[2]

Similarly, most websites and blogs include contact details, so use them. They are a very effective way to reach people quickly.

Persistence is key

Once you have decided who you are going to interview (it could be your own idea or that of your editor, news editor or features editor) and how to contact them, the challenge is to persuade the individual in question to talk to you. It helps, of course, if your publication has an excellent reputation and a healthy circulation (publicists sometimes ask to see a copy of the publication and its readership figures before considering interview requests) and you have a good reputation as a journalist. PRs may want to see some of the pieces you have written in the past before they make their decision. If this happens, choose your material wisely. If you're seeking an interview with a hyper-sensitive celebrity who is used to being garlanded with praise, don't send a hard-hitting profile that doesn't pull its punches.

But how do you secure an interview if you're completely unknown and have a dearth of journalistic assignments and by-lines to your name?

First of all, don't lose heart. Put yourself in your prospective interviewee's shoes and work out what will persuade them to say 'yes'. Figure out why they should do the interview. In other words, what's in it for them? It could be publicity for their new project, the chance to raise their profile or the opportunity to put their side of the story. Author and former *Daily Telegraph* journalist Wendy Holden says some people find it 'therapeutic' to talk to a stranger about their experiences. Indeed, when journalist Miranda Sawyer asked Olympic cyclist Sir Bradley Wiggins in an interview for *Red* magazine if he'd ever had therapy he replied: 'No, I've never had therapy. I do interviews instead.'[3] He was no doubt joking, but whatever the reason for requesting an interview with someone, you need to convince them that *you're* the person they should be talking to – and no-one else.

If you're approaching an individual, company or organisation with an agent, press officer or PR, phone or email the agent to outline your request. Writing a letter is less common these days, largely because of time constraints, but it's worth trying if phone calls, emails and tweets fail to elicit a response. As a child I was hugely entertained by a delightful letter that Margaret Thatcher's husband Denis sent to my mother following her request for an interview. 'The answer to your ever charming request for an interview is, of course, no,' wrote Sir Denis politely but firmly in spidery writing.

Camilla Long, the award-winning *Sunday Times* interviewer, columnist and film critic, usually emails people she wants to interview but in some cases will send a handwritten letter to their home address – 'particularly politicians, who are quite difficult to pin down,' she says. 'Most politicians monitor their emails but if I'm trying to get hold of somebody who doesn't or who has a massive team around them, I just write to their home address.'

Agents and PRs may ask you countless questions before they agree to set up an interview with a well-known figure. If so, write a concise email explaining why you want to interview the individual in question, giving details of your publication and its circulation, a couple of lines about yourself, the amount of time you will need for the interview and when you need to do it by.

'I try to make the case that I am the best person to interview them – either because I have some special interest in the subject or perhaps by some quirk of background that might win their sympathy,' says award-winning freelance Emma Brockes, who writes for the *Guardian* and the *New York Times*. 'You have to try and get them to think of you as a real person and make a connection with them.'

If your interview request is turned down

If your request for an interview is refused don't assume that all is lost. When Phillip Knightley arrived in the UK from Australia he began freelancing for *The Sunday Times*. On one occasion he was asked to follow up a lead about Eton College appointing its own public relations officer for the first time. He failed to get an interview with the PR but to his intense mortification another *Sunday Times* journalist succeeded.

The next week Knightley received the following advice from colleague Nicholas Tomalin, the editor of Atticus (the paper's diary). Tomalin, one of the legendary journalists of his era, was killed while reporting on the Yom Kippur War in 1973.

As Knightley recalled in his memoir, *A Hack's Progress*: 'Tomalin came straight to the point. "You lost that Eton story because you gave up too soon," he said. "An important lesson for journalists – most people are modest or like to give that impression. So when you want to put them in the limelight they'll say no. But they don't mean it. They're waiting for you to ask again, so that finally they can surrender gracefully and modestly. That PR was delighted to be asked to be interviewed for Atticus but he felt he had to say no as a matter of form and he was deeply disappointed when you took his no as final. Lesson: in journalism, no no is ever final."'[4]

In his book Knightley declared that the advice had a 'resounding effect' on his career. One of his later scoops was an interview with the Soviet spy Kim Philby in Moscow in 1988, just before Philby died. Knightley had been corresponding with him for more than 20 years – and his tenacity paid off.

Your place or mine?

Once an interviewee has agreed to do an interview you'll need to fix the time and the place. The chances are that if you're interviewing a well-known figure you won't be given a choice about the location, but if you're able to choose the place yourself always opt for somewhere quiet and peaceful. Keep a note of good places to conduct an interview. My personal favourites in London include the British Library and the Southbank Centre, both of which have loads of room, quiet corners, long opening hours, are open to all and sell tea, coffee and drinks. Other journalists choose bars, restaurants and members' clubs, such as the Century Club in London's Shaftesbury Avenue and the House of St Barnabas in nearby Soho Square, a not-for-profit members' club run to support homeless people in London into work. If you're stuck for ideas it's definitely worth asking journalistic colleagues for recommendations and building up your own list.

If you're interviewing over lunch it's vital to book a quiet restaurant and have a good-quality voice recorder (and/or iPhone). Beware of crowded pubs and cafés, or anywhere with music. You'll pay the price when it comes to transcribing your tape and realise you can't make out a word over the din. If by any chance the location you've chosen turns out to have loud music blaring and children yelling, either ask for a quieter table or move next door.

Experienced journalists tend to choose the same restaurants time and time again, usually reserving a table in the corner where waiting staff know not to disturb them. If you're taking notes as well as recording the interview choose something easy to eat and don't even think of ordering spaghetti, complicated seafood or anything with chopsticks. A well-known journalist told me she always orders scampi, because she can prong it with her fork in one hand while taking notes with the other. 'If I don't eat at all it embarrasses the person I'm interviewing – so I have to order something, even if I don't eat much.'

The Times columnist and interviewer Janice Turner takes a similar approach, ordering something off the menu she 'can tackle with one hand'. She also reckons that lunch interviews are 'more elastic' time wise. After all, she wrote in her column, 'it is hard for a PR to insist upon a rigid hour when service is slow or for your subject to storm out, making a scene'.[5]

Emma Brockes prefers not to interview people over lunch at all. 'When I do an interview over lunch I enjoy myself too much and you're not there to enjoy it,' she says. 'There's an argument that it feels like a more naturalistic encounter but you keep being interrupted and I would rather focus on the interview.

'I think it's a bad idea to have a glass of wine too, because you need to be really sharp and keep your wits about you. I suppose if you were interviewing a *bon viveur* and you felt they would be more likely to relax if you joined them in a glass of wine then you would do it tactically but on the whole I don't.'

Heidi Blake suggests letting your interviewee choose where to meet – 'because they are likely to feel comfortable there'. On the other hand, she adds, it sometimes works 'to take people out of their comfort zone because then they are more on your turf and you can call the shots a little bit more'. She also reckons that taking them 'somewhere really nice' works. 'Take them to a nice environment where they are going to be relaxed and able to enjoy themselves – and more likely to let their guard down and start chatting to you.'

Interviews at home

If you get the chance to interview someone at home seize the chance immediately. Interviewing individuals in their own houses is like interview gold dust. For a start interviewees tend to feel far more relaxed on their home turf. Equally importantly, interviewing an individual at home enables the journalist to observe their taste in interior décor, the family photographs on display and the books and magazines they read – all grist to the journalistic mill. When Emily Sheffield interviewed Victoria Beckham for *Vogue* magazine in 2014 she was granted a fascinating insight into the Beckhams' family life in west London, complete with holiday snaps on the mantelpiece, Damien Hirst butterfly paintings on the walls and a garden with a football net.

'Safely inside, Victoria is welcoming and cheerful, while she ushers sleepy-eyed Cruz and Romeo, both dressed in football strips, to their weekly practice,' wrote Sheffield. '"Work hard, boys," she instructs. She picks up Harper, a gorgeous little thing in a floral-print nightie who is gently twisting her ash-blonde hair under her chin . . .'[6]

The writer Chrissy Iley, who specialises in interviewing Hollywood superstars, remarked on the types of detail journalists can glean when they interview people at home. After interviewing the actor Dominic West for *The Sunday Times* magazine in 2016, Iley described Dominic's arrival home from the school run. 'He's instantly attentive and makes me a coffee. I'm not sure why actors invite journalists into their homes; it seems to be asking for trouble. Who doesn't want to know what their bathroom's like? Or what books they read? Or if they're tidy or chaotic?'[7]

Journalism lecturer and coach Susan Grossman gives a lot of thought to choosing the right location for an interview. In the early years of her career she interviewed the romantic novelist Dame Barbara Cartland at home, with Cartland lounging on the sofa where she dictated her novels to her secretary and a dining table laden with pink meringues. Another memorable interview was with Dame Gracie Fields at her house on the Isle of Capri. As Grossman left the island by boat after the interview the legendary singer stood at the shore and sang the famous songs she'd used to entertain the troops during the Second World War.

'I often ask the interviewee where they would like to be interviewed,' says Grossman. 'If you are interviewing Mary Berry (the food writer and TV presenter) about food it would make sense to be in her kitchen whereas if you are talking to a business leader about work there's no point in interviewing them on a Sunday morning on their sofa with the dog. Tell them in what capacity you are interviewing them (as head of the firm or a lover of fine art, for example) so that they can relax.'

Freelance writer Stephanie Rafanelli offers interviewees the chance to suggest the location too. 'I want the person I'm interviewing to feel comfortable,' she says. 'At their home is the ideal but not always possible so I always ask first if they have a local they'd like to go to. A sense of intimacy is key. Hotel suites are the worst, but sometimes unavoidable.'

When Rafanelli interviewed Julianne Moore for *Stylist* magazine, the Oscar-winning star suggested meeting at her local café in New York. 'I got there 45 minutes early and they all knew her really well,' Rafanelli recalls. 'They were saying things like "Oh, Julie doesn't like the table in the window because of the paps". You can tell a lot about someone from their choice of location and I got a real sense of her.'

Here is the first line of Rafanelli's piece: 'When she blows in with the pre-blizzard wind – in a black mohair beanie and shearling jacket – she is only unsettled because she is six minutes late (for which she apologises profusely).'[8]

She went on to describe the café as 'the extended living room' of Moore's nearby townhouse and said the staff were 'all on first name terms' with her – small details that succeeded in giving the reader real insight into her character.

Asking your interviewee where they'd like to meet sometimes leads to unusual suggestions – and may give you your intro. When Hermione Eyre interviewed Cara Delevingne for *Vogue* magazine in 2016 the supermodel came up with the idea of doing the interview on a trapeze wire.

'Please, Cara. Not the deathslide,' wrote Eyre. 'Cara Delevingne and I are suspended 40ft from the ground, halfway round Go Ape, a high-wire adventure circuit in Battersea Park – her idea of a relaxing afternoon. She leaps insouciantly across wobbly rope bridges and wire-walks gracefully over the tops of trees.'[9]

Similarly, *Sunday Times* journalist Camilla Long interviewed Eddie Izzard on the first leg of his nineteenth marathon for Comic Relief. This was her intro: 'Well, this is a first: interviewing at a run. On the crest of a hill just south of Penrith, Eddie Izzard and I are four miles into his 19th marathon, running a six-mile leg together while he is part of the way through his astonishing 1,000-mile run around Britain.'[10]

When and how long?

Some journalists reckon that interviewees are more benevolent, chatty and relaxed after lunch – so prefer to do afternoon interviews.

Your own deadline may dictate the best time for the interview too. If you work for an evening newspaper, for example, the earlier in the day the better – especially if you're filing a news story for the next edition.

It's customary to discuss how long you need for the interview. Once you've done a few interviews you'll get a feel for the length of time you need although in practice people don't necessarily cut interviews short because you've reached the allotted time. A BBC Radio 5 live presenter once told a freelance journalist that he could spare 15 minutes for an interview. Forty-five minutes later they were still talking and the journalist remarked that he'd been generous with his time. 'I just wanted to be able to get rid of you if necessary,' said the presenter. This doesn't apply, incidentally, to interviews with Hollywood stars, which are tightly controlled and rarely over-run.

This may sound obvious, but when scheduling interviews, exchange mobile phone numbers and emails if you don't have them already, so you can make contact if there are any hitches, i.e. if either of you is late or has to cancel or reschedule.

Doing your research

In a speech at the BBC College of Journalism in 2011 Dame Jenni Murray, the presenter of BBC Radio 4's *Woman's Hour*, said that solid research before an interview is crucial. She was right, although the amount of time you will have to research will depend on your deadline and the publication you are working for. If you're working for an online news organisation you may only have a few minutes. If you're working for a monthly magazine you may have a few days. Either way, the key is to use your time wisely. You need to find out as much as you can about your interviewee before you talk to them – so Google them, read previous media coverage, look at their website, LinkedIn profile, Facebook page, YouTube videos, Twitter and Instagram feeds and/or blog and, where possible, talk to other people who have met them (fellow journalists in your office can be a fount of knowledge). BuzzFeed UK investigations editor Heidi Blake points out that 'people have a big online footprint now' so you can 'get a sense of the nature of the person you are going to talk to' before you speak to them.

Even if you're working on a breaking news story, with limited time and opportunity to do any research beforehand, take a few moments to check key facts and figures. If you're being sent out of the office to report on an incident at an airport, for instance, equip yourself with a few important details before you arrive. How many terminals does the airport have? How many airlines use the airport? How many planes take off and land there every day? How many passengers use the airport in a day/week/month/year?

Don't forget to check your own publication's coverage of the news story. Talk to colleagues with knowledge of the story and use search engines and social media to get up to speed. In this day and age there's no excuse not to have a raft of background information before you start.

Never simply rely on Wikipedia – in fact 'don't rely on *anything* as an infallible source', advises Tony Harcup in *Journalism: Principles and Practice*.[11] Many journalists are hard-pressed for time these days – according to the Reuters Institute for the Study of Journalism at the University of Oxford, the majority of today's UK journalists (86 per cent) believe that the time available for researching stories has decreased in recent years[12] – but do as much research as you can. Even if you are tight for time those five minutes of research will pay dividends in the long run.

Another word of warning. When you read previous media coverage, either online or in print, remember that this should only be a starting point. Rather than relying on someone else's work, you should always check the facts with your interviewee, unless of course they are obvious or common knowledge. If an existing article contains a libellous statement and you republish it you may still be liable. As *McNae's Essential Law for Journalists* points out: 'Every repetition of a libel is a fresh publication and creates a fresh cause of action. This is called the repetition rule. It is no defence to say that you, the publisher, are not liable because you are only repeating the words of others.'[13]

Read as much as you can

For features you will usually have longer to prepare. *Sunday Times* interviewer Camilla Long reads as much as she can beforehand. 'If I can read books that's an amazing starting point,' she says. 'I personally don't think there is such a thing as too much preparation. It's better to be forewarned, simply because there is nothing worse than being fed a whole load of lies that they may have been trotting out in other interviews or thinking that you've got an amazing scoop, only to discover that they wrote about it in their autobiography five years ago.'

If the theme of your piece is a general one – such as the top music festivals in Europe or the future of the farming industry – you will need to find experts who are articulate and willing to help. Talk to colleagues, contacts and PRs, use search engines and ask companies, charities and organisations with expertise in the area you're writing about. Join journalists' groups on LinkedIn and Facebook and ask if anyone has useful contacts or suggestions. In my experience most journalists are delighted to help, mindful of the fact that it could well be them asking for assistance next time round.

If your interview subject is in the public eye – a politician, an actor or a sports personality perhaps – read as many previous interviews, reviews and reports as possible. If they've written an autobiography, get hold of a copy from the publisher. If the interview is timed to coincide with a forthcoming film or TV series ring the relevant film or TV company and arrange to go to a screening. Talk to their fans, critics, agents, directors, partners and friends to glean as much background as you can. Don't skimp on your research just because you've only been granted a short interview either. When Cole Moreton interviewed Sir Richard Branson for the *Mail on Sunday*'s *Event* magazine in 2016 he spent two days preparing for a conversation of 22 minutes. Why? Because, as he explained, if you aren't familiar with your interviewee's background you risk missing the significance and resonance of a key remark.

Don't forget, either, that you're going to be writing a journalistic feature, not an essay or a university dissertation. Once you've done a reasonable amount of research, pause. Imagine you are the editor, features editor or, most importantly, a reader. What would they want to know? Where are the gaps? What are the areas that interviewers haven't covered in the past? What questions hasn't the person answered before? What would readers want to ask if they were in your shoes? These are the questions that will turn your interview with an individual who may have been interviewed countless times before into a must-read, even an exclusive story.

When Piers Morgan was interviewed ahead of the launch of his CNN chat show, he said he always researched very thoroughly. Recalling the interview in *Shooting Straight*, he wrote: 'I would hate to have a moment with a guest where they know you don't know about a key aspect of their life because you haven't bothered to find out. I think as a journalist, I see it as a prerequisite of the job to be very well briefed. Having said that, I love spontaneity and I think on television, with an interview, you can get some of the best moments from silence or from a "Whoa, what did you say?" Anything that makes it suddenly feel unscripted, that makes it go veering off from what the viewer at home assumes is a nice, cosy setup.'[14]

What to ask

Before you do the interview, work out what you need – and want – to know. List your questions and the topics you want to cover. In most cases, your editor's brief will give you the angles you need to cover and your research will highlight the areas you need to talk about. The exact questions, however, are down to you.

If you're working in news a few lines from an editorial written by *Brighton Argus* editor Mike Gilson in 2016 may inspire you. In his piece, entitled 'Why journalists must always be a nuisance', he expressed his concern that journalists have 'forgotten' their primary role. 'That is to obtain information and pass it on to you, our readers,' he wrote, 'to tell you things you didn't know . . . A good journalist must also expose wrongdoing, question our leaders, examine policy, put the powerful on the spot, make a nuisance of themselves.'[15]

Write your questions down on a separate sheet of paper or an iPad ahead of the interview. Don't write them in your notebook – it's useful to be able to see the questions throughout the interview (although some interviewers don't consult them at all). Even if you don't follow your list exactly, simply having a variety of questions at the ready in case your mind goes blank will give you confidence. Some experts suggest numbering your questions and putting the question number next to the answer during the interview. I'm not convinced by this – there's quite enough to think about during an interview without complicating it further. As you get more experienced you might not need to write all your questions down at all but it's helpful to have a prompt or reminder. As mentioned earlier, Camilla Long doesn't consult her list during interviews but takes a moment at the end to check she's covered all the points she wanted to raise.

When you're planning your questions try and think of the shape of the interview. Make an effort to structure it in a logical fashion – i.e. don't jump back and forth in a confusing way. Start with an easy, uncontroversial question. This might include asking an author about the inspiration for their new book, a plot summary (always make it clear that you've read the book but that you'd like them to sum it up in their own words) and the readership they think it will appeal to. A few straightforward questions will get you and your interviewee warmed up and into the flow of the conversation. Leave the more sensitive questions till later on in the interview (but not too late or you risk not getting the chance to ask them at all).

For feature and profile writing it's a good idea to have a few supplementary questions up your sleeve, just in case you run out of questions or the conversation dries up. Camilla Long keeps a file of 'trigger questions' that will 'kick-start' any interview and prompt an interesting response. She doesn't necessarily use them but she's got them to hand if she needs them. They include: 'Is there life after death?' 'Have you ever punched anyone?' 'Have you ever been arrested?' 'What is your earliest memory?' 'If you're very desperate and the person you are interviewing is very, very monosyllabic you could try to get them to go through their day,' she says. 'But that's definitely an "only use in the event of an emergency question."'

Stephanie Rafanelli's favourite questions include: 'How are you like your father?' 'How are you like your mother?' 'What was the hardest thing about that time?' 'I'm a frustrated psychotherapist really,' Rafanelli says. 'You can tell so much about someone from the relationship with their mother and father. These are the dynamics that often inform and motivate their adult life.'

In an interview with the *New York Times* the US broadcast journalist Barbara Walters, best known for hosting TV shows like *Today*, *The View* and *20/20*, once revealed her five 'foolproof' questions. They were: 'If you were recuperating in a hospital, who would you want in the bed next to you, excluding relatives?' 'What was your last job?' 'When was the last time you cried?' 'Who was the first person you ever loved?' 'What has given you the most pleasure in the last year?' Having said that, when the *New York Times* asked how she would answer her own questions she sidestepped them altogether, saying it would take too long.[16]

Before you interview someone take a long, hard look at the areas you want to talk about and the questions you've prepared. Your questions need to be fresh and interesting – the very best you can think of. After all, if you're bored when you ask them the chances are that your interviewee will be bored when it comes to answering them.

If you need some new ideas, take heart from the group of journalists who turned up to interview a man who was planning to do a charity walk around the coastline of the UK. They duly started asking him questions. 'When will you set off?' 'What is your route?' 'How long will the walk take?' 'How many miles will you walk a day?' 'Where will you stay?' 'How much do you expect to raise for charity?' The questions were perfectly valid, but he had answered them hundreds of times before. Then out of the blue someone asked: 'What about your *feet?* At that point the interview shifted into a different gear. The man's eyes lit up with interest – and the story took off like a rocket.

To get you thinking, here are a variety of questions that have worked for journalists in the past (others are mentioned in the 'How I interview' sections of this book). Remember to phrase these suggested questions in your own words and in your own style though. There is no point in using other people's questions like a script; you need, as contestants on TV's *The X Factor* proudly declare, to make each question 'your own'.

'What is your best quality?'
'What is your worst fault?'
'Who has been the greatest influence on you?'
'Do you have a pet hate?'
'What drives (or motivates) you?'
'If money was no object and you could change one thing in the world what would it be?'
'What's your motto?'
'Where do you expect to be in five years time?'
'What's the most important lesson you've learned in your life?'
'How do you handle disappointment?'
'Who is your hero or heroine?'
'What three words would you use to describe yourself?'
'If you knew you were going to die tomorrow, what would you do tonight?'

Another way to come up with great questions is to seek inspiration from the vast array of Q&A features in newspapers and magazines. Below are a few questions writer Hester Lacey asked conservationist and TV presenter Chris Packham for the *FT Weekend* magazine:[17]

'What was your childhood or earliest ambition?'
'How physically fit are you?'
'Ambition or talent: which matters more to success?'
'What's your biggest extravagance?'
'In what place are you happiest?'
'If your 20-year-old self could see you now, what would he think?'

Meanwhile journalist Colin Crummy asked the comedian and writer Katy Brand questions like these for *Stylist's* 5 Minute Philosopher feature:

'What is the meaning of life?'
'What is the difference between right and wrong?'
'Is it more important to be liked or respected?'
'When did you last lie?'

'What is your greatest fear?'
And for a little light relief: 'Quinoa or Quavers?'[18]

In a similar vein, *The Sunday Times* magazine puts interviewees on the spot by asking interviewees a few extra questions as part of its popular 'A life in the day' feature. Recent examples include the following: 'The best advice I was given', 'Advice I'd give' and 'What I wish I'd known'.

Questions don't necessarily have to be clever or sophisticated. The simplest questions often turn out to be the most newsworthy. Mumsnet's innocuous 'What is your favourite biscuit?' flummoxed former prime minister Gordon Brown, who was criticised for sidestepping the question during an online chat in 2009. Since then the question has become a tradition on Mumsnet, with David Cameron declaring that he likes 'oatcakes with butter and cheese' and Boris Johnson opting for chocolate digestives.[19]

Once you've worked out the questions you want to ask you will probably have an excellent feel for what you want to achieve from the interview. If you're worried about forgetting to ask the most important questions it may help to put an asterisk next to them or to underline them. Leave plenty of space on the page so the questions are legible, rather than a messy scrawl that you can't decipher. It's perfectly reasonable, too, to say to your interviewee at the end of your allotted time 'Do you mind if I just check that I've got everything I need?' and consult your list.

Dress appropriately

It's common sense really. Dress in a way that suits your interviewee and the occasion. That means not dressing up to the nines if you're interviewing a sheep farmer in the middle of the countryside (more to the point, take along a pair of flat shoes or boots, the muddier the better) and not turning up in shorts and a T-shirt for an interview at a posh hotel. If freelance writer Stephanie Rafanelli is interviewing a politician, for instance, she won't turn up 'in my most fabulous Miu Miu print trousers'. But, she adds, 'sometimes it's a talking point if you have a great pair of shoes or a scarf on'.

Heidi Blake reckons that it's a good idea to be 'slightly chameleon-like' and tailor your clothes and manner to the person you are interviewing. In other words, she says: 'If you are going to a meeting with an old school tie type, a major general or someone like that, then go booted and suited and look smart. Write to them first on headed notepaper and when you meet them keep a straight back and be formal. If you are going to talk to a millennial who is much more comfortable chatting on social media then they'll be happier if you turn up in jeans and Converse trainers.'

'I'm not saying you should go along and be someone that you're not,' adds Blake, 'but it's good manners to dress appropriately for the occasion so the person you're talking to feels comfortable. It's just about adapting a little bit.'

Lance Samson, my inspirational first editor (and father of the novelist Polly Samson), insisted that journalists should always look smart in the *Mid-Devon Advertiser* news room, whether they were interviewing or not. One day he sent a fellow reporter home for wearing a polo-neck jumper instead of a shirt and tie. 'How could I send you to interview the Archbishop of Canterbury dressed like that?' he demanded. This was highly unlikely considering we were based in a sleepy market town where the most exciting thing to happen most weeks was the planning committee meeting, but we got the point.

What to take with you

Most of the following is obvious but if you're interviewing someone face to face it's a good idea to check you've got everything you need before you set off. Don't arrive looking harassed and stressed or laden down with suitcases or bags of shopping either – it looks unprofessional.

You will need the following:

- Voice recorder/phone – fully charged and ready to go. Many interviewers take two recorders, just in case one breaks down.
- Spare batteries.
- Notebook (plus a spare if the current one is nearly full) – some journalists prefer traditional spiral-bound reporter's notebooks they can tuck in their pockets while others choose A4 versions (you need to turn the pages less often).
- Pens/pencils – nothing screams 'unprofessional' more than if you have to borrow a pen. Obvious as it sounds, choose a pen or pencil that enables you to write fast – a gel or rollerball pen, for instance, that glides over the pages.
- List of questions or crib-sheet.
- Research notes/cuttings – in case you're early and want to glance at them again.
- Headphones and laptop – if time is tight and you have to file quickly you can download your interview and start transcribing on the way back to the office.

- Business cards – these can be helpful if your interviewee is likely to be a useful contact in the future. If you give them yours they are more likely to give you theirs.
- Contact details for your interviewee, including telephone number, email, address and directions on how to get to the interview venue.
- A copy of the newspaper or magazine you write for – interviewees sometimes ask to see an issue, especially if it's a niche publication that they might not have seen before. It's a good idea, too, to be clued up about the numbers of readers and when the piece you're writing might appear.

Interviewing task

It's useful to keep a list of supplementary questions, just in case the conversation with an interviewee dries up or you run out of questions. Write six 'trigger questions' – questions that you will be able to ask when an interviewee you are profiling for a feature is monosyllabic or unforthcoming. File them away afterwards. You never know when you might need them.

HOW I INTERVIEW: SHERON BOYLE

Sheron Boyle is one of the UK's most respected freelance journalists. She trained as a reporter on the *Halifax Evening Courier*, then worked for the *Yorkshire Evening Post* for six years.

She has been a freelance for more than 20 years and specialises in human-interest stories, particularly crime and health. She has thousands of by-lines to her name, from stories about the Yorkshire Ripper and his victims to exclusive interviews with people like Christine Freeman, the police family liaison officer who was with the family of missing nine-year-old Shannon Matthews 'around the clock' from the day the little girl vanished from her home in Dewsbury, West Yorkshire in 2008. It later emerged that her 24-day disappearance was a hoax kidnapping organised by Shannon's mother Karen Matthews.

Ordinary people have extraordinary stories

Unlike many staff reporters and feature writers, Sheron Boyle doesn't follow the crowd. She's a talented self-starter who comes up with her own ideas, rather than being handed stories on a plate by the newspapers and magazines she works for. She doesn't do celebrity interviews either, 'because ordinary people have the most extraordinary stories. I love hearing them and I love telling them.'

Her enthusiasm for people's stories extends to her own family. She was so fascinated by the story of her own grandmother, who was due to sail on the Titanic in 1912 but cancelled her passage, that she wrote several newspaper articles about it. 'She was just an ordinary woman,' says Boyle, 'but it was an extraordinary story.'

'Journalism is a licence to be nosy, a licence to look through the lace curtains,' Boyle adds. 'We get the chance to ask the questions that other people would like to ask but are too polite to. We're lucky because we can do it professionally.'

She believes that spotting stories and then getting people to talk about them are the two key aspects of interviewing.

'I find 99 per cent of my own work and I'm pretty good at spotting a story. That's probably one of my strengths. What fascinates me about criminals is to find out what made them do it and how the people around them cope. I always want to look at the story behind the story.

'I've never hunted with the pack. When the Shannon Matthews story broke I knew all the staffers and all the agencies would be there so I left it. I went to the trial though and saw Karen Matthews give evidence. I wanted to get a feel for what was going on and I interviewed Christine Freeman, the family liaison officer. She was the window into Shannon Matthews's home life – the story behind the story. She was a woman who was doing her job professionally, possibly supporting the mother of a kidnap victim, but her instinct told her that Karen Matthews had something to do with it.'

Another example of how Boyle comes up with ideas for interviews is the case of WPC Sharon Beshenivsky, who was gunned down in the line of duty in 2005. The policewoman had been preparing to celebrate her daughter's fourth birthday on 18 November 2005 when she answered a call to a robbery at a Bradford travel agency. The call had a tragic outcome. Sharon, who had only joined the police nine months earlier, was shot in the chest, while the seven-strong gang escaped with £5,000 in cash.

Boyle's exclusive two-part interview with the policewoman's children, Lydia and Paul, was published in the *Sunday* and *Daily Mirror* on the tenth anniversary of her death. This was the intro to the heart-rending piece: 'When asked what she can remember of her mum, 13-year-old Lydia Beshenivsky shakes her head and looks down. Tears fill her eyes as she gives her heartbreaking reply.

'"Nothing, I have no memories," she says quietly. "I've been cheated, haven't I? Her murderers were heartless."'[20]

'I never covered this story while it was happening,' says Boyle. 'I never covered the trial but I did watch Sharon's funeral on Sky News. I watched her best friend pay tribute to Sharon and I remember thinking "everybody's got a best friend. She must know more about Sharon than anyone other than her husband." So I found Sharon's best friend and interviewed her. I knew every woman would relate to the story of how you cope with losing your best friend. They skipped into school together on the first day, they compared teenage dates and they swapped clothes.'

Boyle usually approaches her interviewees by phone in the first instance ('I rarely write letters') but will sometimes go and knock on their door. She often emails examples of her work to them so they can see the calibre of her journalism.

Before an interview she does as much research and preparation as she can. 'If I'm going to interview someone about their family I tend to write down their names and ages so I get an idea of who's who,' she says. 'If I'm interviewing a family where someone has been murdered I will get all the dates written down because I think it would look shabby to say "I'm sorry to hear that your son died in June 2014", when in fact it was October 2009. It's sloppy journalism. It's important to get your facts straight.'

Boyle does some of her 'best thinking' in the car on the way to interviews. 'I'll mull over what would be interesting. So, for example, when I interviewed the family liaison officer in the Shannon Matthews case I said: "When did your instinct kick in that Karen Matthews was guilty? What was the turning point?"'

Here are a couple of lines from Boyle's interview for the *Sun* with Christine Freeman, detailing the moment Karen Matthews unexpectedly started dancing around her sitting room.

'Immediately, the seed of suspicion was planted in my mind. I've questioned myself since – why didn't I challenge her more and trust my instinct? But I was between a rock and a hard place, because if Shannon had been found dead I'd have felt awful . . .'[21]

Journalism is about people's stories

'I think myself into the position of the reader,' says Boyle. 'What would I want to know? If you're interviewing a mum who's lost a child you might say: "How do you cope? How do you get up on a morning?" My strength and skill is in getting people to talk. For me journalism is about people's stories. I like talking to people and I like getting to know them.'

Boyle makes a point of looking smart and professional for interviews – her Burberry raincoat has seen her 'through many a door-knock'. She also does her utmost to engage people and put them at their ease straight away.

'Journalists are often talking to people at a time of crisis,' she says. 'It could be someone who has lost someone in the Tsunami or has just found out that a relative has been murdered. Most people don't deal with the media and it can be scary for the ordinary punter. They might have experienced the media pack, which I think is quite daunting, so when I turn up they may be jaded, scared and worried that they are going to be splashed across the front pages. It's important to reassure them. They've got to be able to trust you. I did an interview recently and we talked for an hour before I even got out my notebook and pen.'

Boyle rarely uses a voice recorder, preferring to use her Teeline shorthand. She puts an asterisk or a line in the margin next to key phrases, so she can find the material quickly when she is writing the interview up. 'My advice is to use a notebook, asterisk the main or best quotes and go through it soon afterwards. Only tape anything legally contentious,' she says.

She concentrates on building up trust with her interviewees and always lets them take their time when they're telling their story. Her interviews can last up to three or four hours but she never rushes people and if she needs to sign people up for an exclusive she wouldn't dream of getting the contract out until the end of the interview.

'Most people are really nervous so put them at their ease and find something to engage them. If you're interviewing a mum you talk about the kids. If you're interviewing someone from your neck of the woods you talk about that. Don't be afraid of silence either. Silence is a good thing. When you say something like "How did you feel when you found out your husband had murdered your neighbour?" just wait. Don't butt in. Instead of staring at them I look down at my notebook. I've got my pen ready but they need time to think about it and I give them that time. It's about treating them with the respect they deserve.'

Sheron Boyle's top tip

Put yourself in the position of a reader. What would they want to know?

Notes

1 P. Kidd, 'The Ayatollah is behind you', *The Times*. Available from: www.thetimes. co.uk/article/tms-2chjz32gl (accessed 11 October 2016).
2 P. Morgan, *Shooting Straight*, Ebury Press, 2014, p. 47.
3 M. Sawyer, 'Sir Bradley Wiggins: "I've never had therapy. I do interviews instead"', *Red* magazine, August 2016.
4 P. Knightley, *A Hack's Progress*, Jonathan Cape, 1997, p. 100.

5   J. Turner, 'Tactical eating', *The Times*, 29 September 2016.

6   E. Sheffield, 'Victoria Beckham's era', *Vogue*. Available from: www.vogue.co.uk/news/2014/07/04/victoria-beckham-full-cover-interview-august-2014 (accessed 12 July 2016).

7   C. Iley, 'The Interview: Dominic West – "Sex is not erotic when you've got 30 people sticking microphones in your face"', *The Sunday Times* magazine, July 2016.

8   S. Rafanelli, 'Julianne Moore talks to *Stylist* about family, politics and the battle for gay rights', *Stylist*. Available from: www.stylist.co.uk/people/julianne-moore-interview-family-politics-battle-for-gay-rights (accessed 21 May 2016).

9   H. Eyre, 'Back on track', *Vogue*, September 2016.

10 C. Long, 'Eddie Izzard's marathon battle', *The Sunday Times*. Available from: www.thesundaytimes.co.uk/sto/news/uk_news/article182673.ece#prev (accessed 31 August 2016).

11 T. Harcup, *Journalism: Principles and Practice* (3rd edn), Sage Publications, 2015, p. 128.

12 N. Thurman, A. Cornia and J. Kunert, *Journalists in the UK*, Reuters Institute for the Study of Journalism, 2016. Available from: http://reutersinstitute.politics.ox.ac.uk/sites/default/files/Journalists%20in%20the%20UK.pdf (accessed 12 May 2016).

13 M. Dodd and M. Hanna, *McNae's Essential Law for Journalists*, Oxford University Press, 2014, p. 253.

14 P. Morgan, *Shooting Straight*, Ebury Press, 2014, p. 55.

15 M. Gilson, 'Why journalists must always be a nuisance', *Brighton Argus*, 29 March 2016.

16 J. T. Chirban, *Interviewing in Depth: The Interactive-Relational Approach*, Sage Publications, 1996, p. 123.

17 H. Lacey, 'The Inventory: Chris Packham', *FT Weekend* magazine, 4 June 2016.

18 C. Crummy, '5 minute philosopher: Katy Brand', *Stylist*, 27 July 2016.

19 L. Dodds and A. Bennett, 'How every politician has answered Mumsnet's "favourite biscuit" question since 2009', *Telegraph*. Available from: www.telegraph.co.uk/news/politics/11775359/How-every-politician-has-answered-Mumsnets-favourite-biscuit-question-since-2009.html (accessed 5 June 2016).

20 S. Boyle, 'Daughter of murdered PC's heartbreak: "Mum was killed on my fourth birthday – I've been cheated of memories"', *Mirror*. Available from: www.mirror.co.uk/news/uk-news/daughter-murdered-pc-says-mum-6795738 (accessed 7 September 2016).

21 S. Boyle, 'Karen sobbed a confession to her mates. These were not fake TV tears. I stopped the car and arrested her', *Sun*. Available from: www.thesun.co.uk/sol/homepage/woman/real_life/2228957/Family-liaison-officer-tells-truth-about-Karen-Matthews-confession.html (accessed 24 April 2016).

5
The interview itself

The first rule is: be punctual. Make sure you arrive in good time for the interview – even to the extent of being ridiculously early. Plenty of journalists arrive an hour or more beforehand, using the time to go through their questions and do some last-minute research. One well-known interviewer was so strict about timekeeping that she regularly arrived for interviews a couple of hours early. 'I park down the road, check my make-up and have a cup of coffee,' she said. 'It gives me time to go through my notes again and means that I'm never late or flustered when I ring the doorbell.'

Arriving late will almost certainly irritate your interviewee. It's unprofessional and you risk losing precious interviewing time. Worse still, you may lose your interview slot altogether and be forced to go back to the office empty-handed. If you're running late, don't assume that all is lost though. Call your interviewee or, if they have one, their PA or PR, and let them know you've been held up. In most cases they'll be understanding and the interview will still go ahead as planned.

If you're meeting your interviewee at their workplace you may be asked to wait in reception but try to stay relaxed. Settle down in your seat, secure in the knowledge that you have prepared well. Read any literature offered (companies and schools tend to have plenty on display), take in relevant information and listen to the conversations going on around you. You may glean something that comes in useful later on.

Remember to put your mobile phone on silent before the interview (or set it to airplane mode if you're using it as a recorder). Don't smoke (unless invited to) or chew gum.

The start of the interview

First impressions count. Beginners can sometimes be hampered by nerves and a lack of interviewing experience but try to be self-assured and upbeat. However nervous you feel, walk in with an air of confidence (but not arrogance) and you'll find that the interview gets off to a good start. Make sure you smile too – a simple, unforced, pleased-to-meet-you smile, not a fake one. Smiling makes everyone feel better and will also reassure your interviewee. A worried expression or anxious scowl doesn't do anything for anybody.

Some beginners ask whether they should shake hands with their interviewee or not. If your interviewee walks towards you with their hand outstretched then take it without hesitation. If they don't hold out their hand, then it's up to you. In most cases shaking hands is friendly and courteous, although make sure your hand isn't clammy from nerves. *Daily Mail* film critic Brian Viner reckons 'a firm handshake, but not too firm' is ideal.

Introduce yourself straight away and thank your interviewee for agreeing to do the interview. Former *Daily Telegraph* foreign correspondent Wendy Holden says the start of an interview is vitally important and sets the tone for the ensuing conversation. 'You need to put people at their ease,' she says. 'Be open, warm and friendly. That would be my biggest advice.'

What should you call your interviewee? Either take your cue from the person you're interviewing or ask them outright. When Stephanie Rafanelli interviewed Al Pacino in New York she asked whether she could call him 'Al' and he was happy to agree. If you aren't sure how to address them it's best to err on the side of formality and use Mr, Mrs, Ms, etc. You should check their title beforehand, just in case they are Dr, Professor, Sir, Lady or Lord (this will usually be obvious from the cuttings).

Think about the tone of your voice too. It's important to be confident but at the same time, keep your voice calm and measured, especially if you're doing a sensitive interview. Avoid speaking too fast or becoming breathless.

Where to sit

Don't sit down until you are invited to and definitely don't move chairs around without asking your interviewee first. Sitting directly opposite them is probably a mistake whereas sitting at right angles (90 degrees) works well because it's neither confrontational nor cosy. Sitting too far away is inadvisable, mainly because it's more difficult to build up a rapport and your voice recorder might not pick up everything. Avoid sitting side by side on a sofa. It's far too matey for a start, and it's excruciating when your interviewee peers over your shoulder, tries to read what you're writing or comments on your illegible shorthand.

Camilla Long advises against instructing interviewees where to sit. 'Let them do all the leading,' she says. 'If you are giving stage directions you are losing the story. In some senses you need to remember that you are there purely in an observational capacity until you start writing. You just need to watch them behave. If they want to sit on their giant anthracite throne at the end of the room, then let them. If you stop them sitting there you've messed up.'

Building rapport

Your first task is to try and build a rapport with your interviewee, which is easier than it sounds. You've already started by greeting them warmly and thanking them for doing the interview. Now you need to say something that makes them feel relaxed and ready to talk.

One of the easiest ways to do this is to establish common ground at the start, perhaps by mentioning an acquaintance you share or a region that you both know. Other possibilities are commenting on the view from their room or office, admiring a picture or photograph on the wall or saying how much you enjoyed their last book, film or play.

As you become more experienced, another way to establish rapport is to mirror your interviewee's body language and match the way they are sitting. 'When you start the interview your interviewee might be sitting back in their chair with their legs crossed so you might sit in a similar way,' says journalism lecturer Susan Grossman. 'It's not a question of overtly copying them, it's about matching or mirroring their position so they don't feel intimidated.'

Try not to appear hunched up or tense (it makes you look nervous and agitated), but on the other hand don't lounge back with your feet splayed out. The BBC's former economics editor Robert Peston got into hot water with TV viewers when he interviewed former Chancellor of the Exchequer George Osborne at a press conference in China in 2015. One complained: 'I was surprised to see the BBC represented by a man who is not only lolling in a slatternly manner in the interview but was not correctly dressed. Wearing a casual shirt and no tie. This shows no respect to either the man he was interviewing or the viewers.'[1]

Down to business

It's time to get out your notebook or voice recorder. Opinions vary on whether you should ask permission to take notes or tape an interview. Some journalists say that this is a given but others feel that it's the polite thing to do and acts as a formal sign that the interview is about to begin.

Before launching into the interview it's important that you remind your interviewee of what you want to talk to them about. It doesn't matter if they are a business leader doing six interviews a day or someone being interviewed for the first time; specifying the interview subject and angle focuses their minds.

Rather than a brusque 'OK, tell me about your snail farm', a softer and wiser approach would be to explain some of the thinking behind the interview. For example, 'Our readers are very interested in innovation and your snail farm is one of the most unusual ideas we've heard about. It would be very helpful if we could talk about the inspiration for the idea, about your start-up and running costs, the pleasures and pitfalls of snail farming and whether you'd recommend it to other farmers. That sort of thing.'

A combination of charm and purpose

The first four minutes of an interview are critical, so concentrate on achieving a combination of charm and purpose. Remember, too, that some interviewees are nervous and take a bit of time to settle down while others may talk confidently from the outset.

You are – and must be – in charge. You need to do it subtly but remember that you are the one calling the shots. If you don't take charge of the interview from the start you may end up feeling that you are taking dictation or being swept off on a tide of 'useless reminiscence', unable to stop the flow.

BuzzFeed UK investigations editor Heidi Blake points out, however, that while journalists need to be in control of their interviews, they 'don't necessarily need to be visibly in control – because then it can become a bit of a power struggle'.

She insists that while it's important 'not to be too pushy', you may need to be 'quite assertive about directing the conversation to the heart of what you want to talk about and not let them railroad you or go off at whatever tangent they want to pursue'. As she says: 'Quite often as a journalist you find yourself having to do things that in real life would be quite impolite. But you have to be able to suck it up and do it with as much charm as you can. If you think about it, knocking on someone's door and asking them difficult questions is quite impolite, especially if you are focusing on trying to develop a rapport with someone.' Camilla Long made a similar point in a piece she wrote for *The Sunday Times's Style* magazine. 'As babies, we are told nice girls don't ask direct questions. Only the rude girl says, "How much did that cost?" or "Where did you go to school?" or "Why is your dad weird?" But as an interviewer, a large part of my job now involves asking people very unpleasant questions.'[2]

First questions

Planning your questions has been covered in the last chapter but don't feel that you have to stick to them exactly or ask them in a set order. Avoid launching into the interview too abruptly and don't start with a complicated question that your interviewee either can't answer or needs time to think about. If you do that, the interview may well stall before it's got going.

Some journalism tutors advise starting with 'must-know' facts. The thinking behind this idea is that questions like these are safe and easy to confirm. They reassure the interviewee that you're a stickler for accuracy. Also, as a novice interviewer, you may be so exhausted or elated by the end of the interview that you forget to ask these basic facts, resulting in an embarrassing follow-up phone call or email.

My own view is that while you *must* obtain your publication's 'must-know' information (and get the spellings right) this is best done at the end of the interview. If you launch into questions like your interviewee's job title and date of birth at the beginning you will get bogged down in minor details before the interview gets into its stride. You also risk irritating (or boring) the person you're interviewing right at the start.

So how should you begin? If you're covering a news story it's a good idea to go through the chronology of the incident. If you're writing a feature about water leakage, for instance, and have been asked to interview the boss of a water company I would recommend starting with questions like: 'How long have you been in this role?' 'What are your chief responsibilities?' 'What initiatives have you put in place to reduce water leakage in your area?' I would check spellings and basic details once I had established a rapport with my interviewee and had got a decent interview in my notebook or on my recorder.

Whatever you do, don't copy the approach of a young journalist quoted by a novelist in the second edition of *Interviewing for Journalists*.

'"So," asked the young journalist as she sat down at my kitchen table, "what would you say to those people who say that the sort of books you write are written for housewives who are not very well educated?"

'As an opening gambit it fair took the biscuit. Hell, it took the best all-butter shortbread I had bought in for her visit. "Have you," I asked mildly, "read any of my books?"

'Go on. Take a wild guess as to what her answer was . . .'[3]

Empathy, empathy, empathy

Empathy is a quality that all interviewers need. When you're on a deadline to get a story don't overlook your interviewee's feelings and emotions about the subject or event they are talking about. It's imperative to try and understand what they have experienced and how they feel.

'Empathy is vital,' says freelance editor and writer Melanie Whitehouse. 'People think you have to be hard to be a successful journalist but I believe that while a tough exterior helps, a soft interior is a must. How else can you ever relate to the woman who is telling you how her daughter was murdered or that her husband beat her up? You need to develop the ability to win someone's trust in a matter of minutes and you should never abuse that trust.'

In other words, you need to show that you're sympathetic, understanding and compassionate. You're there to do a job, yes, but you need to empathise with the interviewee, especially if they are talking about a trauma, tragedy or bereavement. If in doubt, remember Cole Moreton's advice: 'Your first duty is to the other person as a human being.'

Make it interesting for them

Unless the story is a distressing one, do your best to make the interview enjoyable for your subject. This means engaging them right from the start, listening intently and asking interesting questions. If you don't do all of these things there's a risk that the interviewee will subconsciously switch off, go into automatic pilot and trot out the same well-rehearsed answers they've given time and time again – exactly what you don't want to happen in an interview.

It's only when you are interviewed yourself that you realise that being asked the same questions over and over again is tedious, especially if your answers elicit little or no reaction and the interviewer simply proceeds to the next question without reacting or commenting. Famous people who give frequent interviews often remark on the predictable nature of journalists' questions. Novelist Shirley Conran said that when she travelled across the world to promote her books every interviewer asked her exactly the same four questions – one of which was 'always about the goldfish'. If you don't know what she meant by that remark, take a look at *Lace*, her best-selling novel.

Similarly, former Downing Street director of communications Alastair Campbell declared that the question he gets asked most is: 'What are you up to these days?' Writing in *British GQ* magazine in 2016, Campbell added: 'It's irritating, because it's really a way of saying, "Didn't you used to be important?"'[4]

Make sure your questions are clear and precise, rather than too general. When the Hollywood actor Chris Evans was promoting the movie *Captain America: Civil War* in London in 2016 *BBC Breakfast* presenter Naga Munchetty began her interview by asking him: 'Tell me about the film.' Quick as a flash, the actor replied: 'What would you like to know?'

Interviewing checklist

- Approach people confidently (but don't be arrogant).
- Introduce yourself properly at the start of the interview, giving your name and the publication you work for. The way you launch into an interview will set the tone of the conversation so it's important to concentrate on doing it well.
- Explain why you want to talk to them (this is particularly important if you are approaching people in the street or calling them without warning).
- At the start of the interview ask if they mind if you take notes/record the conversation. Both of you know that you will be doing this but it's polite to check and in my experience no one refuses.
- Never use a clipboard. As Brian Viner says: 'Keep your clipboard in your head rather than on your knee.'
- If you're using shorthand, write the name of your interviewee and the date of the interview in your notebook. If you're taping, give your interviewee's name and the date at the start of the interview. When you've got a stack of interviews to transcribe this can help a lot, especially when interviewees have similar voices.
- Ask clear, concise questions. The shorter the question, the better. Remember Lynn Barber's favourite question, 'Why?'
- Ask your questions in a logical order. If your questions jump about you will confuse your interviewee and interrupt the flow of the conversation. At the same time, don't stick to your list of questions so rigidly that you miss an unexpected follow-up question, startling revelation or new angle. Use your list as a reminder or prompt but don't let it get in the way of a good story. As David Randall explained in *The Universal Journalist*: 'In stories which are about events, your main concern should be to build up a chronology of what happened.' He also suggested that when you get to what he called 'the core action' you should 'slow them right down and get every detail that you can. Ask them what happened at every moment, what they saw, the colours, smells, noises. Ask them where they were

standing, what people were wearing, what they shouted, what the weather was like.'[5]

- Don't waste time by asking questions you can easily research yourself. Or as Cole Moreton puts it: 'Never ask anything you should know already.'
- Don't waste time by asking irrelevant questions. There's always the risk that the interview might be curtailed for reasons beyond your control so use your time wisely. When Polly Vernon interviewed supermodel Gigi Hadid and designer Tommy Hilfiger for *The Times* magazine she flew out to New York on the promise of a 20-minute chat with Hadid and a further 20 minutes with Hilfiger. In the event she got a total of five minutes and seven seconds. The interview was going well but Hilfiger and Hadid were pressed for time. As Vernon reported in her piece: 'It is at this point that a Hilfiger employee winds up proceedings. Hilfiger and Hadid need to be somewhere else. Tommy Hilfiger apologises for the briefness of our interaction. Hadid returns my tape machine. I'm done.'[6] Luckily, Vernon had plenty of material but it's a useful reminder of the need to make the most of your allotted interviewing time.
- Listen to the answers and stay engaged throughout the interview.
- Don't talk about yourself. (This is generally the advice given for news interviews. Features interviews may be different. You often have more time and more flexibility.)
- Don't deviate from the purpose of the interview and don't try to make yourself look clever.
- Empathise. This doesn't mean that you have to like your interviewee but being aware of the likely impact of your questions is important.
- Be charming and polite throughout – even if you disagree profoundly with your interviewee's views. Be sceptical rather than adversarial.
- Respond in the right way. 'If they say something funny, then laugh – whether it's funny or not,' says Brian Viner.
- Recognise a good story when you hear one.
- Recognise a good quote when you hear one. Vivid quotes are the key to a great interview.
- Ask questions that elicit lively replies.
- Avoid questions that elicit a series of closed 'yes' and 'no' answers. Instead, keep the interview moving with responsive questions: 'Really?' 'And what happened next?' The *Guardian*'s Paul Lewis avoids asking binary questions prematurely. 'Early on in my career I discovered I got stuck, from time to time, by asking a source a binary question – one in which there is a straight "yes" or "no" answer – too early on in our conversation,' he says. 'If the answer is "no" – "no" to a follow-up meeting, say, or "no" to handing over a useful document – that can be a problem. Once someone has given you a flat "no", it is very hard to pull them back round for what feels, to them,

like a complete u-turn. They may have only said "no" because you asked them too soon, or because they wanted to figure you out first. So generally I've found it is best to avoid asking that kind of binary question, particularly early on in a conversation. It is better to talk around a subject, and be led by the interviewee, giving you time to get to know them and understand their motivations, while also allowing them to get to know you.'

- Don't ask several questions at once. If you ask a string of questions, your interviewee may forget to answer them all or conveniently avoid the ones they don't like.

- Encourage the interviewee to keep talking but don't rush to fill the gaps in the conversation. Give your interviewee a bit of time and space to think.

- Don't let your interviewee lapse into technical talk or acronyms you don't understand. If they do, ask them to explain.

- Don't be flattered if they say 'what a great (or fascinating) question'. The odds are that it's a tricky question and they need to think about the answer.

- Keep an open mind. The story might not turn out to be the one you expect. On the other hand you might find an even better story.

- Remember that it's not just *what* an interviewee says. It's *how* they say it too. Where relevant, take notes on your interviewee's appearance, expressions, house, office, etc. Use your eyes – even a photograph or painting might reveal something interesting about them.

- Make sure you have all the essential or 'must-know' details. For local newspapers these will include the interviewee's name, age, occupation and address. For specialist magazines a person's age and address may be irrelevant but there will be other essential information. For an education magazine 'must knows' will include teachers' specialisms, the number of pupils at their school and the school's most recent exam results while for a business magazine you'll need to check details like job titles, company turnover and the number of employees.

- At the end of the interview some journalists ask if there is anything else the interviewee would like to add – or as a famous radio broadcaster often asks, 'Is there anything else you'd like to get off your chest?' This may elicit some additional nuggets of information but it doesn't always work. When writer Emma Brockes asked the author and broadcaster Clive James a question like this he replied: 'I'm not doing your work for you!' Cole Moreton sometimes ends by asking his interviewees if he can take a picture as an *aide memoire*. Most people agree to his request, but it might not work for everyone.

- If you have approached your interviewee without any warning (on a doorstep for a news story or for a vox pop) ask them for a contact number and email address – just in case you need to go back to them for further details or for a future story.

- Don't forget pictures. Or as Sally Adams always put it when she was commissioning features as editor of *She* magazine – 'think pics'. Make sure you know what type of photographs your publication needs before you embark on the interview. If you're working with a photographer stay with them while they're taking pictures. You can sometimes get useful supplementary details and quotes at this point. If you haven't got a photographer with you or you're conducting a phone or Skype interview ask your interviewee if they have any high-resolution pictures they can email to you. Bystanders who have witnessed major incidents as they unfold frequently take pictures on their phones and these can give a graphic account of breaking news stories. Alternatively, note down the picture possibilities and give the interviewee's contact details to the picture desk.
- Last, but not least, never forget that the interviewee is the star. Or as Cole Moreton puts it: 'It's never about you.'
- If you do all of these things, fulfil your editor's brief, keep to your deadline and write a professional, well-structured piece you'll be well on the way to producing a first-class story.

Interviewing task

Role play can be a useful way to practise interviewing. Working in pairs, with one student playing the interviewer and one playing an interviewee who wants to promote their new book, rehearse the first two minutes of the interview. The interviewer should introduce themselves, explain the theme of the interview and ask the first few questions. Afterwards, the whole class can discuss what they learned from the exercise, what worked well and what didn't work so well.

HOW I INTERVIEW: COLE MORETON

Cole Moreton started his career at the age of 16, as a trainee reporter on the *Waltham Forest Guardian*. After four years he left to work with refugees in Asia and Africa, returning several years later to do a degree in contemporary writing. When he resumed his journalistic career in the 1990s he joined the *Express*, then worked as an editor and writer for the *Independent on Sunday* for 12 years. He later became chief feature writer of the *Sunday Telegraph*, producing reports, features, analysis and comment on the big stories of the day. He has been a visiting journalism lecturer at the University of Westminster and has also led courses at the Arvon Foundation.

Moreton's moving BBC Radio 4 documentary series, *The Boy Who Gave His Heart Away*, which told the story of what happened when the death of a child miraculously allowed others to live, was highly praised. The story of Martin Burton, the child in question, was also a powerful example of how interviews can raise awareness and understanding of organ donation. As Moreton wrote in the *Daily Telegraph* afterwards: 'I was squeamish about the idea of allowing my heart, lungs, liver, kidney or eyes to be used for others – and even more so about letting that happen to someone I loved – but hearing about what Martin achieved after death has changed my mind completely.'[7] Moreton added that he had signed up to the donor register and urged everyone else to do the same.

Moreton won the interviewer of the year title (popular newspapers) at the 2015 Press Awards for interviews with Anthony Horowitz, Anne Robinson and Brian Sewell, all of which appeared in the *Mail on Sunday*'s *Event* magazine. The judging panel's citation said: 'He is insightful and a master craftsman, producing entertaining and memorable pieces.'

Cole Moreton loves interviewing and believes that there is something 'intrinsically interesting' about everybody. 'I'm nosy and I think that good conversation is one of the joys of life,' he says. 'I prefer to conduct interviews as conversations rather than interrogations. There is an adversarial aspect with some of the more famous, important or notorious subjects but the pleasure of interviewing is meeting people intimately and trying to get to know them.'

'Mum, dad, kids or money'

Like Camilla Long, Moreton fixes 50 per cent of his own interviews and virtually always contacts prospective interviewees by email. He's meticulous about his research, spending up to two days trawling through cuttings, books, documentaries, videos and speeches. He believes that 'mum, dad, kids or money' are the four things that unlock most people and he researches aspects like these carefully, always looking for 'things that they have an emotional investment in'.

'You're looking to be across everything there is to know about their career – but that's not enough,' he says. 'You need to know the "wiki" facts, you need to have read a dozen interviews with them and you need to have checked every news story that they've done over the past year. Those three things are the minimum – but on top of that you're looking for things around the edge – a tweet, a social media thing, a diary piece, a blog, something in a book, something they've said on a chat show.'

Rather than writing out a list of questions, Moreton comes up with a list of a dozen or so single-word subject headings he'd like to talk about. As mentioned in Chapter 3, he's a keen advocate of concentrating on 'the narrative strand' of an interview. 'So if you're interviewing someone whose house has burned down, clearly the best way of doing that is to start from the moment they first smelled smoke and then take it chronologically. Ask them what happened and what happened next. Students forget that narrative strand sometimes – and when it comes to interviewing famous people they forget it even more. They think different rules apply but they really don't. It's just common sense to ask "Why did you do that?" or "How did you feel about this?"'

In the hour before an interview Moreton goes back over his subject headings and memorises them. 'I might have them on an iPad or a piece of paper when I go in but I won't refer to them if I can possibly help it.'

When it comes to the location for interviews Moreton advises choosing somewhere that means something to the interviewee – either their home or somewhere that relates to their profession or what they are trying to say. Hotels, he reckons, are the worst of all, impersonal and bland.

He always gets to interviews early and checks out the location before the person he is interviewing arrives. 'Work out where they have been beforehand and what they need. If they've been hurrying or running late then you need to be as calm as you can possibly be, almost like the host, whereas if they are difficult and sparky, you need to be on full alert right from the beginning.'

Walk around the block

Moreton, a two-voice recorder man, doesn't take any notes at all during interviews – not even about facial expressions or body language. Instead he prefers to walk around the block immediately afterwards and record his impressions of the meeting.

He always tries to find 'common ground' with interviewees. For example, when he interviewed tough guy actor Ray Winstone for the *Mail on Sunday* he asked what would happen if he challenged the star to a fight. Why did he do that? 'For the mischief and because we are a couple of East End geezers,' he says. 'We talked about our grannies and how the East End has all changed.'

Unlike other interviewers he doesn't mind talking about himself if he has to. 'It's a two-way street,' he says. 'People become vulnerable with you if you become vulnerable with them. You don't want to impose yourself but if somebody is describing something you want them to feel that you understand and sometimes it helps to mention your own experience.'

Interviewing Richard Branson

His first interview with Sir Richard Branson took place in 2010, in a tiny cabin on the Virgin chief's yacht, which was moored off the coast of Monte Carlo. The Monaco Grand Prix was taking place at the time, which meant there were no flights available and no hotels. It took Moreton nine hours to travel across France by train, get a taxi to the harbour and a boat to Branson's yacht, only to discover that Branson had limited time. Why spend hours preparing for what turned out to be a short interview? 'Because you need to be able to hear what he is saying,' explains Moreton. 'If he says something that has resonance about his situation and you don't know what the background is you are going to miss it. And you can't afford to miss the mark in an interview.'

Moreton interviewed Branson again in 2016, eliciting some fascinating lines, like the fact that Stephen Hawking was 'desperate' to go to space, that Branson would be 'extremely sad' if Britain left the EU and that 'if my balloon had not come back (during his 1987 transatlantic balloon flight he had to be rescued) I would have kicked myself and my wife would not have turned up at my funeral'.[8]

Another example of the forensic approach Moreton takes to his research came when he interviewed Tiger Woods in New York in 2011 for the first print interview after the golfer's life 'fell apart in late 2009'. As Moreton wrote: 'The rules are strict: there must be no mention of the strange car accident outside his home in Florida, involving a fire hydrant and a golf club, nor the numerous women who subsequently claimed to have had affairs with him.'[9]

Moreton was allotted 15 minutes for the interview and spent a week preparing. Not only that, he had to submit his questions to Woods's team beforehand and was instructed that three-quarters of them must be about EA Sports, the company behind the Tiger Woods PGA Tour computer game. After a fair amount of wrangling Moreton was duly allowed to ask the grand total of three questions 'that weren't about the game'.

When it came to the interview the room was packed. Along with Woods and Moreton, there were six people, all with tape recorders, and a photographer snapping away. By the time 13 minutes and 26 seconds had ticked by Moreton was starting to get worried. 'I had a minute and a half left and nothing had happened. And then Woods suddenly said, almost to himself, "I'm not going to be doing this forever. I may be playing with friends, family, whatever, but at this level?"'

Moreton describes this as a 'kerching' moment. 'The six people around him were recoiling in horror at what he had just said, but they couldn't stop him,' he recalls. 'I knew I mustn't make too much of it. I mustn't say "Oh my God, what did you just say?" Because if I did they'd jump in and say "Right, wipe that out." Inside I was thinking "I've got it" but outside I was cool, cool, cool. I said "Lovely to meet you", went back into the corridor and took a deep breath. "I'm not going to be doing this forever" made headlines all over the world. It's true that he has never played again at the level he was before the scandal and that his career has gone into serious decline since.'

No tricks

Contrary to the widely held view that journalists are trying to 'trick' interviewees Moreton says: 'You're really not. There are times when it gets adversarial and both sides really go for it but most of the time it's about trying to understand the other person and helping them to express what they really think. Often, if you're interviewing an actor about their latest film they don't really care – so you've got to find something they really do care about and help them to talk about that.'

Moreton's number one advice to young interviewers is to 'listen'. If it sounds obvious it really isn't. 'Don't be in too much of a rush to get to the next question,' he says. 'I'm guilty of it myself – even now. Sometimes people are dropping subconscious hints and if you don't pay attention you risk missing something or not picking up on it or not taking it further.

'I've published books and been interviewed by people who sit with their questions in front of them. They say: "What is your book about?" You're in the middle of answering and they're already asking: "So how did you come to write it?" And I'm thinking: "I haven't finished answering the first question. Just listen."'

He also cautions against the temptation to think you are 'buddies' with your interviewee, especially if an interview has gone well. He once did an interview with a celebrity that was supposed to last for an hour. In the event it went on for 24 hours as he roared round the countryside in his sports car, went out to dinner with the star and his wife and stayed the night at their house.

'I was on the phone to a friend who works for a real superstar and I was full of it,' says Moreton. 'There was this pause and he said: "It's never about you." And he was right. An interview is never about you. With very few exceptions you are going to be put back on the boat, like I was after interviewing Richard Branson at Monte Carlo. "Thank you very much. Goodbye."'

Writing is like sculpture

When it comes to writing his interviews Moreton compares it to sculpture. He transcribes most of his own work, then starts to whittle down the thousands of words of transcription, working out the key lines as he goes through it. The whole process – transcribing, writing and teasing the 3,000-word piece into shape – can take the best part of a week.

As Moreton reflects on his assignments he's keen to emphasise the amount of work involved in interviewing at this level.

'The reason I can do what I do and the reason why no end of other journalists with more reputable educations can't do what I do is empathy – that understanding of who the other person is,' he says.

'If you want to do this properly you have to outwork everybody else in terms of hours, in terms of application and in terms of your time. What frustrates me is when young journalists in particular want this to be an ordinary job. It's not. You've got to want to get up in the middle of the night if it suddenly occurs to you how you should have done that intro. This job is a privilege but if you don't want to do all of that you should just stop and do something else.'

Cole Moreton's top tips

Know everything there is to know about the person before you go into the room. Have a conversation. Listen to the answers – and don't be afraid.

Notes

1   G. Mullin and K. Rushton, 'Television dress codes are "nuts" – I don't need a tie to be taken seriously, insists BBC economics editor Robert Peston', *MailOnline*. Available from: www.dailymail.co.uk/news/article-3251910/Television-dress-codes-nuts-don-t-need-tie-taken-seriously-insists-BBC-economics-editor-Robert-Peston.html (accessed 3 June 2016).
2   C. Long, 'What I've learnt from men', *The Sunday Times*, 25 September 2016.
3   S. Adams, *Interviewing for Journalists* (2nd edn), Routledge, 2009, p. 38.
4   A. Campbell, 'Campbell vs Campbell', *British GQ*, September 2016.
5   D. Randall, *The Universal Journalist*, Pluto Press, 1996, p. 43.
6   P. Vernon, 'The smartphone supermodel', *The Times* magazine, 17 September 2016.
7   C. Moreton, 'The grieving mother who gave her son's heart so others could live', *Telegraph*. Available from: www.telegraph.co.uk/women/family/the-grieving-mother-who-gave-her-sons-heart-so-others-could-live (accessed 11 October 2016).
8   C. Moreton, 'Stephen Hawking is desperate to go into space with me . . . even if it kills him', *Mail on Sunday*. Available from: www.mailonsunday.co.uk/home/event/article-3507870/Richard-Branson-talks-spaceflight-marriage-tax-status-future.html (accessed 11 October 2016).
9   C. Moreton, '"I am trying to become a better person. I'm trying to become a better person with my kids, a better father": Tiger Woods opens up', *Mail on Sunday*. Available from: www.dailymail.co.uk/home/moslive/article-1371862/Tiger-Woods-I-trying-better-person-better-father.html#ixzz4920oMteC (accessed 11 October 2016).

6
Interviewing techniques

It sounds obvious, but as Cole Moreton emphasised in Chapter 5, listening is of critical importance during an interview. The main purpose of a print or online interview is to get your interviewee to talk freely – and the best way to do that is to listen. The American writer John Hohenberg once declared: 'No talking journalist ever held a good interview',[1] and this view was echoed by virtually every interviewer I spoke to during my research for this book. A. J. Liebling, an American journalist who wrote for *The New Yorker* magazine for nearly 30 years, put it even more bluntly: 'The worst thing an interviewer can do is talk a lot himself.'[2] Having said that, if an interviewee asks you about yourself don't cut them off in mid-flow. It's far better to give a brief answer than to risk alienating them by being rude and possibly damaging the rapport you've so carefully built up.

As well as devising interesting questions interviewers also need to master the non-questioning skills of eliciting information and quotes. These are:

- listening and encouraging
- observing body language
- using silence
- making statements requiring confirmation or denial
- summarising and moving on.

Many journalists do all of these things without thinking but when you are starting out it can be useful to reflect on them and practise them. Don't focus on them so much that you become unnatural or insincere but using some of these techniques may help you to conduct more thoughtful interviews and avoid the rapid-fire, ping-pong, question-and-answer style often used by TV and radio journalists.

Listening and encouraging

You need to listen hard for fresh angles, surprises or new revelations – and follow them up, while keeping the flow of the conversation going smoothly.

Listening requires an immense amount of concentration and can be exhausting. Many of the interviewers I spoke to said they felt utterly drained at the end of interviews. 'After it's finished, I'm exhausted,' said Cole Moreton.

As well as concentration, being a good listener requires empathy, discipline, understanding and endless patience. If you're tense, indifferent, hostile, impatient or distracted, your mind will wander and you won't be able to listen properly, let alone react to what your interviewee has said and think about your next question.

Listening, however, is not the same as hearing. As Sally Adams put it: 'Good listening is hearing *and* understanding.' In other words, if you are interviewing someone face to face you need to show that you are interested in what they are saying. Ways in which you can do this include using reassuring body language, mirroring the other person's body posture, nodding, tilting your head, leaning forward and smiling. Nodding is particularly effective. If you don't feel natural, watch how others nod, practise it and observe how it looks in a mirror. Nodding too much looks ridiculous and is likely to inhibit rather than encourage your interviewee, so don't introduce it into your interviews until you're happy you've got it right. It has to be natural; otherwise it doesn't work.

Nodding obviously isn't an option in phone interviews but you can show that you're listening by using positive words like 'ah', 'yes', 'really?' and 'of course'. Again, don't overdo it or you will sound false and unconvincing.

Observing body language

Most journalists would agree that the body language of their interviewees says a lot about them, although it's by no means an exact science. If your interviewee folds their arms, for example, it may mean that they are feeling defensive, but then again, it may simply mean that they feel more comfortable sitting that way.

Your interviewee abruptly shifting their posture is more significant. If they have been leaning forward and talking freely but suddenly lean back in their chair and fold their arms tightly across their body, it's likely that something will have caused the change – possibly the subject that either you or they have just mentioned. It's definitely worth following this up.

BuzzFeed UK investigations editor Heidi Blake agrees that a person's body language can tell you a lot about how they are responding to you and to your questions. 'If someone is leaning forward, is clearly engaged, making eye contact with you and gesturing expansively that's a good sign,' she says. 'If they are being a bit more formal all of a sudden, sitting back, folding their arms and narrowing their eyes, it probably isn't.'

The most important aspects of body language for interviewers to bear in mind are:

- appearance
- eyes
- face
- gestures
- feet
- head
- posture.

There is a wealth of information on reading body language, including *The Definitive Book of Body Language* by Allan and Barbara Pease.[3] Most journalists, however, use fairly basic observation skills to 'read' their interviewees so here are a few pointers.

Appearance

The first impression you get of someone is the way they look – but remember that this doesn't necessarily tell the whole story. After all, appearance is something that's fairly easy to change, thanks to hair dye, coloured contact lenses, facial hair and glasses.

A person's physical appearance undoubtedly makes an immediate impact on observers but a warm, engaging manner can soon put eccentric clothes, scuffed shoes or bitten fingernails in the shade. That said, what an interviewee looks like definitely tells you something. It could be, for instance, that their obsession about how they look verges on the narcissistic or that they are wearing sunglasses to appear mysterious and 'cool'. As a journalist, the key is to make a note of your interviewee's appearance but not to let it get in the way of what they actually say.

Your own body language is important too. Leaning forward sends out a sub-conscious message of approval and shows your interviewee how engaged you are, while smiling adds further reassurance. If you're not sure about this, imagine doing the opposite of these things. If as a journalist you slouched back in your seat, frowned, looked bored and didn't give any signs of encouragement you would be sending out completely the wrong message to your interviewee – and the chances are that you wouldn't get a good interview either.

Eyes

'The eyes are the mirror of the soul and reflect everything that seems to be hidden.'[4] Those were the words of the Brazilian novelist Paulo Coelho in

Manuscript Found in Accra and they are well worth remembering when you are interviewing. Good eye contact is vital when you are interviewing face to face, although you should look but not stare. Some journalists believe that if you take your eyes off your interviewee their voice will start to falter and tail away. You should therefore look at the person you're interviewing as much as possible. The only exceptions are when you're looking down at your notebook, checking your questions or perhaps encouraging confessions. Don't drop your eyes when your interviewee looks at you either. They may interpret this as a sign that you're not enjoying their company.

By maintaining eye contact you are signalling that you are interested in what the person you are interviewing is saying. As Elizabeth Kuhnke's *Body Language for Dummies* points out: 'When you want to build rapport with someone, research shows that you need to meet that person's gaze between 60–70 per cent of the time.'[5] Looking at the person you are interviewing also means that you can pick up on the non-verbal cues they are giving you – everything from facial expressions to body posture.

A word of warning on eye contact though. Don't assume that because your interviewee isn't looking at you all the time that there is something amiss. Some people find eye contact difficult or uncomfortable, possibly because they are shy or unsure of themselves.

Face

People's faces can register all sorts of emotions, from fear to happiness, anger to surprise.

Most interviewees, however, learn to control their expressions to some extent, although occasionally the mask will slip and there will be a fleeting glimpse of anger at a question they don't like. The skill is to spot changes of expression, perhaps from a broad smile to tightened lips and jaw, and ask yourself, 'Why?'

Gestures

Hand signals have a bewildering array of meanings so they are worth watching out for. Look out for the following gestures:

- Steepling – where the hands are placed in a prayer-like position, with fingertips together but palms apart – is said to show seniority, superiority and/or confidence.
- Index finger-wagging often reveals an 'I know best' temperament.

- Ticking off points on the fingers of one hand with the forefinger of another ('one, two, three . . .') is said to show an authoritarian nature.
- Twirling a pair of spectacles round and round mimics TV's 'wind up what you're saying soon' hand signal.
- Pushing real or imaginary items away with the hands or flicking imaginary fluff off clothes is often interpreted as dismissing or rejecting what has been heard.
- A hand near the mouth may be interpreted as 'a pale echo' of a hand involuntarily clapped over the mouth after some appalling indiscretion, suggesting anxiety or even deception.
- Hands near the chin are said to show thought.
- Rubbing the back of the neck is sometimes seen as a sign of frustration with someone or something.

Feet

Feet are apparently the hardest part of the body to control. If an interviewee's feet suddenly start to tap or twitch or they shuffle or shift, some people reckon that it's a sign that they want to get away.

Head

Nods and head tilts are a sign of encouragement and approval, so they're far more useful to the interviewer than the interviewee. The position of a person's head can also give a few clues – forward of the body looks rather aggressive, a head held high can suggest superiority and dropped may denote submission.

Posture

In a straightforward, uncomplicated interview an interviewee leaning towards you indicates that everything is going well. If they are leaning backwards or away from you they may either be very relaxed or they may have lost interest and switched off.

Receive *and* send

One of the advantages of becoming proficient at reading body language is that you can use it to communicate with interviewees without them knowing. Here are some useful tips to try:

- Lean towards the interviewee and they'll talk more, sensing that you like them.
- Nod and they'll carry on talking for longer than they would have otherwise.
- If you want to interrupt, lean forward and raise your head and hand slightly to gain their attention. Or try three fast nods; that can work too.
- If they're talking too much, reduce the nods, lean back, look away and sigh softly or adopt a posture that is contradictory to theirs.
- If you suspect they aren't telling the truth, cover your mouth or flick imaginary fluff from your jacket. If you catch their eye, look away for a second.

Using silence

Many journalists are gregarious by nature and find it difficult, almost impossible, to be silent. If you use silence well, however, it pays off. Virtually all the writers I spoke to mentioned the importance of silence. It isn't appropriate during the first few minutes of an interview, of course, but once the conversation has got going and your interviewee has relaxed, then you should try and talk very little.

Focus on not jumping in with another question or comment the instant your interviewee has finished what they are saying. If you count at least four seconds in your head you'll often find that the person will start speaking again. In fact they may amplify their last comment and give you the best quotes of the whole interview. One writer discovered the power of silence when she ran out of questions and was about to panic. To her surprise her interviewee didn't notice and carried on speaking quite happily.

Remember not to overdo the silences though. If you let the silence last too long or become awkward you risk undoing all the excellent groundwork you've laid already.

Making statements requiring confirmation or denial

Questioning ranges from casual checking to out-and-out interrogation. Journalists' questions tend to sit somewhere in the middle of this but one way to get interviewees to talk is to seek confirmation, denial or amplification. It reassures them that you are keen to get your facts right and encourages them to add more detail.

For instance, it's far better to say:

'I'd just like to check how you spell your name.'

Than the more brusque:

'How do you spell your name?'

It's more effective to say:

'I see from the cuttings that you have a flat in Paris.'

Than the more curt:

'Where do you live?'

Summarising and moving on

Summing up a point or area of conversation can be very helpful. If you are interviewing someone who is over-talkative and time is running short you can summarise what they have said on a particular point, restate it and then move on. Use phrases like 'So what you're saying is . . . Now I'd like to ask you about . . .' or 'We've covered the time when you . . . Now, perhaps we can talk about . . .'

Summarising can be very useful at the end of an interview, especially when you want to double-check the details of a story. If you sum up the story in your own words you may find that your interviewee then adds details they may have forgotten to mention earlier on.

Framing questions

Once you have been interviewing for a while the way you frame your questions will become second nature. Experienced interviewers often go into interviews with a list of topics or areas that they want to talk about but when you're starting out it's useful to spend time planning a series of precise questions.

There are three main categories of questions – closed, open and leading. All have their uses, but they need to be asked in the right way and at the right time.

Closed questions

Closed questions are those that can be answered with a simple 'yes' or 'no'. They tend to be questions about fact or opinion that can be answered with a one-word answer or a very short answer. Don't dismiss them out of hand in interviews though. They are useful when it comes to checking essential facts quickly, such as:

'Did you see the accident?'
'Are you going to resign?'
'Does your firm offer apprenticeships?'
'Does your restaurant serve vegetarian food?'
'How many pupils are there on the school roll?'
'Where is this year's award ceremony being held?'

Closed questions will focus your interviewee's mind and speed up their replies – but avoid using too many of them. The danger is that interviewees get used to giving one-word answers and carry on giving the briefest of answers, even when you get to your more in-depth, probing questions.

Open questions

Open questions are those that encourage interviewees to give more detailed and meaningful answers. Here are some examples:

'How did the fire start?'
'What made you decide to become a teacher?'
'What inspired you to write your book?'
'Can you tell me about your relationship with your mother?'
'What was your earliest childhood memory?'
'Why did you launch your business?'

The most common open question, certainly in journalistic terms, is 'How did you feel?' TV and radio reporters use it a lot and are often criticised for doing so but don't be afraid to use it. It is very effective and often produces poignant and moving answers. As Cole Moreton says, 'It's just common sense to ask "Why did you do that?" or "How did you feel about this?"'

Another variation of the open question is the echo question. You can use this when you sense that the interviewee wants to say more but is hesitant.

They say, 'I fell in love with her there and then.'
You pause, then repeat, 'You fell in love with her there and then?'
You pause again, and they add more detail.
They say, 'She was beautiful, generous and I knew I couldn't live the rest of my life without her.'

Here is another example:

They say, 'I was so upset that I cried for a month.'
You pause, then repeat: 'You cried for a month?'
You pause again, and wait for them to add more detail.
They say, 'Yes, I was devastated when we broke up. I couldn't do anything. My whole life was on hold. All I did was lie in bed all day and weep.'

Amplification

Amplification questions are a sub-category of open questions, used to elicit additional details. The aim of these is to get the interviewee to elaborate on what they have just said and to give some vivid examples and quotes. As a journalist, you don't want generalisations or sweeping statements that don't tell you much. You want specifics.

Here are two examples where the journalist succeeds in getting more information out of their interviewee:

'When I took over as the head teacher we had a lot of trouble in the playground at break-times.'
'What sort of trouble did you have?'
'Some of the students threw stones at me and yelled abuse. On one occasion I remember seeing hundreds of the younger ones jumping on top of each other. They were shouting and swearing and I thought to myself, "I've just wrecked my career by coming to this school."'

or

'The street looks much better since we launched our litter patrol but we have had a bit of an issue with graffiti.'
'What sort of issue with graffiti?'
'The other night someone daubed a rude message on the wall of the community centre.'
'What did the message say?'

Leading questions

Leading questions have a bad reputation but are widely used nevertheless. They prompt or encourage people to give the answer wanted or assumed, such as:

'How did you react? Were you furious?'
'How much money was stolen? More than £500,000?'
'You're a millionaire, aren't you?'

Clarification

Get into the habit of clarifying anything you're unsure about or don't understand. It's easy to misunderstand or mishear something that has been said so if you are in any doubt at all check, check and check again. Don't simply assume you'll be able to pick it up on the recording when you transcribe the interview. Your interviewee won't mind clarifying what they have said. They would far rather repeat something and make sure you get the details right than risk it being wrong in print.

I learned this the hard way as a young reporter when I did a phone interview with an American who had recently started an exercise class for plus-size men and women. 'What is the class called?' I asked. 'Big, Beautiful and Thick,' she said. I thought it sounded odd but noted the name down all the same. On the day the piece was published the irate woman rang (very justifiably) to complain. 'The group is called Big, Beautiful and Fit,' she yelled down the phone. It was a salutary lesson for a young reporter.

Short, simple, clear

Rather than endlessly analysing types of questions, the best way to develop your skills as an interviewer is to keep a note of those that work and those that don't.

There's no doubt, as has been highlighted earlier, that short questions are more effective than long ones, simple questions are more effective than convoluted ones and clear questions are more effective than complex ones.

Customise your questions

Make your questions suit the person you are interviewing. People who are more at home with facts and figures, for example, generally loathe hypothetical questions (politicians do too). By contrast, creative types often enjoy questions along the lines of 'What would you do if . . .?'

Another useful line of questioning is to tailor questions to interviewee's interests. If the person you are interviewing is a celebrity who loves cooking, you could ask them, 'If you were planning a posh dinner party who would you invite?' 'What would you cook?' If the person is a brilliant footballer or cricketer, you could ask them, 'Who would be in your world 11 to play against Mars?' Don't use questions like these too often though and choose the right moment to ask them. If you're in the middle of a serious conversation about a celebrity's latest film or TV series they won't be impressed to be asked a light-hearted, fanciful question about their culinary skills. There's also a risk that the celebrity might take too long to answer, using up too much of your valuable interviewing time.

Avoid interrogation

Don't interrogate your interviewee unless it's absolutely necessary. After all, if an interviewee objects to your tone they're perfectly within their rights to end the interview there and then and walk out altogether.

Author and broadcaster Clive James once said that adversarial interviews are over-rated and I tend to agree. He took a more subtle, nuanced approach to interviewing, which he discussed with a *Daily Telegraph* interviewer in 1996.

'I ask him whether his interviewing style is deceptively gentle or just gentle. "Just gentle. I'm not very good as a probing interviewer – too easily embarrassed. I believe in bowling under arm, instead. That way they take a big swing at it and get caught out."'[6]

Don't be embarrassed or judgemental

If you are interviewing someone about a sensitive subject – such as money, sex and/or relationships – don't be coy, embarrassed or critical. Try not to look shocked or disapproving (even if that's the way you feel); it may affect the interviewee's trust and confidence and make them reticent about telling you more.

Be straightforward, don't use euphemisms and avoid judgemental language. It's more effective to take a matter-of-fact approach. 'Every journalist I've met who has done a sex interview began by thinking it would be difficult and discovered the only problem was shutting the interviewee up,' said Sally Adams. 'You usually learn more than you expect, sometimes more than you wish.'[7]

Softly, softly

Skilled interviewers can ask almost anybody anything and get a reasonable response. How do they do this? By asking tough questions in a polite, charming way.

If you need to ask important questions that you suspect your interviewee will not wish to answer, approach the subject gently. If you meet refusal, anger or aggression, veer away from the subject (with an apology if that's your style) and return to the subject later.

If you want to ask questions that you know will cause trouble it is best to leave these until the end of the interview (not till the very last minute, or you might not get the chance at all). Then, if the interviewee walks out you can still write the story.

Fair warning

Warning your interviewee that you're going to ask a difficult question can be very effective. Because they are prepared, the sting goes out of the question and they feel more able to answer. Here are a few examples:

'I hope you don't mind me asking but journalists always use people's ages. How old are you?'

'This may sound rude but you've said that you are very disorganised. So how did you manage to edit a dictionary?'

'This may be a difficult question to answer but you were a top-flight businessman, running a company with a multi-million-pound turnover. Why did you ruin it all by . . .?'

Flattery

Flattery is a powerful tool, but be careful not to overuse it. When used well, though, flattery can make people feel important and valued and with luck gets them to drop their defences.

If you're interviewing someone about a new fashion collection or a play that's just made it to the West End complimenting them on their achievement is likely to make them relax and open up. This can work well at the start of an interview and has the added bonus of showing that you have done your research properly.

Interviewing task

When you're writing a profile, describing a person's body language and demeanour can be just as revealing as using quotes to show what a person is actually like. Take a recent interview you have conducted and rewrite the first five paragraphs without quoting the person you interviewed at all. Working in groups, discuss whether you think this is effective.

HOW I INTERVIEW: SUSAN GROSSMAN

Susan Grossman is a former BBC broadcaster, travel writer and magazine editor. She began her career as a researcher for *Which?* magazine and now works as a journalism lecturer, writing mentor and career and workplace coach. She runs pitching clinics for freelance journalists, lectures worldwide and works with students in groups, one to one and via Skype. She launched JournoAnswers, a Facebook group for journalists, in 2015. Her website is www. susangrossman.co.uk.

'Do your research.' That's one of the most important parts of the interviewing process, says Grossman. 'Make sure you spend time thinking about what you want to get out of the interview. If you approach an interviewee and show your ignorance in the first two or three minutes of the interview they are going to be irritated. They will be annoyed that you haven't bothered to find out about them beforehand and as a result they're unlikely to share interesting things with you.'

As well as researching the person you are interviewing as thoroughly as possible before you speak to them, Grossman believes that journalists can establish a rapport with interviewees in a whole host of ways – from praising their work to listening intently (and demonstrating that they are listening by maintaining good eye contact).

'The quickest way to build a rapport is by praise and flattery,' she says. 'This will make the person you are speaking to want to engage with you. You might start an interview by saying "I read your paper on X or I saw your broadcast on Y." They then start to think that you understand what they do and that you're someone they can talk to.'

Empathy is important too – in fact Grossman describes it as 'the biggest tool you have to enable people to feel safe with you'. She admits, however, that empathy is something that cannot be taught. 'You've either got it or you haven't, but remember that if you look bored during an interview there is no way that someone is going to be convinced that you understand how they feel or want to open up to you. It's important to be aware of the importance of empathy so it can be helpful to watch people's reactions to bad news on TV and observe how some are genuinely empathetic while others are simply pretending to be empathetic.'

Another tip Grossman gives her students is to work out what they want their interviewee to say. If you use a word in your question that you'd like your interviewee to include in their answer they often do just that. She cites the example of David Frost's 1993 interview with Nelson Mandela, when Frost asked Mandela if he ever got 'bitter'. Piers Morgan reported Frost's memories of the interview in his book, *Shooting Straight*. 'How did you get through 28 years, wrongly incarcerated, and you're not bitter?' asked Frost. Mandela replied, 'David, I would like to be bitter, but there is no time to be bitter. There is work to be done.'[8]

Grossman believes that journalism students and trainees can learn a lot from watching celebrated TV interviewers in action – from David Frost to Jeremy Paxman. Former *Newsnight* anchor Paxman is perhaps best known for his interview with home secretary Michael Howard in 1997, when he asked the same question – 'Did you threaten to overrule him?' – a total of 12 times. The *Guardian* later described it as 'a masterclass in persistence, even if it led to a very uncomfortable stalemate'[9] and it has gone into interviewing lore. Paxman admitted in his autobiography that 'it had been an unusually tetchy encounter'. Some people felt his interview had done politics a 'disservice' but Paxman disagreed. 'If as an interviewer you ask a question,' he wrote, 'it is your duty to get an answer.'[10]

Interestingly, Grossman doesn't advise her students to emulate Paxman. 'If you want to get the best out of someone you wouldn't apply the Paxman technique,' she says. 'I think his attraction as an interviewer was how much he interrupted and how uncomfortable he made people feel. That isn't a good interview. It's good television – and there's a difference. It's pretty predictable that if you are going to be rude to somebody they are not going to like it. It won't make someone open up. It's going to make them angry.'

Let them say what they need to say

Many interviewees set out to take control of interviews and insist on making the points or soundbites that they (or their PRs) have prepared in advance. Grossman's advice on this is unequivocal. 'You might find that the person you are interviewing has no intention of listening to your questions,' she says. 'They have got three points they want to make and regardless of what you ask they are going to make them. Your skill as an interviewer is to let them do that first and get it off their chest. People who want to be interviewed always have an agenda, whether it's their new book or a new piece of research, so let them say what they need to say. You can then start asking questions that involve them having to think about the answers and get into the areas you really want to know about.'

Another strategy that Grossman finds effective is to ask questions that require interviewees to reflect on the past or to recall memories. 'If you ask someone a direct question and they have prepared an answer they will say the answer,' she says. 'But if you ask them about something to do with nostalgia or memory they will physically stop – because they haven't got the answer and they need to think about it.'

Grossman says the most common anxieties of student interviewers are about the questions to ask and the fear of 'looking stupid'. She believes that novices can gain confidence through role-play – by two students playing the interviewer and the interviewee and one person observing the strategies that work best.

She is also a firm believer in paying attention to how a person looks, to their clothes, their body language and their personality as well as what they say. In her classes she uses the example of a *Financial Times* interview with the French philosopher Bernard-Pierre Lévy to illustrate how much journalists can say about a person without even quoting them. This is how the interview, conducted by the writer John Thornhill, starts: 'Universally known as BHL, the 59-year-old writer is, depending on your point of view, either the dashing darling of hopeless causes or a flashy dilettante, more concerned with promoting himself than the needy. Certainly he has a genius for stirring controversy.'[11]

The article goes on to describe the writer's apartment in Paris, the clothes he wore, his pauses, his arm movements, what distracted him, the pictures on his walls and the fact that his maid served him tea from 'a giant, antique silver teapot' – a series of fascinating details that paint a vivid picture of the interviewee long before he is quoted in the seventh paragraph.

Could you say that again?

Other questions that Grossman is often asked by students include the problem of how to maintain eye contact with your interviewee while making notes and checking the next question on your list. Grossman herself prefers to record interviews rather than take notes, although she writes down key points. When she interviewed the Queen's cousin, the society photographer Lord Lichfield, she used a tape recorder and scribbled notes. 'He stopped in the middle of the interview and said: "Why are you doing both?" "In case one of them doesn't work," I said.'

'I have no compunction in telling my students that if you hear a soundbite that you really know is going to be the one you can say "Hold on a minute, I'm just making a note of that." Or "Could you say that again?"'

'Some students think it's really bad form to show your vulnerability but I think it actually affirms to the person you are interviewing that you like what they said. In my view they will be quite flattered that you have asked them to say it again.'

Listen to the press pack

Grossman takes a huge amount of time and care in working out the best questions to ask. She advises students to ask themselves: 'What does your audience want to know at *this* minute about *this* situation?' Students can learn a lot, for instance, when someone at the eye of a political storm gets out of a car in Downing Street and hurries into Number 10. 'Listen to the question the press pack shouts,' says Grossman. 'It's always the one thing the public wants to know at that precise moment.'

She often gets students to practise interviewing by sending them out into a specific location, with instructions to get a soundbite from somebody. Whether it's an old woman in a wheelchair or a young gardener planting tulips in a park, it is an excellent way to learn how to spot good quotes and tell a story about the place in question. Another source of good quotes is the Brainy Quote website, which includes everything from Groucho Marx's 'I refuse to join any club that would have me as a member' to David Frost's 'Television is an invention that permits you to be entertained in your living room by people you wouldn't have in your home.' Keep a list of quotes you admire and the good ones will leap out at you.

Susan Grossman's top tip

Never promise your interviewee that they can read back or see what you have written about them. If they ask you to do this, say, 'It's not our editorial policy to do that' or 'I'm the interviewer, not the editor.'

Notes

1   J. Brady, *The Craft of Interviewing*, Writer's Digest, 1976, p. ix.
2   J. Brady, *The Craft of Interviewing*, Writer's Digest, 1976, p. 58.
3   A. and B. Pease, *The Definitive Book of Body Language*, Orion, 2004.
4   P. Coelho, *Manuscript Found in Accra*, HarperCollins, 2013, p. 64.
5   E. Kuhnke, *Body Language for Dummies* (2nd edn), John Wiley & Sons, 2012, p. 86.
6   *Telegraph*, 'Obnoxious? Me? Clive James continued'. Available from: www.telegraph.co.uk/culture/books/sportbookreviews/4704024/ObnoxiousMe-Clive-James-continued.html (accessed on 5 June 2016).
7   S. Adams, *Interviewing for Journalists* (2nd edn), Routledge, 2009, p. 55.
8   P. Morgan, *Shooting Straight*, Ebury Press, 2013, p. 118.
9   M. Smith and J. Randerson, 'Jeremy Paxman's top 10 Newsnight moments', *Guardian*. Available from: www.theguardian.com/media/2014/apr/30/jeremy-paxmans-top-10-newsnight-moments (accessed 31 August 2016).
10 J. Paxman, *A Life in Questions*, William Collins, 2016, p. 272.
11 J. Thornhill, 'Sons of Sartre', *Financial Times*. Available from: https://next.ft.com/content/5c945872-2608-11dd-b510-000077b07658 (accessed 18 April 2016).

7
Vox pops and other interviewing opportunities

One-to-one interviews are by no means the only interviews you will be required to do as a journalist. There are a host of other ways to gather material for news stories and features – from vox pops to press conferences – all of which require first-rate interviewing skills.

Vox pops

The term comes from the Latin phrase *vox populi* and means 'the voice of the people'. In short, editors use vox pops to provide a snapshot of public opinion. They are a cheap and easy way to fill a page with the views of a cross-section of people who have been interviewed in the street about current topics – anything from their opinions on the state of the economy to the latest *EastEnders* storyline. Over the years I have been commissioned to do vox pops on smoking, alcohol, swearing, museum charges and the price of fuel. A local paper even sent me to a nearby shopping centre to interview people about their favourite types of sandwich filling.

As well as being a good source of copy, vox pops are an excellent way to practise your interviewing skills. You soon learn to get people's essential details (name, address, age, occupation, etc.), precise answers and short, snappy quotes. You can also jettison interviews that don't work because the answers were dull or irrelevant (as long as you have gathered enough material from other interviews along the way).

Before you embark on a vox pop, compose a few pertinent, interesting and open-ended questions. Avoid questions that produce 'yes' or 'no' answers. If you are sent to the local railway station to ask passengers for their views on train fare rises, for instance, you'll need to ask where they commute to, how long the commute takes, how much they pay now, how much they will have to pay in the future and what they would like to tell the rail company in question.

Choose a spot where you're likely to find the journalistic equivalent of a captive audience, such as people waiting for a bus or queuing to get into a club. Shopping centres and street markets can be productive locations but bear in mind that if they are private property you'll need prior permission and if you don't have it you may be moved on. Unless you're desperate and there's no one else in sight, don't approach people laden with shopping or harassed parents looking after small children. If you're doing a vox pop on the increase in train fares it's a sensible idea to stand outside the railway station – but don't try and talk to people who are rushing for their train.

Make sure you choose a variety of interviewees so you get as many different opinions and perspectives as you can. There is no point in speaking to five or six people with exactly the same point of view. You need a mix of opinions, not just to provide a balance but also to make a compelling piece. Take heed of a warning from Nicholas Jones, the former BBC industrial and political correspondent. Writing in a 2016 blog post he said that vox pops can be unrepresentative, especially as they tend to be conducted in the late morning or early afternoon, when many people are at work.

'A major flaw in the practice is that most daytime shoppers or public house customers tend to be retired or self-employed, local tradesmen and the like, a sample that is invariably unrepresentative of the population at large,' wrote Jones. 'This time constraint tends to exclude most if not all those of working age.'[1]

How to get started

Once you've chosen the best place to do the vox pop, approach people confidently, notebook and/or voice recorder in hand. As with conventional interviews, never use a clipboard. If you do, everyone will assume you're doing market research and will probably avoid you. Smile, be positive and say you're a journalist straight away, adding your name and the publication you work for at the earliest opportunity. Explain the story succinctly and tell them that you want to hear people's views. It's worth adding that your questions won't take long – and make sure they don't.

Here are two possible opening lines:

'Hello. I'm a journalist for the *Evening Sentinel* and I'm writing a story about the rise in rail fares that's just been announced. We're keen to hear people's views so I wondered if you would mind giving your reaction?'

'Hello. I'm an *Evening Sentinel* journalist and I'm interviewing people about the rise in rail fares. Would you be willing to talk about it?'

Ask for their opinions first and get them talking. Once you're happy with what you've got, ask for their name. Make sure you know the style your publication uses for vox pops before you leave the office. Some publications simply use names and ages, others use occupations and the areas where interviewees live too. If you're working with a photographer they will need to get a head and shoulders shot of the people you have spoken to. Wait until you've got what you need before asking politely if they mind having their picture taken. In our 'selfie' obsessed age most people are happy to oblige. The photographer will in all likelihood make a note of their names but it's worth jotting down a few details so you can match your copy to the picture if required.

Ring rounds

These are a variation of the vox pop – but are done on the phone. Rather than approaching strangers at random in the street, you'll be calling specific people about specific subjects. You could be ringing teachers to ask them about their views on changes to the curriculum or calling estate agents to find out about house prices in your area.

Once again, introduce yourself and your publication, give details of the story you are covering and explain that you want to hear people's views about it. Keep a note of individuals who are helpful – you may want to contact them again in the future.

Following up a press release

Some publications, especially those with very few staff, print press releases verbatim. It's far better, though, to use a press release as the starting point for your own story – rather than simply using the words of the PR who wrote it (who is likely to have their own agenda).

Read the press release thoroughly, work out the best angle for your own publication, spot where the gaps in the story are and then decide who you'd like to interview. If you source your own quotes rather than using quotes from the press release (which may have been decided by committee rather than the person they are attributed to), your story will be stronger and more authentic as a result. PRs are keen to get coverage so they will almost always be happy to put you in touch with relevant people to interview.

Press conferences

Forget the rowdy scrums seen on TV and in films like *Notting Hill*. They are long gone. These days press conferences are tightly controlled by PRs and tend to run like clockwork. Make sure you arrive early, introduce yourself to the PR team and check the exact format of the event. You'll also need to find out if speakers will be available for one-to-one interviews after the press conference – and if so, for how long?

Take any handouts on offer, although PRs sometimes prefer to give them out after the press conference to ensure journalists sit through the entire event.

Even if you get a detailed press release, *always* take notes. You get livelier quotes this way and speakers often reveal unscripted details that don't feature in the handout at all.

Sit at the front. When you ask a question give your name and the publication you are working for. Don't be afraid to ask simple questions – or to check something you either don't understand or are unfamiliar with. However much you fear appearing stupid or uninformed in front of your fellow journalists, it's far more important not to appear stupid in print. 'Don't be afraid of your instincts,' adds *Evening Standard* crime editor Justin Davenport. 'If you're think-ing "why hasn't someone asked this?", ask it, because the chances are that it's a good question.'

All the same, don't take up valuable time with irrelevancies that you should know already or can research perfectly well for yourself. A successful showbiz writer says she and her fellow journalists bristle in their seats when ill-prepared journalists ask celebrities ludicrous questions. Then again, different journalists have different priorities. As a news reporter for the *Evening Standard* I covered numerous press conferences at the Wimbledon tennis championships. Year after year serious-minded tennis correspondents from around the world wanted to discuss the technical minutiae of players' serves and volleys while reporters from the UK tabloids were far more interested in quizzing them about their love lives.

There's also the conundrum of when to ask your prized question at a press conference. Many journalists loathe the thought of asking their best question in front of the rest of the press pack. They'd far rather talk to the main speaker one to one in the hope of securing a scoop, so it's worth waiting around afterwards to try and get an exclusive chat. 'Take advantage of a one-to-one interview following a press conference if this is on offer,' says education correspondent Dorothy Lepkowska. 'Or find out from the press officer in advance if this is going to be possible. You might have an angle on a story that you want to ask about but you don't want to alert other journalists to what it is.'

If the only opportunity to ask your key question is during the course of the press conference wait until the event is nearly over. There is always the faint possibility that people's attention will be flagging and they might miss your amazing question.

Interviewing task

Choose a controversial subject from the week's news and think of a suitable angle for a vox pop in your local area. List three possible locations to conduct the vox pop and compose a question that is likely to elicit some informative and intriguing responses. With the permission of your editor or journalism tutor/trainer, choose one of the locations and conduct the vox pop you have discussed. Write it up as a blog and either publish it on your own website or that of your college or university.

HOW I INTERVIEW: WENDY HOLDEN

Wendy Holden spent ten years at the *Daily Telegraph*, covering stories around the world, including the Iran-Iraq War, the first Gulf War and the Middle East conflict. She also had a stint as the paper's acting New York bureau chief. She is now an author and ghost-writer; her books include *Born Survivors*, *In the Name of Gucci*, *Shell Shock* and *Five Minutes of Amazing: My Journey through Dementia*.

As a journalist Holden often wrote pieces that were up to 1,000 words long. These days she writes books that are 100,000 words long. She firmly believes, however, that the roles of journalist and author have a lot in common.

'The techniques are very similar, except you have more time as an author,' she says. 'As a journalist I would turn up and interview someone for an hour if I was lucky, whereas for a book I speak to people on and off for several months. I live with them and really get under their skin. It's a kind of deluxe version of journalism.'

Although she has longer to research and write her books, Holden puts her journalistic experience to excellent use. She generally records her interviews but also relies on the 120 wpm Pitman's shorthand that she learned as a trainee reporter. As she talks to her interviewees she puts a star or asterisk by the key points and focuses throughout on how she can best tell their story.

'At journalism college we were always told we should see a story in terms of an inverted triangle, with the salient points of the story at the top,' she says. 'You gradually taper down to the bottom, with the less important points at the end. A book is an hourglass shape. You have the salient points at the front and an eye-catching opener. The book tapers down and then flares out so you have a strong denouement.'

Put people at their ease

Holden says that the first and most important thing during an interview is 'to put people completely at their ease' and to be open, warm and friendly.

'People are quite often terrified. The idea of a journalist coming in and asking prying questions about their lives can be daunting and frightening. Smile immediately, give them a warm handshake, make sure you have lots of eye contact and a really open and friendly demeanour, so they immediately feel "this is someone I could talk to. This is someone I could open up to."

'If you arrive in a grumpy mood or make it seem like you're in a hurry or on a deadline or that this isn't a story that particularly interests you they will immediately pick up on that. They'll sense your antipathy and it will be a bad interview.'

Holden adds that even though it sounds obvious, journalists *must* listen. 'Don't make it about you,' she says. 'Make it all about them. And be sure to leave the silences. When someone stops speaking don't immediately jump in with the next question. Wait a minute. Take a breath. Give pause for thought and let them fill the silence, because it quite often happens that when you leave silences the most important things come out.'

Unlike some interviewers she believes that in certain circumstances it can be helpful to share details of your own life with interviewees.

'If someone was talking about the loss of a loved one in the course of an hour-long interview, I wouldn't necessarily talk about my own losses,' she says. 'But if I was spending a lot of time with them I might share that I've also experienced the loss of a loved one, as we all have. Empathy is very important in an interview and you can show it by showing that you've experienced something similar.'

She says that 'practice makes perfect' when you're interviewing. 'The more you do it, the more at ease you feel doing it and the more comfortable you are.'

If you feel the interview isn't going anywhere she says that it is important to try different tacks and to 'keep plugging away'. Then again, 'people sometimes don't want to talk and you can't force them to, no matter how open, warm and friendly you are. That's their prerogative and you have to accept it – and ultimately your news editor has to accept it as well.'

Interviewing people *in extremis*

Holden is a natural interviewer and over the years she's interviewed many people who have suffered heartbreak and trauma in their lives. They include three survivors of the 1988 Piper Alpha disaster, one of the world's worst oil-rig accidents, in which 167 workers died off the coast of Aberdeen.

'A trauma counsellor who had been employed by the oil company said "you can talk to these people on one condition – that you carry on listening for as long as they want to talk. It's incredibly therapeutic for them to talk to a complete stranger. They may get very emotional and they may want to tell you more than you've got time for but I don't want you to cut the interview short." I've never forgotten that. There have been several occasions when I've interviewed people *in extremis* or after terrible events have happened to them and their families and there is an extraordinary outpouring of emotion to a complete stranger. I think it's sometimes easier for people to open up to a stranger than to open up to their immediate family members. There is emotional baggage attached to families whereas with a journalist you walk into their lives, they tell you their stories and then they dry their eyes and move on.'

Some of the most emotional interviews Holden has conducted during the course of her career were for *Born Survivors*, her book about three young women who were sent to Auschwitz II-Birkenau in 1944. The women didn't know each other but they were all newly pregnant and faced an uncertain fate without their husbands. Alone, terrified and bereft of many of their loved ones, all three knew that their only chance of saving their unborn babies from almost certain death was to hide their pregnancies from the Nazis. Against the odds, the three babies survived the Holocaust and their stories form the basis of *Born Survivors*.

When Holden travelled to Tennessee to interview the aunt of one of the babies who survived she knew that the conversation would be traumatic for the elderly woman.

'She hadn't ever spoken about her experiences before and from the moment I arrived she was in floods of tears. Her niece had come along to chaperone the interview and it was clear to me that it was too distressing for her. I knew I was going to be there for three days so I cut the interview short and said: "We're not going to talk about this any more." We had cups of tea and biscuits and chatted about life in general – about living in Tennessee, her family and her cat – and she was completely at ease. At that point I got up to go and she said: "But I haven't told you anything. I feel stronger now. I can tell you now." And then she sat down again and told me everything. I had won her over and she felt comfortable in my presence. It was all down to trust. Trust is the key to the whole thing.'

Keep your voice calm

Holden makes sure that the people she interviews feel comfortable with the situation.

'It's very important to keep your voice calm and to deliver your questions slowly,' she says. 'As soon as you become breathless or let your eyes dart around the room, either because you're nervous or because you're in a hurry, that anxiety transfers to the interviewee. If I sit and talk quite slowly, use hand gestures and eye contact and give the sense of "there's no hurry" the interviewee immediately has a sense that "this is going to be OK, this is going to be relaxing". And if they relax they are going to say more.

'For the hour you are talking to them, or even the ten minutes on the phone, it's important to make them feel as though they're the only person in your universe. You are there to listen to them and ask the questions – and that is your only focus.'

Like other writers she says that it is 'a great privilege' to tell people's stories. 'Every day is different as a journalist. You're meeting different people all the time and you could be interviewing anybody from a member of the royal family to the victim of a terrible disaster. You may be the only person they've spoken to about what they've experienced. You are a chronicler of their history and it's important to embrace it.'

One of her most memorable interviews was with Queen Noor of Jordan in 1990, at the height of the Gulf War. Queen Noor (the wife of King Hussein of Jordan, who died in 1999) rarely gives interviews but Holden put in countless requests and her persistence paid off.

'It was one of those occasions when I deliberately didn't get my notebook out for the first 15 minutes,' recalls Holden. 'My father had known King Hussein so I was able to tell her that. At one point the King walked past so she brought him into the room to introduce me and he remembered my father very fondly. I was told I would only have 45 minutes but I ended up having four hours and got an exclusive interview which ran in the *Telegraph*.'

Holden secured many exclusive interviews by thinking ahead, arriving early and always being a step in front of the pack. 'It's important to think outside the box,' she says. 'Don't have the pack mentality. Put yourself in the shoes of the person you want to interview. Think what they might want from the interview, when they might be available to talk and how they might feel about the interview.'

Off the record

When it comes to off-the-record comments Holden is unequivocal. 'If it's off the record, it's off the record. If it was something major I would try and come back to it. I might say: "Can we just go back to that point? I think it's pretty salient to this story. Is there a way you could word it that you would be comfortable with?" Don't jump in straight away and say "I really want to include that", because it will alienate them. Wait till the interview is almost over and then come back to those key points that you want to explore or expand.'

At the end of an interview Holden makes sure that she's leaving with the knowledge that she will be welcome back. 'When it comes to ghosting projects I've stayed friendly with every single client I've ever worked with,' she says. 'Journalism is similar. Even in the space of an hour you can build up a relationship with somebody and you never know when you might need to talk to them again.'

Wendy Holden's top tips

Give the people you interview every reason to trust you and use whatever weapons you have in your armoury for that. Maintain eye contact, smile and be open, warm and friendly.

Note

1   N. Jones, 'Pub regulars hardly a representative sample for European Union referendum vox pops', Nicholas Jones blog. Available from: www.nicholasjones.org.uk/article-categories/29-media-ethics/320-pub-regulars-hardly-a-representative-sample-for-european-union-referendum-vox-pops (accessed 18 August 2016).

8

The twenty-first-century tools of interviewing

Today's journalists need to be multi-skilled. As well as conducting interviews and writing them up, you may be required to tweet the best lines from your piece, upload a podcast or even produce a short video. As John Dale reported in *24 Hours in Journalism*, his account of a typical day in journalism: 'Now employers want trainees who have all the traditional "print" skills, including subbing and layout, *plus* the ability to make and edit videos, *plus* the skills to put stories, pics and videos, and links, on a website.'[1]

Cole Moreton is an excellent example of the multi-skilled journalist. When he worked for the *Sunday Telegraph* he pioneered new forms of multimedia storytelling. He often recorded short videos after a traditional-style interview and these would be posted online with his feature. 'We would do the interview and then take the two or three best quotes and record them with a really non-intrusive camera,' he says.

Always try and think of audio and video possibilities when you're interviewing. In 2014 the *Financial Times* commissioned Brian Viner to learn how to become a horse-racing commentator for the paper's *FT Masterclasses* series. 'The firm message at the end of my masterclass is not to give up the day job,'[2] he wrote afterwards. It made a fine piece but in retrospect Viner reckons it would have worked even better if his commentary had been posted with the online version of his feature.

Citizen journalists (private individuals who act as news reporters) need twenty-first-century interviewing tools too. Often the first to arrive on the scene as stories unfold, they produce podcasts, blogs, videos and pictures on a variety of online platforms, including text, pictures, audio and video.

In this intensely competitive media landscape many journalism students may end up working as citizen journalists, perhaps combining this with another job.

If you are interested in this type of journalism, good interviewing skills will stand you in good stead and mark you out from the crowd.

Shorthand or voice recorder – or both?

Every print and online journalist I interviewed for this book emphasised the importance of quoting people accurately, a finding borne out by a report published by the Reuters Institute for the Study of Journalism at the University of Oxford in 2016. 'Almost all UK journalists (95%) disapprove of altering or fabricating quotes,' said Alessio Cornia and Neil Thurman, co-authors of the chapter on ethics and standards.[3]

In order to quote accurately you need to have an accurate record of your interviews, so one of the first decisions you need to make when you're interviewing is whether to use shorthand or a voice recorder – or both. Lynn Barber and Camilla Long, two of the UK's most highly regarded journalists, don't use shorthand, but other writers, Wendy Holden, Justin Davenport and Sheron Boyle among them, reckon that shorthand is an important skill for journalists and use it for every interview.

Each approach has its advantages and disadvantages but there are two enduring principles. First, I've never met a journalist who regretted learning shorthand (although a few expressed regret that they'd let their speeds lapse). Second, there's no 'best' method of recording an interview. It all depends what you're after. If it's a 1,000-word profile of an up-and-coming celebrity, complete with revelatory quotes, plenty of description and needing to be filed in a week's time, then a voice recorder and notebook used in tandem will probably work best. If you've been asked to write a 200-word news story within the hour, then phone your interviewee and take down what they say in shorthand. There won't be time to transcribe a recording.

Hunter Davies, the veteran journalist and author, prefers to use a notebook and pen. In his highly readable collection of interviews, *Hunting People: Thirty Years of Interviews with the Famous*, he explained that he went to shorthand lessons when he started on the *Manchester Evening Chronicle* but didn't keep it up. 'The big advantage to me of a notebook, as opposed to tape,' he wrote, 'is that I am editing as I go along. I jot down only the good stuff, the flavour, people's speech mannerisms . . . I jot down details of their clothes, their face, the setting, conversations with other people, any interruptions, especially interruptions. All interviewers are dying for the unexpected, to give us colour, show the subject in a different light.'[4]

Shorthand

Pros and cons

For:

- minimal, inexpensive equipment – a notebook and pen is all you need
- works almost anywhere and is unaffected by noisy backgrounds or battery failures
- immediately accessible, with no need to play back
- acceptable in law
- interviewees (and bosses) are impressed – looks good on CVs
- about four to five times faster than longhand.

Against:

- takes time to learn, especially to reach speeds of 100 wpm and over
- reduces eye contact
- may look old-fashioned to some interviewees, particularly celebrities
- works best when transcribed quickly
- unlike a digital recording, is not verbatim
- chance of errors in both note-taking and transcription.

What the experts say

The National Council for the Training of Journalists (NCTJ), the body that accredits journalists' training, describes shorthand as 'a key skill for journalists', and trainees who take the National Qualification in Journalism (NQJ) are required to have 100 wpm shorthand.[5] NCTJ chairman Kim Fletcher told BBC Radio 4's flagship *Today* programme in 2009 that in his opinion shorthand is 'more necessary than ever'. 'If you have a shorthand note you can find the quote very quickly,' he said. 'You go in with a tape recorder, or a digital recorder, and if you've spent an hour in there with your recorder you've got an hour of tape to go through. That takes quite a long time.'[6]

There are several types of shorthand, including Pitman's, Teeline, Gregg and Speedwriting, but Teeline is probably the most commonly used by journalists. It was invented in 1967 by James Hill, who maintained that 'if you can write, you can write Teeline'. Formerly a Pitman's teacher, he developed Teeline to make learning shorthand easier and faster. He died before his system became widespread but its potential was recognised by Harry Butler, the NCTJ's shorthand consultant, who saw that trainee journalists could achieve 100 wpm in a fraction of the time it took to learn other shorthand systems.

Freelance journalist Nilufer Atik learned Teeline more than 18 years ago and says she couldn't manage without it. 'I know it's deemed the old-fashioned approach but trust me, it saves a lot of time,' she says. 'Instead of transcribing, you read it as you would read print, plus shorthand notes are legally admissible in court as evidence. I tend to record interviews just as a legal record when needed, but always take shorthand too so I can write features up directly. Sometimes the old ways are the best ways.'

Heidi Blake, investigations editor of BuzzFeed UK, learned shorthand during her training at the *Daily Telegraph*. After a six-week course she improved her shorthand speed by using a website with recordings of people talking at speeds of up to 120 wpm. She'd take notes using her shorthand and then check she could read it back.

Blake finds her notebook 'a useful tool' when interviewing sources. 'When you are a young reporter trying to persuade people to reveal stuff to you, the biggest obstacle is persuading people that you are a serious individual they can trust and you're not a fly-by-night 22-year-old who doesn't know they are born. So going in and quite visibly doing something very professional like shorthand is a mark of your profession as a trained journalist. It shows that you know what you are talking about and it really helps. People feel that they are dealing with a professional. I totally recommend learning it if you can, especially if you have to file in a hurry.'

She believes that taking notes impresses some interviewees. 'Some people love it when you sit down and write down everything they say. It makes them feel important. Some sources arrive all ready to tell you everything they know. They have really worked themselves up about something and say things like "Have you got that down? Make sure you make a note of that."'

Blake also uses her notebook to signal interest in what her interviewees are saying. 'If someone is telling you something interesting and you want to know more, you show them you're writing it down. It tells them that you're interested. But if you put your pen down and sit back, it tells them that it's not interesting. And if you close your notebook it tells them that the interview is over now.'

Longhand

Pros and cons

If you haven't learned shorthand and don't want to use a voice recorder then writing in longhand is the only alternative.

For:

- simple
- fine with a very slow speaker (but even so it will be hard to keep up)
- just about suitable for statistics and short facts.

Against:

- slow, and the odds are that you will have to ask your interviewee to pause so you can catch up or repeat details
- unimpressive – shorthand and/or voice recorders look far more professional
- relies heavily on memory, which is not ideal
- not good for lively, vivid quotes or for interviewees who speak fast
- only to be used as a last resort – it's far better to learn Teeline if you possibly can.

Voice recorders

For long interviews, most journalists prefer to use digital recorders, although many (but by no means all) take notes as well. Stephanie Rafanelli doesn't take any notes during interviews. She believes that using a notebook changes the mood of the conversation. Holding eye contact is very important and in her view taking notes makes an interviewer's body language more rigid and less relaxed too.

If you are conducting a sensitive or controversial interview it's advisable to record the conversation. If elements of your interview are disputed at a later date you can then produce a transcript of the recording (this will be discussed in greater detail in Chapter 12). *The Times* did this after Andrea Leadsom, a candidate for the Conservative Party leadership in 2016, challenged the contents of an interview she'd given to *The Times* journalist Rachel Sylvester. The recording showed that the politician had been reported accurately. As Katharine Viner, editor-in-chief of the *Guardian*, wrote afterwards: 'After telling *The Times* that being a mother would make her a better PM than her rival Theresa May, she cried "gutter journalism!" and accused the newspaper of misrepresenting her remarks – even though she said exactly that, clearly and definitively and on tape.'[7]

Pros and cons

For:

- provide proof of what was said
- quotes are verbatim, with no gaps
- enable you to concentrate totally on your interviewee
- enable you to maintain excellent eye contact (if the interview is face to face and not on the telephone)

- most interviewees forget they are being recorded and talk freely
- if the interviewee is a fast talker you don't have to ask them to speak more slowly to get their quotes down
- interviewees who know they have been recorded rarely question the accuracy of quotes (although there have been notable exceptions)
- it is possible to interview in transit and while you are walking along (when using shorthand might be difficult)
- easy to save on your computer afterwards.

Against:

- unless you use a notebook at the same time, you can't record details such as the expression on the interviewee's face, the colour of their eyes and the state of their desk (some journalists record these immediately after the interview)
- not always suitable for interviews with large groups, when you need to keep track of who is saying what
- there's a risk that the recorder might fail or batteries may go flat (hence some interviewers use two recorders)
- some recorders don't work well in crowded places, especially when there is a lot of background noise
- recordings take hours to transcribe and you may have to listen to certain parts over and over again
- with so much recorded material there can be a risk of over-quoting the interviewee and using inconsequential words and details.

Choose the best voice recorder

There are a multitude of digital voice recorders to choose from so ask your colleagues for recommendations and buy the best you can afford.

Many of the journalists I interviewed for this book said they use two devices – either two digital recorders or a digital recorder and a smartphone (set to airplane mode so there's no interference). Why? Because they want to make absolutely sure that nothing goes wrong, although virtually all of them admitted that they'd experienced panic-stricken moments when their recorders had failed.

My own calamity came when I interviewed Paul Weller for *Woman's Own* magazine. As we sat companionably on a bench in a leafy London square the singer talked in depth about his days with The Jam and The Style Council. I had no idea until later that my recorder had died midway through. Luckily I'd taken shorthand notes as well so disaster was averted. These days I use a digital recorder or iPhone, plus a shorthand notebook.

During the interview

To avoid voice recorder disasters keep a weather eye on your device during the interview. Try not to make this obvious but check the recording light is on right the way through the conversation.

The *Daily Mail's* Brian Viner, who uses two recorders, always takes a surreptitious look at his voice recorders at the start. 'In the whole kerfuffle of sitting down with somebody you can hit the wrong button, so check they are both working,' he says. 'Make sure your tape recorders are good enough to blot out any background noise because that's a nightmare – and have them at different angles.'

Taping the interviewer

It's not inconceivable that an interviewee might produce a voice recorder of their own – so don't be thrown off your guard by this. The late Labour MP Tony Benn always taped his own interviews, as the political journalist and broadcaster Andrew Rawnsley recalled following the politician's death in 2014. Interviewing Mr Benn in the early days of his career, wrote Rawnsley in the *Observer*, was 'an intimidating experience for a young reporter, not least because when I set up my tape machine, he plonked down a recording device of his own'.

Rawnsley clearly got off lightly. He added that when a colleague conducted an interview with Mr Benn the politician 'suddenly drew from a cupboard a magnetic device and waved it over the reporter's machine, erasing the tape'.[8]

Transcribing

Almost every journalist hates the laborious process of transcribing – from the endless time it takes to the irritation of listening to your own voice for hours on end. Indeed, some loathe it so much they farm the job out to transcription services, such as Rev, UK Transcription and a start-up company called Trint, a browser-based platform that 'converts any audio or video file to text in minutes'. There are plenty of freelance transcribers too. Indeed some freelance journalists themselves offer transcription. Prices vary – a straw poll at the time of writing found that freelance transcribers charge between £1 and £1.50 per recorded minute for their services – so it's worth asking other journalists for recommendations. Some writers use voice recognition software, with varying degrees of success.

Just as journalists take different approaches to interviewing they have a variety of transcription styles too. Some cut down on transcription time by only transcribing the sections they think they will need for their article. Others transcribe every word of their interviews, arguing that listening to the whole conversation a second time round helps the writing process. 'One of the points of transcribing is that you can hear the moment again,' says Cole Moreton. Brian Viner agrees. 'I always do my own,' he says. 'I have farmed them out once or twice but what you don't get there are those little moments when you hear a catch in their voice or a hesitation or a reminder of something.'

Classical music journalist Ariane Todes finds transcribing a chore but insists on doing it herself. 'I usually prioritise speed over accuracy in the first run-through, as it's easy to fix spelling afterwards – although I do make sure that the quotes I'm probably going to use are correct,' she says. 'Usually I transcribe all of it, as I have a blog, so if I can't use everything I can sometimes make the leftovers into something for that. If I don't have time to transcribe everything I find that it helps to write in the timings of the recording, which at least makes it easier to go back to the right spot on the tape. Otherwise you have to listen to the whole thing again.'

Multimedia courses

As more and more online magazines and newspapers expect journalists to add multimedia content to their stories, consider taking a specialist course, especially if you are a freelance journalist and want to add more strings to your bow.

There are a variety of short courses and workshops on offer, teaching skills like how to record audio interviews and shoot video using your smartphone, how to edit clips on a smartphone and create a video news story and how to use social media sites to launch videos and blogs online. If you don't have the time or funds to take a course there are plenty of tutorials on YouTube. You can use your smartphone and experts say it's perfectly possible to learn the basics of shooting great video and video-editing in 24 hours. Here are a few simple tips to help you record a video interview:

- Don't shoot vertical video. Today's world is widescreen – so shoot your video horizontally.
- If you are conducting the interview by yourself try and get hold of a tripod if you possibly can. It looks professional and you will avoid the inevitable camera shake.
- If you don't have access to a tripod hold your smartphone or camera to one side. As with other interviews, it's important to maintain eye contact with your interviewee.
- If you are using an external microphone make sure that it is as close to your subject as possible. If you are shooting video with an iPhone, it works

best to place a second iPhone close to your interviewee to record the audio.

- You can invest in professional lighting but if this isn't an option make sure you film in a well-lit location.
- When it comes to asking your questions, keep them short, snappy, direct and precise.
- Ask 'open' questions, giving the interviewee the opportunity to give vivid, interesting answers. If you're interviewing a debut author who is predicted to become a literary superstar, for example, you might ask: 'The critics have described your first novel as "witty and unputdownable". What was the inspiration for the book?' If you're interviewing a head teacher whose pupils have achieved top grades in their exams you might ask: 'Your students have all got into their first choice of university this year. What is the secret of their success?'
- As with print interviews, don't rush to fill silences. Interviewees will often fill the silence with a great quote – and remember that you can always edit the silence out of the recording later.
- Keep the video clips short. As the journalism trainer and writer Brendan Martin said in the second edition of *Interviewing for Journalists*: 'The nature of the internet is brevity, speed and instant communication. You would be far better uploading a single 15-second soundbite within minutes of your interviewee saying it than waiting hours or even days to edit, polish and upload a five-minute package.'[9]

Interviewing task

Today's journalists need to be up to date with the latest technology. If you haven't done so already, view online tutorials on shooting and editing video, data journalism and Photoshop. The more skilled you are, the more employable you will be. You should already have started your own blog so write a blog-post about the twenty-first-century journalism tools that are making a difference to you.

HOW I INTERVIEW: BRIAN VINER

Brian Viner trained with Reed Business Publishing. He then spent five years on the *Ham and High*, as the *Hampstead and Highgate Express* in London is affectionately known, working his way from cub reporter to features editor. He was the *Mail on Sunday*'s award-winning TV critic from 1995 to 1999, followed by a 13-year stint as a feature writer for the *Independent*. His weekly sports interview for the *Independent* was the longest running weekly interview in national newspaper journalism in the UK at the time. Since 2013 he has been the *Daily Mail*'s film critic. He has written several non-fiction books, including *The Good, the Dad and the Ugly: The Trials of Fatherhood* and *Tales of the Country*.

Brian Viner reckons he has interviewed around 1,500 people during his career – everyone from Hugh Hefner to Zara Phillips. He once interviewed Cliff Richard for a feature called 'Out to Lunch', only to find that the singer preferred to do the interview at home and hadn't eaten lunch since 1964. 'Instead he asked his assistant to bring us coffee and biscuits,' wrote Viner in a subsequent column. 'So "Out to Lunch with Cliff Richard" turned out to be "In for Coffee and Jammie Dodgers with Cliff Richard". And he didn't even have a Jammie Dodger.'[10]

Viner points out that while there are some hard and fast rules when it comes to interviewing, everyone does it differently 'depending on who they are and the experiences they've had'. He, for instance, believes that interviews should generally be as informal and relaxed as possible, with the interviewer doing their best to establish a rapport right from the start – 'not being deferential exactly, but being respectful and polite,' he says. 'I thank them for finding the time to do the interview, tell them roughly how long it will be and explain why I am there and who I am writing for. If you can establish a common bond it can be helpful, such as a mutual friend or if they live in a place where you used to live. An interview is inherently an awkward and artificial situation so you have to do what you can to change that and make it seem entirely natural that the interviewee, having never met you before, will start talking to you about their children, their health, whatever it might be.'

Breaking the ice

Unusually, Viner sometimes presents his interviewees with a gift – 'not everybody,' he says, 'but if I think it might help break the ice and get me off on the right foot'. He presented Frank Warren with a bottle of Puligny-Montrachet because he'd read that the boxing promoter liked white wine and when he interviewed Prince Philip at Buckingham Palace he presented him with two packs of smoked butter. Viner later wrote in his column: 'A friend of mine runs the Organic Smokehouse in Shropshire, and had told me that when the Queen and Prince Philip passed their stall during a visit to Ludlow farmers' market a few years previously, one particular item had intrigued Her Majesty. "Smoked butter!" she exclaimed in amazement, and walked regally on, only to return a moment later to say, again, "smoked butter!" A packet was duly slipped to a lady-in-waiting, and a couple of weeks later my friend got a call from the Palace asking for more. Apparently Prince Philip was most partial.

'And so it was that I became almost certainly the only person ever to walk across the forecourt of Buckingham Palace with a briefcase containing two tape recorders and two packs of smoked butter. I told the Duke's delightful press officer of my plan, and she suggested that it might be best to wait until the interview was over. "I believe Mr Viner has something for you, sir," she duly said as the old boy got to his feet, which was my cue to remind him of his trip to Ludlow.

'Unfortunately, as I reached into my case, I realised that even on one bar, the electric fire had had a disastrous effect. Yet there was nothing else in there I could give him, apart from a month-old boiled sweet. The royal eyebrows shot heavenwards as I self-consciously handed over my gift. "Smoked butter!" he said in a kind of strangulated voice, as if he had never seen it before in his life, and doubtless wondering why a chap should talk to him for 45 minutes about cricket, soccer, rugger and carriage-driving and then give him two slightly melted packs of smoked butter.'[11]

Explore new territory

Viner believes that thorough preparation is respectful to interviewees and enables the journalist to do a better interview. 'You don't want somebody telling you something they've already told 30 other interviewers,' he says. 'What's the point of that? You want to explore new territory.' He emphasises, too, that it can be helpful to look at decades-old cuttings. 'Go back as far as you want,' he says. 'You can sometimes pull out some really good nuggets.' He adds, however, that journalists don't have to know everything about their interviewees. 'There needs to be some sort of mystery. Otherwise you'll sit there and think "I've heard all of this before" and your disinterest will probably come across.'

When Viner interviews sports personalities he always talks to specialist writers on his paper first. Similarly, he might have a chat with a theatre critic ahead of an interview with a Shakespearian actor. 'It can be helpful to ask them what they would ask. Equally, if you're struggling to decide which way you are going to take an interview then ask your wife, husband or neighbour what they'd like to know about the person.'

He arrives up to 90 minutes early for interviews, especially if he is travelling by train. How you dress is important too, he says. 'Don't turn up in a tatty pair of jeans if you're interviewing somebody who would be offended by that, but equally, don't overdress either. Don't necessarily wear a suit if you're going to a football training ground where everyone else is going to be in shorts.'

A mental list

Viner goes into interviews with 'a mental list' of the questions he wants to ask. 'I try not to use a physical list or have a book open in my lap,' he says.

'Sometimes it's helpful to have a crib-sheet but I try very hard not to refer to it too much.

'I think novice interviewers make the mistake of being too rigid about the questions they have written down or thought about beforehand. You might ask someone "Which school did you go to?" and then the interviewee says: "I went to such-and-such a school but I had to take a year out because my mother died when I was 12." Some interviewers are so interested in the next question on their list that they immediately ask "And did you go to university after school?" And the whole thing about their mother dying has gone. You have to listen to the answers and sometimes mentally tear up your questions so you can follow the path that they take you on. Then the interview becomes more of a conversation.'

Questions about parenthood (such as 'How has becoming a parent changed your attitude to your career?') often produce illuminating answers but he cautions against asking questions that provoke a long silence while your interviewee mulls over their answer. 'Don't sit down with someone and ask them "What are your five favourite films?" You'll waste ten minutes while they try to think. Send them questions like that in advance or ask them to have a think about it and call them later on.'

On a similar note, he says that it's important not to waste time during the interview by making small talk for too long. 'A bit of small talk is good at the beginning,' he says, 'but ten minutes into your valuable hour you don't want to be still talking about the train journey they've had.' He tries to avoid talking about himself too much. 'Don't make the mistake of thinking that the interviewee wants to hear about you when they are there to talk about themselves. You don't ever want to play back the tape afterwards and hear too much of yourself.'

He generally finds that hour-long interviews give 'more than enough' time to draw interviewees out – and enough material to write a 2,000-word feature. 'Sometimes I'd have to get 2,000 words out of ten minutes with a cosseted sports star, standing outside a changing room. On the other hand I've done interviews that have gone on for three hours over lunch or dinner. That is way too much material for a newspaper article but the best bits might come after two and a half hours.'

Check your batteries

Viner uses two good-quality dictaphones – 'there's nothing worse than listening back afterwards and not being able to make out a word,' he says. 'You feel ghastly.' He tests the batteries beforehand and ensures there is sufficient space left for new recordings. Like most journalists his dictaphones have occasionally failed.

During the interview he rarely takes notes but always double-checks the recording afterwards. 'I have a little listen on the way home and make sure the interview is all there. If you can't really hear it then at least it's fairly fresh in your memory and you can jot everything down. If you come back to it a week later you'll have forgotten the whole thing.'

No copy approval

He never offers copy approval but admits that when interviewees ask him not to use certain details it can be 'a bit of a grey area'. 'I've done quite a few interviews over the years where they have followed me out and said "Please don't use what I said about such-and-such", without having said at the time that it was off the record. If someone says at the time "this is off the record", you should respect that; otherwise you get a really bad reputation. But if someone doesn't say "this is off the record" and then retrospectively asks you to make it off the record it would entirely depend on what it was.'

He recalls an interview with a high-profile footballer whose autobiography had just been published. When Viner quoted a line from the book, the footballer replied: 'To be honest, mate, I haven't read it.' The publicist asked Viner not to use the remark and he agreed. 'He was supposed to have written the book and here he was saying he hadn't read it. I said "OK, fair enough". It would have ruined my reputation with the publisher and I probably wouldn't have got any more interviews through them. So you just have to be sensible about it.'

Interviewing Michael Winner

No one has ever walked out of an interview with Viner, although he had a testing moment with film director Michael Winner.

'We sat down at his favourite Italian restaurant in Notting Hill and I was doing my usual, trying to establish a rapport and be friendly and twinkly. He wasn't having any of it. He said: "I want you to write down on this napkin that you give Michael Winner copy approval and that you will send the interview to him before it is published. If you don't sign it then I'm leaving right now." I had no reason to think he was bluffing so I signed it. But in the course of the next hour and half we got on so well. He was funny and very entertaining and after a while he tore the napkin up. So, starting from a very abrasive point we reached a point where he thought: "I can trust this guy."'

Viner has often done interviews with publicists sitting in. 'This happens especially with actors,' he says. 'Very often you are accompanied into the interview by a fussy PR who says "you can't talk to so-and-so about their affair or pregnancy or drink-driving charge." My advice is to completely disregard that because quite often you find that the person you are interviewing will talk about anything. It's a bit of a gamble but it's important not to be too hamstrung or constrained by PR directives.'

If interviewees are 'uncooperative, rude or bolshie', Viner refuses to be unnerved. 'You can make a virtue of it,' he says. 'You can turn something that seems like a negative at the time of the interview into a positive when you are writing the piece up. It's never wasted.'

Don't let awkward silences develop

While Viner listens attentively to each answer he's always thinking about his next question too. 'Sometimes the person will finish answering a question and there can be an awkward silence. You can generally tell the difference between somebody who is trying to search for the right word and somebody who has actually finished what they are saying. Don't let those awkward silences develop, even if you have to plug the gap with something inane. It's worth doing that rather than letting the conversation fizzle into silence. Be patient. Sometimes you can be 20 minutes into a 40-minute interview and you're thinking "I haven't really got anything worth writing". You have to bide your time and it will come. Be patient and don't panic.

'While I'm interviewing I always keep half a mind on how I'm going to write it. There are always moments where you think: "I've got my intro, I've got the real selling point." I'm almost writing the piece in my head as they are talking.'

Brian Viner's top tip

You've got to be a good listener.

Notes

1 J. Dale, *24 Hours in Journalism*, John Dale Publishing, 2012, p. 85 (italics in original).
2 B. Viner, 'Racing commentary with Simon Holt', *Financial Times*. Available from: https://next.ft.com/content/baa089a6-f1b6-11e3-a2da-00144feabdc0 (accessed 3 June 2016).
3 N. Thurman and A. Cornia, 'Ethics and standards', in N. Thurman, A. Cornia and J. Kunert, *Journalists in the UK*, Reuters Institute for the Study of Journalism,

2016, p. 53. Available from: https://reutersinstitute.politics.ox.ac.uk/sites/default/files/Journalists%20in%20the%20UK.pdf (accessed 11 October 2016).

4   H. Davies, *Hunting People: Thirty Years of Interviews with the Famous*, Mainstream Publishing Company, 1994, p. 16.

5   NCTJ Level 5 National Qualification in Journalism (NQJ), National Council for the Training of Journalists (NCTJ). Available from: www.nctj.com/journalism-qualifications/National-Qualification-in-Journalism-NQJ? (accessed 11 October 2016).

6   A *Quick Shorthand Test*, BBC Radio 4. Available from: http://news.bbc.co.uk/today/hi/today/newsid_8356000/8356176.stm (accessed 11 October 2016).

7   K. Viner, 'How technology disrupted the truth', *Guardian*. Available from: www.theguardian.com/media/2016/jul/12/how-technology-disrupted-the-truth (accessed 11 October 2016).

8   A. Rawnsley, 'Tony Benn: charismatic leader of the left damned by warm Tory praises', *Observer*. Available from: www.theguardian.com/commentisfree/2014/mar/16/tony-benn-labour-politics (accessed 11 October 2016).

9   S. Adams, *Interviewing for Journalists* (2nd edn), Routledge, 2009, p. 111.

10 B. Viner, 'Wimbledon is weird: that's why it sums up England perfectly', *Independent*. Available from: www.independent.co.uk/voices/columnists/brian-viner/brian-viner-wimbledon-is-weird-ndash-thats-why-it-sums-up-england-perfectly-2017134.html (accessed 11 October 2016).

11 B. Viner, 'Brian Viner: the day I tried to butter up the Duke of Edinburgh', *Independent*. Available from: www.independent.co.uk/voices/columnists/brian-viner/brian-viner-the-day-i-tried-to-butter-up-the-duke-of-edinburgh-2093396.html (accessed 11 October 2016).

9
Interviewing by telephone, email, text and Skype

While every journalist I interviewed agreed that interviewing face to face is always preferable they agreed that it isn't always possible. When time is tight, your interviewee is hundreds of miles away and the news desk budget won't run to a train fare, you may have to do your interviews by telephone or via Skype, FaceTime, email or even text.

Interviewing on the telephone tends to be harder than face to face because it's more difficult to establish a rapport. It's by no means impossible though. Journalists like highly respected freelance Sheron Boyle often use the phone for major interviews and see it as an effective means of communication. Boyle is based in West Yorkshire and when she wrote a series of stories for the *Sunday People* about the deaths of ten babies and children (the youngest was three days old and the oldest was seven) at the Bristol Royal Hospital for Children she did every single interview on the phone. Boyle's series had a huge impact. As she reported in the *Sunday People*: 'after reading one of our stories, NHS top doctor Sir Bruce Keogh answered a parent's plea to act. He met parents and, in February 2014, agreed to set up an independent inquiry, led by health lawyer Sir Ian Kennedy.'[1]

Looking back on the series, Boyle says that a journalist's telephone manner and ability to engage with people on the phone are 'vital' to getting a strong interview. Some of her interviews with the Bristol families were two hours long.

'I introduce myself and say that I'm a journalist who writes for the nationals and for magazines,' she says. 'I say: "I'd really like to have a chat with you about your story." If they are hesitant I might say: "Can I just have a chat and then you can decide one way or the other?"'

'With the Bristol families I'd be on the phone for two hours and then I'd write it up immediately. They'd lost babies and had been fobbed off by bureaucrats, by medics and by hospitals and I took some pride in helping them. That's our job.'

Recording telephone calls

While Sheron Boyle uses shorthand for telephone interviews, some journalists prefer to record them. I record longer phone interviews and always ask people's permission to record first. You shouldn't encounter a problem with this, as long as you explain that you are a journalist. As McNae's Essential Law for Journalists points out, it is legal in the UK to record a phone conversation, 'even if the other is unaware this is being done'. It adds, however, that 'a journalist who fails to declare in such a call that he/she is a journalist may breach the code's ban on subterfuge and misrepresentation, unless the "public interest" exception applies and it seems reasonable to conclude there is no other way to obtain the information.'[2]

There are a variety of apps to enable you to record phone calls, including TapeACall and Call Recorder, although you can also put your phone on speaker-phone and record the interview or even type the quotes straight into a Word document. It is worth experimenting with different methods to find out what works best for you. I use TapeACall, an app that only works once the telephone call has started. I therefore take a moment to ask the interviewee if they mind me recording the interview and then merge the two calls. No one has ever objected and it works well.

Telephone interviews

Telephone interviews are widely used by newspaper, magazine and online journalists. They are time efficient and enable you to reach your interviewees quickly and professionally. If you're writing a piece that requires you to talk to a number of people, you can interview everyone in the space of a few hours whereas if you interviewed them all face to face it would probably take days.

If you are working in news the chances are that you'll routinely be required to ring people without warning, perhaps to check out the details of a breaking story or to talk to an expert. If you have more time and the person is proving difficult to get hold of, it is often worth emailing interviewees first, outlining what you need and then fixing a time to interview them on the phone. This also gives your interviewee the opportunity to collect their thoughts and find additional information.

Establishing a rapport is harder on the phone than in person but it can be done. When the interviewee answers the phone, make an effort to sound warm and friendly. Explain who you are, give the name of your publication and ask if they can possibly help you with a story you are working on. If the story is an upbeat one, try to make your voice sound 'smiley'. This may sound contradictory but the late BBC broadcaster Brian Redhead was brilliant at doing this. Indeed the BBC Radio 2 presenter and journalist Jeremy Vine commented on it in his 2013 book, *It's All News to Me: How I Got Locked Inside the BBC for 25 Years*. 'Working on *Today*, I watched as Brian Redhead broke into a smile every time the red light told him his microphone was on: you could hear the smile in his voice.'[3]

If you are doing a phone interview for a feature, ask your interviewee to describe where they are and what they are doing there. If you're talking to a novelist who has written her latest book in the wilds of the countryside or an actor who is sunning himself by a pool in the south of France, you'll be able to give your readers a more vivid picture by weaving the details into your story. Don't, however, give the impression that the interview was conducted face to face if it wasn't. As Chris Frost explained in the second edition of *Reporting for Journalists*: 'If you use the phone for an interview, it would be unethical to give the reader or viewer the impression that the interview was done face to face. The Press Complaints Commission (PCC) warned in 1992 that such practices could give rise to complaints of publishing inaccurate and misleading material.'[4]

Not everyone likes interviewing on the phone though. Journalism lecturer and coach Susan Grossman tries to avoid phone interviews for anything other than a quick response. She prefers to use Skype or FaceTime, largely because she says that being able to see the person she is talking to makes it easier to establish a rapport.

'In a phone interview you have got to outline your intent as early as possible,' says Grossman. 'Say something like "I've rung you because I need two or three quotes about why you set this laboratory up" or "I'm doing this interview because I'd like to talk to you about your potential move to the Foreign Office." Get to the point quickly and make them feel comfortable.'

Unlike Sheron Boyle, she's sceptical about the likelihood of getting your best interviews on the phone. 'Nobody is going to give you shocking, revealing stuff on the phone,' Grossman says.

Skype and FaceTime

Skype and FaceTime can be effective interviewing tools. Provided that both parties have got decent broadband you can conduct a very successful interview without moving from your desk. When author and journalist Wendy Holden ghost-wrote *Sex, Love and Fashion: A Memoir of a Male Model*, she conducted all her interviews with male supermodel Bruce Hulse (known as 'The Incredible

Hulse') on Skype. 'The intention was to say hello on Skype and then fly out to Los Angeles to interview him,' she recalls. 'But the trip was cancelled so I Skyped him back and said "This is working OK. Can we do the whole book this way?" We did the whole book on Skype and when I finally met him in person it was like I'd known him all my life.'

Now Holden frequently uses Skype and FaceTime for interviews, although she says it's important to observe certain conventions. 'You use the same techniques as interviewing in person, like smiling and being empathetic, but make sure you look at the camera and if you're taking notes look up frequently.'

Another word of advice is to make sure your office doesn't look a tip. Holden works from her office at home and ensures that it's quiet, the door is shut, the view behind her is 'smart and bookish' and no one walks in midway through with a pot of tea. 'I turn off all the phones so they don't ring and interrupt the flow. There's nothing worse than when the interviewee is just at the point of saying "yes, I did kill her" and the phone rings or the dog comes in.'

Susan Grossman uses Skype for teaching as well as interviewing and believes it works well – as long as you use the video camera and maintain good eye contact.

'To begin with I was wary about how I would be able to make the same sort of connection on Skype as I would in real life,' she says. 'You need to see the person you are talking to though. Once you do that you can almost forget it's Skype. You can see people's faces, how they react, their surroundings – you can see an awful lot of things in fact.'

Interviewing by email or text

Interviewing by email or text is probably the least appealing option – unless you have absolutely no alternative.

If you approach a PR or showbiz agent for an interview with a star and they ask you to send a list of questions for their client to answer by email or even text, try and think of another way of doing the interview. 'Go to their book launch and find them in person,' says Susan Grossman. 'What I really dislike are the Q&A interviews that a lot of newspapers and magazines run these days. They don't tell the story at all. It's more about "how quickly can we fill this page?"'

Establishing a rapport by email or text is far more difficult than face to face or on the phone. The only advantage of interviewing in this way is that you may be able to contact people all over the world and in totally different time zones.

Some people are far happier to be interviewed by email or text because they can think about their answers first and answer the questions in their own time. In my experience, one of the many disadvantages of interviewing in this way is that interviewees' answers tend to be brief, formal and often a little lifeless. But if there is no alternative, they are better than nothing.

If you are sending an email to an interviewee it's best to address them formally in the first instance. 'Dear Mr Brown' is preferable to 'Hi John' and 'Dear Lady Bracknell' is better than 'Hey Augusta'. Think carefully about the subject line and make it interesting enough to make sure that the recipient will open it. If you are sending an email to someone who is interviewed frequently, simply typing 'interview request' or 'media opportunity' in the subject line won't guarantee that they read the email. Check that your email is spelled and punctuated correctly and remember that once you have pressed 'send' the recipient of the email is perfectly at liberty to forward it to whoever they choose. In other words, get the email right before you send anything.

When it comes to emailing your questions, the best way to elicit interesting answers is to write interesting, original and open-ended questions. Camilla Long is particularly good at this. Here are some of her questions, emailed to women in the news for the 'Camilla's Weekly Roast' online column she wrote for *Times Woman*:

'What would be the first thing you'd do if you were prime minister for a day?'
'Can you remember where you were when Princess Diana died?'
'What's the first thing you eat in the morning?'
'Do you think you are paid enough?'
'When was the last time you went topless?'[5]

Video interviews

As mentioned earlier, print journalists are increasingly being asked to file audio and video reports to be posted online, alongside their written interviews.

Interviews for audio and visual use rely on the same techniques as written interviews but there are a few key differences, particularly when it comes to the questions. Broadcast interviews largely consist of open questions, i.e. questions that will prompt interesting answers rather than a simple 'yes' or 'no'. If your publication is keen to use a small video or audio extract of an interview you need your interviewee to say something vivid and lively – and that is down to the rapport you have built up and the thought you put into your questions.

Interviewing task

Find an issue you'd like to investigate – anything from crime levels in your area to style bloggers. List the key people you'd like to talk to and discuss this with your journalism tutor or trainer. Once you have their agreement, set up interviews with the relevant people and write a blog, record a podcast or produce an audio package.

HOW I INTERVIEW: HEIDI BLAKE

Heidi Blake, the investigations editor of BuzzFeed UK, started her journalistic career at *Nouse*, the University of York's student newspaper, where she wrote long-form features about refugees in York, sex workers at university and transgender students. She later became editor of *Nouse* and was named Student Journalist of the Year at the 2007 Guardian Student Media Awards. 'I learned to understand the thrill of breaking stories,' she says. 'We felt we were representing the students and giving them a voice. I am a journalist now because I did all of that.'

Blake won a place on the *Daily Telegraph*'s training scheme on the strength of her student newspaper cuttings and has never looked back. Her training included secondments with the Press Association in London and the *Yorkshire Post* in Leeds, where she got a scoop about ContactPoint, a government database that held information on all children under 18 in England. It was created in response to the abuse and death of eight-year-old Victoria Climbié and was shut down in 2010. 'I managed to find out that the database had been beset with huge technical glitches and that the government had had to take the whole thing offline,' recalls Blake.

After her training Blake was offered a job as a general news reporter on the *Daily Telegraph*. She believes that her experience of 'being sent out day in, day out, just knocking on doors, talking to people and trying to persuade them to open up' helped to hone her interviewing skills. 'You develop an understanding of what works and what doesn't,' she says.

Blake joined the *Daily Telegraph*'s investigations team, before moving to *The Sunday Times* Insight team in 2011 (Insight editor Jonathan Calvert described her as 'the most talented journalist I have ever worked with'[6]). Her reporting credits at *The Sunday Times* included the award-winning investigation into alleged bribery by Qatar to win the 2022 World Cup. She became BuzzFeed UK's investigations editor in 2016.

In an interview with *The Drum* in 2016 BuzzFeed UK editor-in-chief Janine Gibson said her aim was to make BuzzFeed into 'a consistent top tier, scoop-getting, disruptive, serious investigative part of people's lives'.[7] With that aim in mind, Heidi Blake has played an integral role in pushing BuzzFeed stories up the news agenda.

Blake, who leads a team of four at BuzzFeed UK, prides herself on being a journalist who gets results. She occasionally does conventional interviews but more often interviews sources she has built up over time 'for the purposes of extracting information from them' – information that usually won't be attributed to them.

'A lot of the time it is a much more nebulous process of getting to know somebody over a long period, perhaps over drinks or lunch, building up a relationship of trust, persuading them to trust me with information and piecing together a picture of what that person knows and what they might be able to reveal to me,' she says.

When Blake and BuzzFeed news reporter John Templon exposed evidence (in a joint year-long investigation with the BBC) of 'widespread match-fixing' by players at the upper level of world tennis their reports were the result of months of journalistic digging.

As the first article, published in January 2016, explained, the investigation into men's tennis by BuzzFeed and the BBC was 'based on a cache of leaked documents from inside the sport – the Fixing Files – as well as an original analysis of the betting activity on 26,000 matches and interviews across three continents with gambling and match-fixing experts, tennis officials, and players.'[8]

Blake developed the match-fixing investigation by approaching a number of sources inside world tennis. 'The aims in talking to them were to find out exactly what they knew about the problem of match-fixing in tennis – what had happened, what evidence might be out there that we might be able to lay our hands on and how much they had access to it,' she says. 'Ultimately my goal was to find the greatest amount of evidence of the problem and to get access to some documentation.'

Building up sources' trust takes endless patience and time. In the early days Blake chats to possible sources 'in a very informal way', scoping out what they know and what information they have and gradually getting them to elaborate.

'I think it's about reading the person and understanding what is motivating them to have a conversation with a journalist. We are generally investigating things because we think it's really important that this information is brought to light and that the public ought to know about it. So I feel it's my mission to persuade people to hand information over as much as possible, but I also have a responsibility to assure the source that they will be protected and that I won't do anything to jeopardise their position or identify them if they don't want to be identified – and then follow through on that assurance.'

When it comes to persuading sources that divulging information is the right thing to do, Blake says that it's a combination of building up trust, showing that you take your responsibilities as an investigative journalist seriously and that you have 'a deep knowledge and genuine passion' for the subject.

She cites the example of *Boston Globe* investigative reporter Sacha Pfeiffer, who was played by Rachel McAdams in the Oscar-winning film *Spotlight*. 'There's a moment in the film which really resonated with me, where the reporter is interviewing someone who has a great deal of knowledge about the way the Catholic Church covered up the sex abuse scandal in Boston. He intimates that he knows things and says: "I really shouldn't be talking about this." She says: "I really think you should." It's that moment where you are trying to show people that they have a moral duty to talk about this stuff while reassuring them that you are not going to expose them if they do.'

Showing that you're a person of integrity is crucial, she says. 'This isn't a particularly helpful thing to say to journalism students at the start of their careers but it helps to have a bit of background. I say to my sources: "I take source protection really seriously. If you look at my previous work you'll see that I've reported on a lot of stories involving confidential sources and whistleblowers who have given me a lot of information and none of these people have ever been exposed."'

Another tip she learned long ago about interviewing sources as an investigative journalist is to see her sources repeatedly. 'It develops trust because they see you over and over again and your message and interest are always consistent,' she says. 'Normally there is an incremental process of disclosure, so they tell you a little bit and then they see you again and realise that you didn't run away and immediately publish everything that they said to you. You held on to it. So they see you again and tell you a little bit more. They dip their toes deeper and deeper in the water and then ultimately they say: "I do have these documents and I'm willing to show them to you."'

These days Blake and her team often communicate with their sources via WhatsApp, Telegram, Signal and other encrypted messaging services. 'We are constantly sending little titbits of information back and forth and building up that kind of chatty rapport,' she says. Approaching people informally like this, she believes, is less intimidating than sending them a formal email with an official signature at the end.

When a story is time-sensitive she might have to speed up the investigation. 'Sometimes you've got a lot of time but sometimes you need to say: "We must get a move on. I really need those documents by next week." It can be useful to put a little bit of pressure on, but not if it's going to freak them out and they are going to go to ground. I guess it's a matter of reading how the person seems to be responding. Sometimes you need to get tough and say: "Listen, you're sitting on some serious evidence of wrong-doing here. Are you comfortable with that?"'

Tailor your approach

Blake firmly believes that the best strategy when dealing with a source or interviewing someone is 'to read that person and tailor your approach'.

As she says: 'Listen more than you talk and be constantly attuned to their reaction to things. What is their body language like? Do they seem uncomfortable? Be aware of the dynamic in the conversation, because you need to be aware of things shifting. You can sense when someone is slightly loosening up and telling you more and more. Or are they stiffening up and getting more guarded? In that case whatever you're doing isn't working so you have to adapt slightly and be a bit chameleon-like.'

She prefers not to go into interviews with loads of prepared questions. 'I like to have a general idea in my mind of the things that I'm really interested in. I open up the conversation and go with the flow and listen and respond to what the person in front of me is saying. I'm really fascinated by people and that helps a lot as a journalist. Sometimes I meet journalists and I think "You're not listening, you're just talking. You're not opening your eyes to the world around you very much."'

The best moment during an interview, she says, is when she makes a breakthrough of some kind. 'It's really thrilling finding stuff out and gradually persuading people to tell you more and more. It's exciting when you think to yourself "I've just made a big leap forward in the investigation. That person has just told me something that I didn't know about before." There's the feeling that you've got it, it's in the bag, but you mustn't show it.'

Is interviewing for an online publication different?

The differences in working for an online site as opposed to a traditional media organisation have been much debated but Blake says that while the 'mode of delivery is different', the way she interviews for BuzzFeed 'is not significantly different' to how she interviewed for the *Daily Telegraph* and *The Sunday Times*.

'The actual central part of the job, is the same,' she says. 'We are looking for investigations that take on matters of major topical interest and our goals are to try to effect real change.

'The difference is the platform and the delivery. BuzzFeed distributes stories mainly through social media channels. We have a website but most of our readers come to us through social media. We are much more plugged into an immediate conversation about a story as soon as it's published. You get instant exposure to what people are saying. Journalists always wonder when they publish a story what people are saying about it over breakfast. This way, you actually see it happening in real time on social media.'

Nevertheless, sites like BuzzFeed are constantly looking for new ways of sharing content, such as Facebook Live, where instead of writing up an interview the video is streamed live on Facebook.

Essential qualities for an investigative journalist

'You need to be obsessive – someone who gets stuck into a particular topic and is fascinated by it,' says Blake.

'You need to have tenacity and the ability to insert yourself into all sorts of little corners of the world where you're not supposed to be poking around. You have to have a bit of a killer instinct when you find out that something is wrong – and you need to be tough about chasing it down. And then you have to have a bit of mischief and sparkle and kind of enjoy the high jinks of it all.'

While excellent writing skills are a bonus she also reckons that having 'a nose for a story' is the most crucial thing, along with the ability to empathise with your sources and be approachable. Investigative journalists often have a news background, which means they can spot good news-lines and have the ability to write stories quickly when required.

A profound bond of trust

Many of Blake's investigations take months, even years, and she says that while she isn't a patient person, 'sometimes you do just have to wait'.

She makes a point of staying in contact with her sources. As she says: 'Once someone has leaked you a lot of information or told you a lot of things, a profound bond of trust has been formed. You've asked a lot of them so I feel I have an ongoing commitment to them. Also, someone who came into possession of very interesting information once might get some very interesting information another time so it's always worth keeping in touch.'

Heidi Blake's top tip

Read and respond to the person in front of you, minute by minute, second by second. Observe their facial micro-expressions – like a glimmer in their eye that makes you think 'you're tempted to tell me something' or 'you're guarded' or 'what I just said didn't go down well'.

Notes

1   S. Boyle, 'Grieving parents' fury over children's hospital deaths: How many will die before we get truth?', *Sunday People*. Available from: www.mirror.co.uk/news/uk-news/grieving-parents-fury-over-childrens-5670620 (accessed 11 October 2016).

2   M. Dodd and M. Hanna, *McNae's Essential Law for Journalists*, Oxford University Press, 2014, p. 18.

3   J. Vine, *It's All News to Me: How I Got Locked Inside the BBC for 25 years*, Simon & Schuster, 2012, p. 68.

4   C. Frost, *Reporting for Journalists* (2nd edn), Routledge, 2010, p. 157.

5   C. Long, 'Camilla's weekly roast', *Times Woman*. Available from: http://nuk-tnl-deck-prod-static.s3-eu-west-1.amazonaws.com/projects/0fe473396242072e84af28 6632d3f0ff.html (accessed 11 October 2016).

6   D. Ponsford, 'Insight editor Jonathan Calvert: 99% journalism "not about trawling through databases, it's talking to people"', *Press Gazette*. Available from: www.pressgazette.co.uk/insight-editor-jonathan-calvert-journalism-not-about-trawling-through-databases-its-talking-people (accessed 11 October 2016).

7   I. Burrell, 'BuzzFeed to Fleet Street – "We're figuring out the future of journalism"', *The Drum*. Available from: www.thedrum.com/opinion/2016/06/09/buzzfeed-fleet-street-were-figuring-out-future-journalism (accessed 11 October 2016).

8   H. Blake and J. Templon, 'The tennis racket', BuzzFeed. Available from: www.buzzfeed.com/heidiblake/the-tennis-racket?utm_term=.nfxdz6v2a#.hiLqd1Ll6 (accessed 11 October 2016).

10

Interviewing the famous – and infamous

Society's obsession with the rich and famous shows no sign of abating. News publications around the world run interviews focused on every aspect of celebrities' lives, from who they are dating to the contents of their fridges.

Celebrities often get a bad press when it comes to interviews but don't assume that they are all difficult. Freelance writer Stephanie Rafanelli, who describes interviews as being 'like a good-natured joust', says: 'It's a cliché that all famous people are tricky. I've never found that to be true. The most legendary are often the most charming. If you treat them with respect, but without deference, you will often get the best out of them.'

Rafanelli's point is a good one. One of my first showbiz interviews was with Morrissey, the singer and songwriter, who I interviewed for *Woman's Own* magazine at the height of his success with The Smiths. We did the interview over lunch at J Sheekey in London's Covent Garden and I found that despite his sardonic image he was a delight to interview. He told me how his mum always believed in him (even when he decided he wasn't cut out for work) and that as a child growing up on a Manchester council estate he preferred staying in and listening to Billy Fury records rather than going out to play with the other children. Even then, he refused point-blank to settle for mediocrity. 'It sounds quite dramatic but I would never be content to straggle midstream,' he told me. 'I always felt that if I couldn't have what I wanted, I would rather have absolutely nothing at all. Perhaps that's why I always thought that I would be impossibly successful or incredibly inconsequential.'

There's no doubt, however, that interviewing celebrities is getting more and more challenging, largely because both they and their PRs make countless stipulations and demands before agreeing to go ahead. These can be anything from writer approval (that's why some celebrities are interviewed time and time again by the same journalists) to question approval, copy approval, photographer approval, picture approval and even clothes approval.

Exclusivity is another issue. Many publications will refuse to run an interview if one of their rivals is planning to publish or has already published a similar piece. Stephanie Rafanelli always checks that the interviews she has been offered are exclusive and if so, how many days exclusivity she has. 'People often forget to talk about that side of things because they are so happy they've got an interview,' she says.

Rafanelli is also adamant that interviewers should never promise things they can't deliver, such as telling interviewees they are going to get a magazine cover when they probably aren't. 'I think sometimes people will blag just to get the interview,' she says. 'I just wouldn't do that. You will always lose more than you gain, including your reputation.'

Interviewees who issue instructions

Another potential problem is that many famous names trot out the same old lines time and time again, making it tricky for interviewers to write anything new. Not only that, some PRs are so keen to control the running of interviews that they send out extraordinary lists of instructions and demands.

One of the best-known lists came from will.i.am's team (will.i.am, aka William Adams, is a member of The Black Eyed Peas and a coach for TV's *The Voice UK*). The star was being interviewed by the *Daily Telegraph*'s Harry Wallop, who said he was handed a list of instructions entitled 'Tips for maximising your interview time with will.i.am'.

Describing the list in a piece for the *Telegraph*, which appeared in April 2016, Wallop wrote: 'It informs me that I cannot discuss his income or net worth and includes the advice, "If he asks you to repeat or restate a question, this indicates that you need to ask crisper, more direct questions," along with various "fact checks."'[1]

The PR team even advised on exactly *when* questions should be asked, although the star seemed 'appalled' when Wallop told him about the guidance he'd been given. Wallop posted some of this on his Twitter feed, including the line: 'Start off with 1–2 warm up questions, and then get to the heart of what you really want to ask. Because he can sometimes give very lengthy responses, don't hold your most important questions until the end of your time allocation.'[2]

Questions in advance

Some publicists ask journalists to send a list of questions in advance. Sometimes this is the only way to gain access to a celebrity but Stephanie Rafanelli refuses to do this. Why? 'Because a) the publicist will edit them and say "you can't ask this", "you can't ask that", b) you need to have an interview strategy and keep that a secret and c) you will get a really stilted interview. The person will over-prepare and come back with wooden, PR answers. It's essential that they are as natural and spontaneous as possible when they respond. If I'm asked to send a list in advance I say that I never write questions. I say: "My interview technique is very spontaneous and goes with the natural flow of the conversation. However, these are the topic areas."'

Journalist and author Wendy Holden takes a similar view. 'I try to resist because in many cases it doesn't allow you to deviate from the questions,' she says. If the interviewee (or their PR or agent) insists, she goes along with the request but 'sneaks a few extra questions in' during the conversation.

The writer Sean Langan gave an idea of the difficulties journalists are up against when they interview celebrities in a *Spectator Life* piece in 2016. Langan, who was kidnapped by the Taliban in 2008 and whose story featured in a film about war reporters called *Whiskey Tango Foxtrot*, had been commissioned to interview Tina Fey, the star of the movie. He spent a week trying to interview her in New York, only to get a few brief words at a party at the Museum of Modern Art. 'I have to admit it wasn't my greatest interview,' Langan wrote. 'The one I did in Afghanistan with a suicide bomber went much better. I actually managed to ask him more than one question before he blew himself up.'[3]

Tips on interviewing the famous

Nigel Farndale, who writes for publications like the *Observer*, the *Financial Times*, *The Spectator* and *Country Life*, once asked chat-show host Michael Parkinson what attracted him to becoming an interviewer. 'It's the best job in the world,' Parkinson told him. 'You get paid to meet your heroes.' There's undoubtedly a lot of truth in that but make sure you aren't so overawed at meeting someone you've long admired that you forget to ask pertinent questions.

Farndale offers a raft of useful advice about interviewing celebrities in his col-lection of interviews, *Flirtation, Seduction, Betrayal: Interviews with Heroes and Villains*. The book features profiles of Elton John, Stephen Hawking, Steven Spielberg and Stephen Fry although Farndale admits he would rather interview 'a paranoid professor, depraved novelist or vainglorious politician over a Hollywood actor any day'.

He says that when he interviews well-known names, 'I try to imagine what the world is like from the famous person's perspective, try and identify with their problems and disappointments, put myself in their tasseled Gucci loafers. I often find myself asking the men I interview about their relationships with their fathers – how they measure up, what values they have in common, whether they were close – because however successful a man becomes he still often craves paternal approval.'[4]

Another effective line of questioning, says Farndale, is to ask people you interview about the difference between 'their public and private personas' or how they would describe themselves 'physically and psychologically'. He adds, however, that this strategy doesn't always work. When he asked broadcaster and former *Sunday Times* editor Andrew Neil this question, he replied: 'That's your job.'

Should you talk about yourself?

Another decision that journalists often have to make during celebrity interviews is whether to talk about themselves. Opinions vary on this but the general consensus is that if a celebrity asks you a question about yourself you should probably answer it – just to be polite.

When Stephanie Rafanelli interviewed the Hollywood actor Ethan Hawke, he wouldn't start the interview until he'd asked her a few questions about herself. 'It depends on the interviewee but I've always found it helpful to talk about myself a little bit,' she says. 'Sadly, journalists have terrible reputations so when you are meeting someone who either hasn't been interviewed before or is very famous and has been interviewed a million times you have to break down the barrier of their perception of you as a journalist.

'"Journalist" has become a dirty word and they sometimes think that you are out to get them or to twist their words. What you need to do is to get them to see that they are dealing with you as a person and not just as a faceless journalist.'

Author and former *Daily Telegraph* journalist Wendy Holden agrees. 'It's helpful to make it slightly reciprocal,' she says. 'It's not that you want to spill the beans about your entire life but when I'm working with someone I might share some of my life story with them.'

Interviewing task

Freelance writer Stephanie Rafanelli (see the 'How I interview' section below) takes the utmost care in writing celebrity interview requests. She believes that it's important to explain why she wants to interview the individual in question, why the timing is good and why they should talk to her rather than anyone else. Choose a famous person you would like to interview and compose an interview request that might persuade them to talk to you.

HOW I INTERVIEW: STEPHANIE RAFANELLI

After studying English at the University of Manchester, Stephanie Rafanelli did a journalism course at the London College of Printing (now the London College of Communication). She spent eight years working on documentaries for the BBC, Channel 4, ITV and Discovery Channel, during which time she gained access to and interviewed members of the Sicilian and New York Mafias, a silent order of nuns (she was nominated for a Royal Television Society award for directing her film), a Nigerian prostitute ring and the leader of an exorcist cult.

She was features director of *Harper's Bazaar* magazine for five years, before leaving to go freelance. She now does big-name interviews for publications like the *Telegraph* magazine, the *Guardian*, *The Times*, the *Sunday Telegraph*, the *Observer* and the *Evening Standard*'s *ES* magazine (her interviewees include Cate Blanchett, Marion Cotillard, Penélope Cruz, Dolce and Gabbana, Ryan Gosling, Ethan Hawke, Nicole Kidman, Julianne Moore, Al Pacino and Kristin Scott Thomas). She was highly commended in the interviewer of the year category at the 2015 Press Awards.

Stephanie Rafanelli firmly believes that interviewing is built on establishing good relationships. Her interviews are often the result of months of painstaking research and preparation, whether she's tracking down contacts who might be able to put her in touch with a mafia hitman or meeting publicists face to face to secure an exclusive chat with the best-known actors in the business.

'You need to establish a relationship of mutual respect and trust right from the beginning,' she says. 'If you show etiquette, respect, intelligence and good research when you are putting in your interview request, it will stand you in good stead.'

Before even submitting an interview request Rafanelli puts a huge amount of time and energy into researching the person she wants to interview. She reckons that if journalists show they are 'intelligent, informed and interested' they stand a far better chance of getting the interview.

Dealing with publicists

When she emails a potential interviewee or their publicist, she doesn't simply type 'interview request' in the subject line. Instead, she composes a very specific email that will stand out from the crowd.

'You want to make them open the email so it needs to be as well-thought-out and informative as possible,' explains Rafanelli. 'You need to say why you want to interview them, why this particular timing is good, why they should choose you and the publication and what's in it for them. It might be the chance for them to tell their side of the story and often, when it's a sensitive subject and interview, it's not disingenuous to say that it might help other people to hear their story.'

If it's a celebrity interview, the star's publicists will also want to know if their image will be on the cover, if there will be a photo-shoot, who the creative team will be, the number of pages planned, the running date, the deadline for the interview and how long the writer needs for the interview.

'You must put yourself in the person's shoes,' says Rafanelli. 'Why would they want to do the interview – and why would they want to do it with you? Also, and this is really important, send two or three relevant examples of interviews you have done. Make sure you choose these carefully, with their psychology in mind.'

Further down the line – not in the first email – it's important to talk about exclusivity. 'You'll need to talk about this just as you are sewing up the interview. Journalists often forget to do this because they are so happy they've got a positive response. But you need to check that the interview is an exclusive – or if you are running it before someone else, how many days exclusivity you will have.

'Sometimes people will blag just to get the interview but I just wouldn't do that. Never ever promise something you can't deliver, such as saying it's going to be a cover when it's not going to be a cover. If you can't deliver, you'll have alienated the publicist – and they'll remember it the next time you want to work with them or interview one of their clients. Always keep the long game in mind.'

The 90-minute interview

Rafanelli asks interviewees for 90 minutes of their time, largely because she prefers to use the first part of the interview (between 10 and 20 minutes) to establish a rapport and gain the interviewee's respect.

She never gives copy approval and rarely agrees to 'off' topics. 'If someone says "no personal questions" I say I want to do a rounded, in-depth portrait of the person, that any questions I ask will be done in a respectful way and that there is no obligation to answer them.' She doesn't like publicists sitting in, mainly because it changes the dynamic of the interview. 'This should be avoided at all costs,' she says. 'It's an interview killer. I usually get the editor who has arranged the interview for me to make sure they don't. If a publicist sits in you feel watched and judged and you end up having a three-way conversation. They often jump in and stop their client answering something they would have felt happy to answer.'

She warns that lunchtime interviews require a decent amount of time. 'If you've only got 45 minutes lunch is really distracting. You spend a lot of that time ordering and eating. Also, if your interviewee has just flown in from LA you want to think about what time is going to be best for their jetlag.' She advises against drinking alcohol. 'Your reactions will be dulled and you'll be likely to miss something. I understand that there might be camaraderie if you're drinking while they're drinking but you've got to be so on the ball. I personally couldn't do it, nor go in with a hangover or a lack of sleep either. You've got to be sharp – forensic even.'

Location, location, location

When it comes to the location of Rafanelli's interviews 'at home' is the ideal. 'It very much depends on the type of interview but if it's a trauma interview with a non-famous person I would always offer to go to their house. I want them to be as comfortable as possible. Interviews at home with high-profile people are more rare but if you do get one you can tell 75 per cent about them from their house. There is so much information there. Even a lack of interior style is revealing.'

Rafanelli often asks celebrities to suggest a location for the interview themselves but says that the key things are that the place is quiet, not too brightly lit and not too exposed – somewhere that you can 'establish intimacy'. 'If the person is famous you don't get that much choice but you don't want to be sitting by the window. Never interview during hair and make-up, in the studio after a shoot or in the back of a cab either – unless this is only one part of the interview or part of an on-the-hoof reportage story. You don't want to be in a situation where you're not getting their full attention. You want to relate to someone as a human being and have a conversation where you are both equals.'

Preparation and research

'I'm all about preparation and research,' says Rafanelli. 'Time permitting, I read every interview they've ever done, everything they've ever said, see all their films. I also read around everything. I'll read about the director of their latest film and research who that director has worked with. I'll look at where they've lived – what type of place is it and who lives there? At the very least I always spend a full day researching. This allows me to write questions that are different from the same old, same old they've been asked a thousand times before – questions that make my interviewees think. They are like gentle scalpels that get under people's skin very quickly. It's like being a detective investigating a person's life. You can make connections about their motivations, their obsessions, their foibles, how they reacted in a certain situation – things that will help you understand them and inform your questions. That way you will never be on the back foot. That is the last thing you want to be.

'Fifty per cent of my interviewees say thank you for being well prepared and well researched. It's important because you gain respect from them in the first ten minutes. They are interviewed by so many people, and asked the same poorly researched questions over and over again. Show that you are intelligent and well-informed. Be *interested* and *interesting* and you will stand out. If you've read enough of their prior interviews you'll know when you're getting a stock answer that they deliver by rote. You'll know when you are boring them.'

Reading so widely also gives Rafanelli an idea of what kind of interviewee the person is going to be. When she did her research for an interview with a well-known British actress she realised that the star had sometimes 'stone-walled' interviewers when she got bored. 'I knew that I had to get her respect and had to engage her by showing that I'm smart and that I'd researched her. I suspected that she had a smart sense of humour underneath it all and I "got" her by making her laugh about a drunk at the bar behaving badly. After that I kept her attention with intelligent questions and she relaxed and opened up.'

Memorising questions

As she goes through her research Rafanelli thinks hard about the questions she wants to ask. She usually comes up with five topic areas and writes questions relating to each one. She always works out her first question by asking herself: 'Do I want to show them that I'm intelligent? Do I want to make them laugh? Do I want to show them that I'm not out to get them as a matter of course, that I'm not just here to get a scoop about their private life?'

Unlike many other interviewers she learns her questions – and the links between them – off by heart. 'I don't learn them word for word,' she says, 'but I learn the areas and the flow of logic. It's lucky I've got a good memory. I would liken it to preparing for an actor's performance. I'm just the best version of myself that I can be. So I prepare, prepare, prepare, write my script, memorise my script. Then I throw away my script and improvise.'

The crucial point is that even though she memorises her questions in advance she doesn't necessarily stick to them during the actual interview.

'It's like having a safety net. If you stick rigidly to your script you're going to throw the whole interview away – because you need to have enough room to listen and follow a lead or for something crazy to happen. Then again, if you only allow yourself to be spontaneous you may come away from the interview and find that you haven't covered the points you need to cover. So for me it's always a tension between asking the questions that I want to ask and at the same time being flexible enough to go with the flow. Bad journalism is going into an interview thinking "this is what I've read about them, this is the way they are", and then going back to the office and writing the piece you've read a thousand times before. You want to reveal the unexpected about them.'

Don't be late

Rafanelli always arrives at least half an hour early (even for the interview I did with her at the British Library in London). 'I am half-Italian so being casual about time is my inclination,' she says. 'But if you arrive late you've blown it. You're going to be backtracking and apologetic when you need to be going in a position of strength and facing them as an equal. This really helps when asking those difficult questions.

'The other reason for arriving early is that I like to read my questions through again – and find the spot in the room that has the best *shui*. It can make or break an interview if you sit at the bar with other people listening to you as opposed to a really good alcove that's private, where there's a good energy and no one is listening in. I always say to the subject: "Are you happy here or do you want to move?"'

Interviewing Al Pacino

Rafanelli is always warm and polite during interviews – and definitely not starstruck. 'I'm nervous before every interview I do because I'm primed. It means I'm not complacent. I want to get the best out of my 90 minutes. I've trained for it like an athlete, I've done my research, done my questions and now I'm ready to do the performance. As soon as I meet the person I'm interviewing the adrenalin kicks in and I'm away.'

She felt nervous before she interviewed Al Pacino for the *Daily Telegraph* in a New York restaurant. She'd arrived 45 minutes early and sat at the bar, with a 'plate of chips' (crisps in the UK) in front of her. She kept her eye on the door but much to her dismay got a message from Pacino's publicist saying that the actor was already in the restaurant (she suspected he had used a back entrance). She introduced herself, apologised (without overdoing it) and it became a good opener. 'I said, "I put on a red hat so you couldn't miss me and I managed to miss you. And now you've caught me eating chips like a Brit. Do you eat chips at all?"'

Looking back on the interview, she says that 'being cheeky was an ice-breaker. I wouldn't be impertinent, but sometimes with a famous person it helps if you treat them like everyone else. It's good if you can surprise them, wake them up and show you're not going to bore them. It's also about being myself. It works for me but it may not work if it's not your natural style. It will depend on the interviewee and you must always go on instinct.'

Her approach paid off. Pacino loved the red hat and gave her a fascinating interview. He also volunteered to speak to her for another hour the next day while he was driving. Here are a few lines from the opening paragraph of Rafanelli's piece: 'I assume he will be hidden in an alcove. But there he sits quietly waiting, elegantly dishevelled in his civilian uniform: black suit, louchely arranged silk scarf, a full head of electrified bed hair. After four decades of exponential "legendary" status, he simply owns the room by doing nothing at all.'[5]

Gain their respect

Rafanelli believes that it's important to show interviewees that 'they are dealing with you as a person and that you're not just a faceless journalist'. She says that many celebrities assume journalists will twist their words so it's important to gain their respect and trust. One way of doing that is to talk about yourself a little – but only when it's appropriate.

'Al Pacino hates being interviewed and it was when I talked about myself that he opened up more,' says Rafanelli. 'Interviews are all about strategy and instincts.'

Above all, Rafanelli says that interviewers should listen intently. 'You have to listen *all the time*. If the person is telling you an anecdote and you're thinking about your next question and assuming you'll pick it up on the dictaphone later you miss so much. You need to have clarity – and if you're not listening, you're not really there.'

No notes

Rafanelli sometimes uses two voice recorders for her interviews (she tends to place them apart from each other so there's no risk of interference) and doesn't take any notes at all, largely because she thinks it's distracting to the interviewee and means that she can't maintain eye contact. Immediately after the interview, once she's alone, she'll make notes about her interviewee's body language, eye contact, expressions and the way they interacted with her.

'You have to maintain eye contact all the time and keep the flow and the pace,' she says. 'I always check the length of the interview at the start because it means I can pace the conversation. For the first ten minutes or so I'm not going for quotes. I'm gaining their respect, establishing a rapport. Once I get down the line I can ask almost anything because I've built this environment where they feel comfortable with me. I've established my voice and my tone with them and it's easier to ask the questions I need to ask.'

She's adamant that the interviewer must always keep control of the interview and mustn't avoid asking challenging questions.

'I would say that you can ask people anything. It's how you do it. You should always ask something that is personal in a very respectful way – and in a way that flows as part of the conversation. If you are embarrassed and uncomfortable about the question then they are going to be embarrassed and uncomfortable too.

'You've got to be prepared to ask the difficult and personal questions but don't let it be something that is just titillating. Let it be something that is revealing. Do it in a respectful, sensitive way. You are there as a representative of the public and therefore you have to ask certain questions – but I don't give interviewees the impression that they owe it to me to tell me, that it's my right to know simply because they are famous. Unless I'm interviewing, say, a politician, I don't think that attitude pays off.

'It has also worked for me to show that I'm not gagging to dig into an interviewee's private life. When I interviewed Mila Kunis, who never talks about her partner Ashton Kutcher, I asked her about her political views and avoided the issue. When she saw that I wasn't there simply for gossip she began to mention him and to open up about him. Being counterintuitive is a risky strategy, but it can work.'

Rafanelli prides herself on not doing a 'hatchet job' on her interviewees. 'I think it's cheap to do that as a *modus operandi*,' she says. 'It's fairly easy to go in, rile them up and then you've got a story with an angle like "they were rude, defensive, egocentric". But you've also shot yourself in the foot because you've shut them down, you've learned nothing more about them. People are far more complex that that. It's easier to be rude about someone. It's harder to tell a more nuanced story about them. I like to paint an honest, realistic, detailed portrait of my encounter and the person I find them to be. You should always be fair and honest, whether you like them or not.'

Transcribing – the worst job

When Rafanelli worked at *Harper's Bazaar* she often asked assistants to transcribe her interviews but these days she does it herself, even though it's laborious and time-consuming.

'Transcribing is the worst thing in the world,' she says, 'but it is really useful because you can re-listen afresh and you sometimes pick up new stuff, including pauses, changes in intonation, the repetition of a word they like to use, which is revealing. Nicole Kidman used "wah" a lot when she was expressing emotion and Björk used "normcore". I referenced both of these in my intros as a way into their psychology.

'However painful it is listening to yourself it will improve your interview technique. I sometimes jump in too early, for example, and kick myself for it. You also end up knowing your material really well, which is very important when you come to write. You'll get Truman Capote-like recall and have everything at your fingertips.'

Stephanie Rafanelli's top tips

Never think you can freestyle an interview. You want to give the impression that it's a conversation – but actually it's not. I feel like I'm split in two when I'm doing an interview. Part of me is holding the conversation and empathising with the interviewee. The other part of me is being a forensic observer. I'm about depth, not speed. I'm about getting to know someone. I'm just not that interested in gossip, and I think that shows. I'm about ferreting inside a character.

Notes

1   H. Wallop, 'will.i.am on Trump, Tom Jones and being put in the friend zone', *Telegraph*. Available from: www.telegraph.co.uk/men/the-filter/william-on-trump-tom-jones-and-being-put-in-the-friend-zone (accessed 11 October 2016).

2   H. Wallop, Twitter. Available from: https://twitter.com/hwallop/status/7163753 44236912642 (accessed 31 August 2016).

3   S. Langan, 'Tracking down Tina', *Spectator Life*. Available from: http://life. spectator.co.uk/2016/03/tracking-down-tina (accessed 1 May 2016).

4   N. Farndale, *Flirtation, Seduction, Betrayal: Interviews with Heroes and Villains*, Constable, 2002, p. 5.

5   S. Rafanelli, 'Al Pacino interview: "Being an outsider is part of being an artist"', *Telegraph*. Available from: www.telegraph.co.uk/film/danny-collins/al-pacino-interview (accessed 22 May 2016).

11

How to manage challenging, difficult or sensitive interviews

If you are working in news (and sometimes features too) you will be required to report on terrible tragedies, crises and life-changing events. That means you'll be tasked with interviewing people who have suffered huge trauma in their lives. You may, for instance, have to interview a widow whose husband has been murdered or doorstep a family who have been involved in a drug abuse scandal.

There are strict ethical guidelines about dealing with difficult and distressing interviews. All journalists, whether they work in print or broadcast media, are required to follow the relevant code of practice and should make sure they have a thorough working knowledge of it. The *Editors' Code of Practice* (regulated by the Independent Press Standards Organisation (IPSO)) lists the rules that 'voluntarily subscribing newspaper and magazine industry members have pledged to accept'. The code has 16 clauses that set out ethical standards on the following: accuracy, privacy, harassment, intrusion into grief or shock, reporting suicide, the welfare of children who become the subject of journalism, anonymity for children in sex cases, making inquiries at hospitals, crime reporting, clandestine devices and subterfuge, victims of sexual assault, discrimination, financial journalism, confidential sources, witness payments, criminal trials and payment to criminals.

The clause pertaining to cases involving personal grief or shock, for example, specifies that 'enquiries and approaches must be made with sympathy and discretion and publication handled sensitively'.[1]

Reporting on events like 9/11 or the Paris bombings of 2015 poses multiple challenges. Talking to people who have witnessed conflicts, riots, natural disasters and terrorist atrocities and who may have been injured and bereaved is one of the most difficult things you will have to do as a journalist. These are occasions when qualities such as empathy, compassion and patience are more important than ever. You will in all likelihood also be working to tight deadlines and having to amass a huge amount of information very quickly.

Having said that, some of those who have lost loved ones in traumatic circumstances say that telling their stories can be helpful in coming to terms with what they have been through. Writing about the challenges of interviewing those who have experienced violence and tragedy, journalist and film-maker Gavin Rees said: 'Skilled journalists who have learnt how to listen without passing judgement and who understand how to help structure a victim's narrative are likely to augment an interviewee's sense of security. They are also likely, of course, to get better information and material that is more quotable.'[2]

It is a good idea to familiarise yourself with the NUJ's *Code of Conduct*, which sets out the main principles of UK and Irish journalism.[3] The code includes a clause stating that a journalist 'does nothing to intrude into anybody's private life, grief or distress unless justified by overriding consideration of the public interest'.

When to ask difficult questions

When it comes to asking tricky questions – the ones that celebrities and politicians try to avoid like the plague – the general consensus is that you can't do it right at the start of the interview, and you can't wait till the very end.

Most interviewers agree that the ideal time to pose the toughest questions is three-quarters of the way into the interview.

'You can't do it last because they always expect that – and wherever possible I don't ask them the tough questions straight away either,' says freelance writer Cole Moreton. 'I think that everybody has got something they need to say about the project they are working on and in fairness you want to let them say everything they need to say, however long that takes. But once that's done you can move on to the other stuff. There's nothing worse than trying to ask a series of questions that they perceive to be difficult or intrusive when they have got something at the back of their mind that they want to say.'

Moreton has covered everything from 9/11 to the death of Nelson Mandela during his career but is probably best known for his interviews with the rich and famous. He insists, however, that he prefers interviewing non-celebrities. 'It's a lot easier and more satisfying to talk somebody through telling their extraordinary story than to coax an actor into saying something provocative about his latest play,' he says.

One of the pieces that he is most proud of was with Maxine Hilson, whose cyclist husband Tony died at the hands of a motorist who took her eyes off the road for 18 seconds to look at her satnav. Moreton interviewed Tony Hilson's widow for the *Sunday Telegraph* after the driver was found guilty of dangerous driving and given an 18-month prison sentence.

'The interview took three or four hours because as you would expect, she kept breaking down,' recalls Moreton. 'You have to be gentle and you have to say: "Look it's OK, we can take a break." In a situation like this, where you're interviewing someone who is bereaved I want to say: "Look, I'm on your side. If you don't want to do it, let's not do it but if you do want to, let's go for it wholeheartedly."'

When it came to writing the piece, Moreton wrote the intro in real time, as if over 18 seconds, to bring home the length of time that the driver had looked away from the road. 'Close your eyes and count to 18,' he began. 'Imagine looking away from the road and driving blind for that long, at 40 miles per hour. It's a terrifying thought.'[4]

As mentioned earlier, he firmly believes that if someone gets upset and dissolves into tears during an interview then 'your first duty is to the other person as a human being'. He adds: 'If someone went to a very dark place in an interview I would offer them the chance to stop and collect themselves. I can think of one particular example where I asked someone a question about their mother that completely by accident touched a terrible raw nerve. It was a perfectly normal conversation over coffee in the middle of the morning at the Groucho Club in London and the person was in floods of tears. I said "Look, we can stop this if you want" and she said "No, I want to talk about this." It was a sensational interview – but only because I offered to stop it.'

Phrasing difficult questions

Don't panic at the thought of asking tough questions. If an interviewee has been caught up in a scandal they won't be surprised to be asked about it (although they might not be as forthcoming as you'd like). Make sure you've done your research in advance and think hard about how you are going to broach the subject. Whatever you do, don't leave the interview without asking the questions that you need to ask.

The *Daily Mail's* Brian Viner says that it is key to spend time beforehand working out how you are going to phrase the difficult questions. It is often helpful, he advises, to start the question by saying something along the lines of 'It must drive you mad that . . .' or by quoting something that has been written about the interviewee in another publication.

'If you know that it's a question that is possibly going to make your interviewee's hackles rise, think about how to phrase it and couch it and make sure that it comes up at the right time,' he says.

'Don't start with the difficult question and risk them saying that the interview's over before it's even begun. The moment to ask is when you feel that a rapport has been established. Wait until you've got enough in your tape recorder or notebook, so if they terminate the interview at least you've got something.'

Monosyllabic interviewees

Even if your approach is professional and your questions excellent you will inevitably encounter the occasional interviewee who is uncooperative, monosyllabic, evasive or reluctant to answer questions.

In a situation like this don't give up and bring the interview – or non-interview – to a close. There are still a few strategies you can try to get your interviewee to be more forthcoming.

- *Persist with questioning.* If your interviewee doesn't want to answer the question it may be a good idea to move to the next subject. You can always return to the question later, perhaps with a reminder that this is a valuable opportunity to set the record straight, tell their side of the story or dispel persistent rumours.
- *Keep them talking.* Keep your cool, keep your head and keep them talking. Even if they don't say very much you can still glean enough to write a story.
- *Suggest/guess.* This can be an effective way to wheedle a bit of detail out of your interviewee. If a company boss, for instance, says they'd rather not discuss 'the actual budget' you could ask: 'Would between £300,000 and £400,000 be a safe guess?'
- *Hint at dissatisfaction.* If an interviewee is unforthcoming and you are using a notebook you can signal your frustration by putting the cap back on your pen and closing your notebook – or in extreme circumstances, by switching off your voice recorder. Another strategy is to say: 'I'm obviously asking the wrong questions. Can we start again?'
- *Wheedle and needle.* This doesn't always work but a skilled interviewer can sometimes get someone to talk by saying something along the lines of 'Oh come on, you can tell me . . .'
- *No comment.* If your interviewee refuses to answer a particular question one approach is to point out how bad this will look in print.
- *Play 'Grandmother's footsteps'.* This requires judgement and delicacy. Having established what your interviewee doesn't want to talk about you creep up to the subject again and again, veering away at the last minute. The theory is that after a while they'll eventually agree to discuss it.

- *Get tough.* If your interviewee has been particularly difficult and you can afford to antagonise them you might consider asking a hostile question. This is a high-risk strategy but ask it with a smile and *never* lose your temper.
- *Use an anecdote.* Remind your interviewee of an anecdote you found in the cuttings. They may seize the opportunity to retell it, or even better, come up with a new one.

Ploys not to fall for

If you're asked for your opinion by an interviewee try to avoid giving it. This is often an experienced interviewee's way of flattering you, attempting to get you on their side and avoiding probing questions.

As mentioned earlier, some interviewees attempt to sidetrack tricky questions by asking you questions about yourself. If someone tries to do this, the best tactic is to answer briefly and then carry on with the interview. Some interviewers deflect all personal questions but in certain cases it's easier and quicker to give a short answer and then get back to business.

Polite at all times

If you are faced with a difficult or challenging interviewee, don't lose your cool. Always be polite and courteous.

The award-winning journalist Sue Lloyd-Roberts, who died in 2015, demonstrated the importance of this throughout her career.

Lloyd-Roberts reported from war zones around the world and exposed human rights abuses in some of the most evil regimes. When *Woman's Hour* presenter Jane Garvey interviewed her for BBC Radio 4 Garvey remarked that she was always 'exquisitely polite'. 'You meet some hideous people in some desperate circumstances but you never lose your sense of decorum,' said Garvey. 'It's a tactic that pays off.' Lloyd-Roberts agreed with this. 'It's definitely a tactic that pays off,' she said. 'I think it makes people reveal more.'[5]

What if the person stops the interview or walks out?

This happens rarely but if the interviewee either stops the interview or threatens to walk out the best strategy is to apologise, recover your composure and move on. If they walk out there is very little you can do, other than talk to the publicist or try and persuade them to reconsider. The one consolation is that moments like these make good copy.

If an interviewee loses their temper at your line of questioning Brian Viner believes that the best thing to do is to say sorry and change the subject. 'It can be intimidating,' he says, 'but the fact that they've got cross can give you a line for your piece. It's always interesting to see where their tender bits are.'

He recalls an interview when a famous cricketer got angry when he asked about his son's sporting record. 'He got so cross that I was able to make a virtue of it in the piece. It wasn't wasted. You can always turn something that at the time of the interview seems like a negative into a positive when you're writing.'

Inexperienced interviewees

Some interviewees are unused to dealing with the press so you need to handle them with care.

When you fix up the interview explain who you work for and why you want to talk to them. They are far more likely to be cooperative and helpful if they know what to expect. But while it's fine to give them an idea of what you want to talk about, avoid going into too much detail. If you give them too much information in advance there's a risk you might get boring, over-rehearsed answers. As outlined earlier in the book, if they insist on having a list of questions beforehand then you'll have to comply. But when it comes to the interview itself don't be afraid to ask additional questions too.

Start with a question on a safe subject that you know they can answer with ease. Get them relaxed and talkative before getting to more controversial or sensitive areas.

Don't worry too much if they insist on other members of the family or friends being in the room during the interview. Anecdotes and colour from others can often be very useful. If the interview is about a delicate subject, try and persuade the interviewee to talk on their own. You can always send the others out to make cups of tea or find photographs while you talk.

Mental illness and suicide: media guidelines

Sensitivity is required when writing stories about mental illness. *Time to Change*, a programme led by the mental health charities Mind and Rethink Mental Illness and funded by the Department of Health and Comic Relief, has produced a useful guide for journalists (available at www.mind.org.uk/news-campaigns/

minds-media-office/how-to-report-on-mental-health). *Time to Change* works with the media 'to encourage realistic and sensitive portrayals of people with mental health problems' and says that 'when done well, news stories can be a tremendous tool'. It adds that 'well written news stories about mental health can raise awareness, challenge attitudes and help to dispel myths'.[6]

The guidelines stress the importance of choosing the right language to describe people with mental health problems. They also encourage journalists to make sure that individuals are 'genuinely prepared' to be interviewed.

When reporting on suicide, journalists must follow guidelines set out in the *Editors' Code of Practice*. Regulated by IPSO, these stipulate that 'when reporting suicide, to prevent simulative acts care should be taken to avoid excessive detail of the method used, while taking into account the media's rights to report legal proceedings'.[7]

The charity Samaritans has published media guidelines for reporting suicides. This document is updated regularly and includes the advice that inappropriate language should not be used, 'such as referring to a death as someone having "committed suicide"'.[8] It also advises media organisations to think about the impact that their coverage might have. The media guidelines add: 'Your story might have an effect on vulnerable individuals or people connected to the person who has died. Providing information on how to contact appropriate local and national sources of support can encourage people experiencing emotional problems or suicidal thoughts to seek help. It can save lives.'

Interviewing children

Children can be a delight to interview but the guidelines are very strict. The first thing you must do is make sure you are familiar with the *Editors' Code of Practice*, which states the following:

    i) All pupils should be free to complete their time at school without unnecessary intrusion.

    ii) They must not be approached or photographed at school without permission of the school authorities.

    iii) Children under 16 must not be interviewed or photographed on issues involving their own or another child's welfare unless a custodial parent or similarly responsible adult consents.

    iv) Children under 16 must not be paid for material involving their welfare, nor parents or guardians for material about their children or wards, unless it is clearly in the child's interest.

    v) Editors must not use the fame, notoriety or position of a parent or guardian as sole justification for publishing details of a child's private life.[9]

There is also a section in the *Editors' Code of Practice* on children in sex cases. This states that:

1. The press must not, even if legally free to do so, identify children under 16 who are victims or witnesses in cases involving sex offences.
2. In any press report of a case involving a sexual offence against a child –

   i) The child must not be identified.
   ii) The adult may be identified.
   iii) The word 'incest' must not be used where a child victim might be identified.
   iv) Care must be taken that nothing in the report implies the relationship between the accused and the child.[10]

For further information about interviews with children take a look at a booklet called *Interviewing Children*, written by Sarah McCrum and Lotte Hughes of Save the Children.[11]

Interviewing sensitive sources

Investigative journalists often spend months cultivating sources and persuading them to expose wrongdoing. Paul Lewis, the *Guardian*'s San Francisco-based west coast bureau chief, previously ran investigations as special projects editor in London and has some useful interviewing tips for journalists working on sensitive investigations.

'I always think it makes sense to meet a contact in a destination of their choosing,' he says. 'Not only is it more convenient for them, but it enables them to choose somewhere where they feel comfortable. That's important. Putting people at ease, being upfront about what you're trying to find out, and ensuring that there is sufficient time for the person you're speaking to not to feel rushed are all crucial first steps.

'In 2011, the *Guardian* conducted research into the England riots in a partnership with the London School of Economics (LSE). The project was called *Reading the Riots*[12] and involved in-depth, detailed and neutral interviews with hundreds of rioters and police officers. There was a lot of skills sharing and mutual collaboration with our academic partners in the project and the journalists among us learned a great deal from the social scientists and sociologists, who had a very different approach to interviewing. The emphasis in social research is on non-leading interviews, in which the interviewer strives to be led by the interviewee, so as not to dictate the trajectory of the discussion, and avoids leading questions. So rather than ask: "Did you enter the store to loot?" the question would be "Tell me why you entered the store". You might be surprised by the answer.'

Lewis says that the research altered his interviewing style. 'We learned how to use neutral prompts, encouraging interviewees to tell us more, to allow them to roam in their discussion, even when they were going down paths that we, as interviewers, did not initially think would be especially fruitful.

'The experience changed the way I interview in a journalistic context. Too often reporters approach a subject with a pre-existing idea of what the answer is and a sense of the types of questions needed to elicit that response as quickly as possible. This is partly understandable. Journalists work under deadlines and sometimes the answers we need – How many people died in the fire? What time did the train crash? – are relatively straightforward and factual. But on the whole, and where time permits, I think it is always preferable to strive to be as open as possible and led by the interviewee, interrupting as little as possible, directing the flow from time to time and always carefully listening. I've found that I'm often surprised by the things people tell me. They end up responding to questions I never would have thought of asking.

'The kinds of prompts that often work are questions that just keep the ball rolling, such as: "Can you tell me a little more about that?" When someone makes a bold claim or statement that requires unpicking, I tend to go with: "In what way?"'

Interviewing in pairs

The idea of two journalists interviewing one person may sound odd but two-handed interviews are more common than you might think.

They may be imposed on you by a PR – perhaps because time is limited and the interviewee reckons that the best solution is to talk to feature writers from, say, a newspaper and a monthly glossy magazine together. As you're not direct competitors this is feasible, although not altogether desirable. Another scenario you may encounter is when you are interviewing someone so prestigious that your editor decides to join you. Third, some publications make two-handed interviews a regular feature. Rachel Sylvester and Alice Thomson often interview politicians together for *The Times*, for example.

In each instance it's very important to work out together beforehand how you intend to share the questioning and who will start. If you are from different publications it may be a good idea to plan the topics you intend to cover – in order to avoid the questioning veering wildly from one subject to another. The alternative is for each of you to interview for ten minutes at a time.

Problems sometimes arise if one interviewer breaks the agreement to share interviewing time equally and hogs the questioning. If this happens, the best tactic is to interrupt the other journalist and say politely but firmly, 'I think it's my turn to ask a few questions now', and launch straight into your next question.

You may find that you are doing a two-hander with a journalist from a totally different publication. Perhaps you are working for a teen magazine and want to ask a young actor about his fashion style whereas your opposite number is from a serious arts publication and is more interested in quizzing the star about his love of Shakespeare. Once again, try and meet five minutes before the interview so you can agree on the shape of the interview and when the interview starts be polite, charming and assertive.

Staying safe

Journalists frequently have to work alone so it's important to be vigilant at all times. Always inform your news, features or commissioning editor about the face-to-face interviews that you are doing. Tell them who you are interviewing, when you are meeting and where – and always keep your mobile phone with you. If you have any reservations about the doorstep you've been asked to do, especially if it's one where there are unlikely to be other journalists, don't go alone. Take a photographer or another reporter with you. If you're a freelance journalist, perhaps without a firm commission for your piece, tell friends and family exactly where you are going and what you are doing.

Distressing news stories and court cases can stay with you for a long time afterwards. If you have been affected by a story you have covered as a journalist speak to colleagues and seek help as soon as possible.

Interviewing task

Read the *Editors' Code of Practice* and make sure you understand the key points. The code is available in a mobile phone friendly format, so journalists can consult it in all circumstances.

HOW I INTERVIEW: DOROTHY LEPKOWSKA

Dorothy Lepkowska is an award-winning freelance education journalist. She started her career on the *Nuneaton Tribune* and went on to work as an education correspondent for the *Birmingham Post, Times Education Supplement, Evening Standard, Daily Express* and *Daily Mirror.*

Lepkowska believes that the most important qualities you need as a journalist are a genuine interest in what people have to say and empathy. As she says, when you are interviewing someone who has suffered a personal tragedy or crisis 'you need to think for a minute what it would be like to be the person you're interviewing. Understand that they might be feeling wary, scared, grief-stricken or whatever – but remain professional, as you still have a job to do.'

Your facial expressions and body language are important too. 'Look like you're listening,' says Lepkowska. 'In face-to-face interviews I always stop writing at some point and look at the person I'm interviewing and just listen. Don't worry about missing writing something down. You can come back to it later and ask them about this again and then get your notes written down.'

When she is interviewing she always judges people's moods and uses the appropriate tone of voice. 'Don't go in loud and hard on someone who must be feeling vulnerable,' she says. 'Let them finish what they're saying before interjecting with another question. Often the interviewee will say something that prompts a supplementary question. Don't throw them off their train of thought by jumping straight on this point as you might miss some good quotes from the original question. Put a mark next to your notes that this is something you want to come back to.'

When it comes to questions Lepkowska never starts a question by saying 'I assume that . . .'

'Assume nothing,' she says, 'unless they've given you a strong hint that this is what they're thinking. It's far better to use something like "From what you've said, am I right in thinking that . . .?" This gives them the option of saying yes or no, and the opportunity to explain better.'

She also highlights the importance of getting interviewees to explain or clarify points that aren't clear.

'Don't be scared of admitting you don't know something and need them to explain more fully,' she says. 'This isn't a sign of weakness or ignorance. On the contrary, you're showing that you want to tell their story accurately. Always ask for an explanation of something you don't understand. You can't inform the reader properly if you haven't understood yourself. And you can't be expected to know everything.'

> **Dorothy Lepkowska's top tip**
>
> When you are interviewing someone who has suffered a personal tragedy or crisis you need to think for a minute what it would be like to be the person you're interviewing. Understand that they might be feeling wary, scared and grief-stricken.

Notes

1 Editors' Code of Practice Committee, *The Code in Full*. Available from: www.editorscode.org.uk/index.php (accessed 10 August 2016).
2 G. Rees, 'The trauma factor: reporting on violence and tragedy', in *Journalism: New Challenges*, eds K. Fowler-Watt and S. Allan, Centre for Journalism and Communication Research, Bournemouth University, 2013, p. 422. Available from: https://microsites.bournemouth.ac.uk/cjcr/files/2013/10/JNC-2013-Chapter-25-Rees.pdf (accessed 20 May 2016).
3 National Union of Journalists, *Code of Conduct*. Available from: www.nuj.org.uk/about/nuj-code (accessed 11 August 2016).
4 C. Moreton, 'It took satnav 18 seconds to tear two families apart', *Telegraph*. Available from: www.telegraph.co.uk/news/uknews/crime/10293094/It-took-satnav-18-seconds-to-tear-two-families-apart.html (accessed 11 October 2016).
5 J. Garvey, 'Interview with Sue Lloyd-Roberts', *Woman's Hour*, BBC Radio 4. Available from: www.bbc.co.uk/programmes/b07nn8br (accessed 18 August 2016).
6 *Time to Change: Media Guidelines*. Available from: www.time-to-change.org.uk/sites/default/files/imce_uploads/TtC%20Media%20Leaflet%20NEWS%20(2).pdf (accessed 10 August 2016).
7 Editors' Code of Practice Committee, *The Code in Full*. Available from: www.editorscode.org.uk/index.php (accessed 10 August 2016).
8 The Samaritans, *Media Guidelines for Reporting Suicide*. Available from: www.samaritans.org/sites/default/files/kcfinder/branches/branch-96/files/Samaritans%20Media%20Guidelines%20UK%202013%20ARTWORK%20v2%20web.pdf (accessed 11 October 2016).
9 Editors' Code of Practice Committee, *The Code in Full*. Available from: www.editorscode.org.uk/index.php (accessed 10 August 2016).
10 Editors' Code of Practice Committee, *The Code in Full*. Available from: www.editorscode.org.uk/index.php (accessed 10 August 2016).
11 S. McCrum and L. Hughes, *Interviewing Children* (2nd edn), Save the Children, 2003. Available from: www.savethechildren.org.uk/sites/default/files/docs/INTERVIEWING_CHILDREN.pdf (accessed 10 August 2016).
12 *Guardian* and the LSE, *Reading the Riots: Investigating England's Summer of Disorder*. Available from: www.theguardian.com/uk/interactive/2011/dec/14/reading-the-riots-investigating-england-s-summer-of-disorder-full-report (accessed 21 August 2016).

12
After the interview

Many journalists feel a sense of relief when the interview is over, especially if it has gone well and they've got an excellent story on their hands – perhaps even a scoop.

The first thing most journalists do after interviews is check that they've got everything down in their notebooks and/or on their voice recorders. As mentioned earlier, once freelance Cole Moreton has said goodbye to his interviewees he makes a point of recording his overall impressions of them and the conversation. Observations like these often prove very helpful when it comes to writing your piece.

Disasters

If you switch on your recorder and discover that you don't have a record of the interview, don't panic. Take several deep breaths and think back to the moment you walked into the room to meet your interviewee, or the moment you were put through to them on the telephone. Closing your eyes often helps you to concentrate.

Write down your first impressions of the person. What were they wearing? What did the room look like? How did they greet you? Think back to what you said and what their response was. Make a note of everything you can think of. You'll be amazed how much you can remember, especially if you do it straight away. You obviously won't be able to quote the interviewee directly from this material but you may have enough information to write a basic story.

The preferable option is to phone your interviewee and ask if they could do the interview again (yet another reason to make sure you have their contact details). At the very least, check missing facts and spellings with them. Remember though, that a repeat interview, while essential, is unlikely to be as successful.

If the person you interviewed is famous, don't assume that they'll refuse to redo the interview. Take heart from the experience of *Daily Mail* film critic Brian Viner. When his recorder failed early in his career during an interview with Melvyn Bragg, the broadcaster generously agreed to do the interview all over again. Similarly, feature writer Deborah Ross suffered 'a tape malfunction' when she interviewed the actress Dame Judi Dench in 2016. In her feature for *The Times* magazine Ross described how she rang Dench's agent 'to ask if she might call me as some of our chat was missing and I wished to recap. I was not hopeful, but she phoned the next day – from an Isle of Wight ferry, I think – and that was an act of great generosity, pure and simple.'[1]

Saving interviews

Save yourself extra anxiety by saving the recording of your interview the moment you can. Many journalists make extra-sure that their interviews won't go astray by emailing their recordings to themselves and/or backing them up to a cloud storage service such as Dropbox, iCloud or Google Drive.

Journalists who rely solely on their notebooks avoid voice recorder mishaps. The equivalent, however, is losing your precious notebook, so if you've done a brilliant interview, don't let it out of your sight.

A host of famous writers have admitted to losing their work in the past. T. E. Lawrence rewrote *The Seven Pillars of Wisdom* three times, admitting that one rewrite was necessary because he lost his manuscript while changing trains at Reading railway station. The poet Dylan Thomas kept losing *Under Milk Wood* in pubs, although luckily it kept being salvaged. And novelist Jilly Cooper left the manuscript of *Riders*, one of her best-known books, on a London bus. Interviewed by journalist Elizabeth Day for the *Observer* in 2011 she recalled: 'It was awful, awful. I'd finished the first draft, I went out to lunch and then I got the bus home – the number 22 bus – and I left it behind. Everyone was very kind and the *Evening Standard* put out an appeal. That was 1970, I think.'[2] The manuscript was never found and it was another 14 years before she started writing the novel again.

Transcribing

Your news editor or features editor will have told you when your story is scheduled to run and when they need it by (if they haven't, ask them). If the story is required immediately it's best to write it directly from your notebook rather than taking time to transcribe your notes. This is far easier than it sounds.

When I worked for the *Evening Standard* in London, the paper published three or four editions a day and news reporters frequently had to file their copy a few minutes ahead of the deadline. Get in the habit of working out possible intros in advance. It concentrates your mind on the key points of the story and you can always ditch your draft intro later on if you come up with something better.

If your interview isn't required straightaway you'll have time to type up your notes before writing the story. Some journalists only transcribe the essential quotes but others find it easier to type out everything, just in case they need more material later on. Don't worry about typing neatly. As long as the transcript is legible it doesn't have to look beautiful. One tip is to highlight the most important lines in bold or a bright colour, so they are easy to find in the mass of words.

Interviewers who use shorthand should grab the first opportunity to transcribe their notes. If you can't decipher your shorthand, write down the letters and sounds you *can* make out. Rather than poring over the missing quotes, leave the problem outlines for a while. You'll be surprised how easily the sense leaps out at you from the page when you read your notes a second time. Incidentally, if during an interview you note down a word or phrase you fear may be difficult to decipher later on, spell it out in the margin as soon as possible, perhaps during a pause in the conversation. It will save time when you're transcribing the interview.

If you're playing back a recording with an excruciating amount of background noise on it, play it over and over again, with the bass turned to its lowest setting and the treble to the highest. When I interviewed a distinguished Harvard academic over the phone on a crackly transatlantic line this worked superbly. As if by magic I could suddenly hear exactly what the professor was saying.

If you're not on a tight deadline, now is also the moment to update your contacts online (or in a contacts book if you find it easier). Make a note of your interviewee's email addresses, telephone numbers, home and work addresses, details of partners, PAs and work associates, so you'll be able to contact them again.

Are there any gaps?

After you've transcribed your notes, read them again more analytically. What gaps are there? How can you fill them? Are there questions that remain unanswered? Who might be able to help?

If you find gaps or discover facts and quotes you are unsure about and need to check with your interviewee, call them back as soon as possible – when the interview is still fresh in their mind. Don't leave it for weeks on end before contacting them. They may be hard to reach, unable to remember the details of the conversation or even change their minds about the interview. Having said that, in my experience most interviewees (apart from celebrities, who are notoriously difficult to get hold of) are happy to provide additional details.

At this juncture you should also consider how the story will play in print. Is it potentially libellous (in which case you will need to discuss it with your editor and check it out with a lawyer)? Does anyone you have named need to be accorded the right to reply? Should you check the details with a third party to ensure that the story stands up and is accurate?

If you haven't already done so, compare what you've been told during the interview with what you discovered in the course of your research. Are there any discrepancies? Do the statistics and chronology agree? What follow-up interviews are needed (if any)? Make sure your story is as watertight as possible.

Checking the details

Never knowingly print anything false. In other words, always strive to be accurate and fair. Accuracy is the cornerstone of journalism, or as journalism tutor and editor Sally Adams put it: 'This sounds moralistic, but accuracy is the basis on which respect and reputations are built.'[3]

If you are writing online content, don't take a 'post now, correct later' attitude. Make sure you get the details (facts, spellings and punctuation) right first time. For a daily reminder of the importance of this take a look at newspapers' corrections and clarifications columns, which encompass everything from factual inaccuracies to grammatical mistakes. Here is a example from the *Guardian* in 2016: 'We confused the singular criterion with the plural criteria yet again in an editorial about the Labour party leadership . . . that ended with the sentence "Readiness for that mission, not abstract tests of ideological purity, should be the criteria on which the leader is chosen."'[4]

Copy and quote approval

Showing copy to interviewees before it is published is complete anathema to many journalists. They regard it as utterly unthinkable. Some writers, however, do let their interviewees see the copy before publication – either because it's part of the agreement (this often happens with celebrities), because they want to avoid potential trouble or, in the case of a complex, technical subject, because they want to ensure that the facts are correct. In certain cases, writers will either read the quotes to interviewees over the phone or email them what they have said (rather than sending the whole piece). Any discussions about whether interviewees will have copy and/or quote approval, however, should take place before the interview itself, not retrospectively. If you're unsure what to do, check your publication's policy with your commissioning editor.

On the whole, copy approval depends on the type of journalism you are engaged in. BuzzFeed UK investigations editor Heidi Blake, for instance, says you should 'never give copy approval' but education correspondent Dorothy Lepkowska advises that if you work for a specialist magazine it will be necessary in certain circumstances.

'Working for in-house publications often means having to agree to copy approval because there are members or professionals that the organisation doesn't want to upset,' says Lepkowska, who has worked for the *Evening Standard*, *Daily Express* and *Daily Mirror* during her award-winning career.

'I've had my stuff completely rewritten in the past by a teacher for the sake of it, not because it was inaccurate. I would have minded less if she had done a good job. I've also had a head teacher deny that what I'd written was what he said to me in the phone interview, but when he made amendments it was to add to his original comments rather than redact them – so I hadn't actually got it wrong after all. This wasn't lost on the commissioning editor.

'It's important always to make clear that you would like interviewees to confirm that the comments attributed to them are accurate and do not misrepresent them and *that is all*. I often transcribe their notes and then send just those comments, and nothing else, for copy approval. This removes any doubt as to what you're asking of them.

'With regard to editing, I might also send quotes for copy approval if I've edited them – to ensure that I haven't changed any tone or meaning, or misrepresented them. I only do this when people have got themselves into a muddle, mixed their metaphors or something like that. Usually they're pleased that they're now coming across better than they did originally. People are often anxious or nervous about speaking to journalists too so it's worth keeping that in mind.'

Piers Morgan took a robust stance on copy approval when he was editor of the *Daily Mirror*. As he told interviewer Charlotte Edwardes in *The Times* magazine in 2016: 'We had a war on airbrushing and copy control at the *Mirror*. Richard Madeley and Judy Finnigan did a 1,000-word interview and they asked for 820 words to be changed. So we ran both interviews, one next to the other.'[5]

Writing your story

This book focuses on interviewing rather than writing up interviews but having said that, it's crucial not to lose sight of the fact that once you have done the interview your task will be to craft it into a readable news story or feature.

Hunter Davies explained in his collection of interviews, *Hunting People: Thirty Years of Interviews with the Famous*, that he preferred to mull over his interviews for a day or so before writing them up.[6] Other journalists, even those with longer deadlines, opt to write their story while the interview is fresh in their mind. Don't, whatever you do, let a string of interviews mount up in your notebook or on your voice recorder before writing them. The longer you leave them, the harder they will be to write.

Description

If you are writing a feature and you can't work out how to begin, one strategy is to imagine taking the reader inside the interview room with you, metaphorically speaking of course. Describe the setting of your meeting, explain the scene that greeted you and write about your interviewee's appearance and demeanour. Take care, however, not to make personal or derogatory remarks about the way your interviewee looks. Stick to the facts.

'You've got to create an impression of what it was like,' says Brian Viner. Similarly, Stephanie Rafanelli often uses a situation from her interviews as an intro. After interviewing the actor Colin Farrell for the *Telegraph* she began her profile with the moment they went outside for a cigarette break.

'Colin Farrell is magnetic: this much we know,' Rafanelli wrote. 'Indeed, there is something about his energy that seems to attract the metal of life – intensely good, at times intensely bad, and sometimes a little random. This is how we end up, standing in the rain.'[7]

The novelist Truman Capote (best-known for *Breakfast at Tiffany's* and *In Cold Blood*) was one of the most talented writers of the twentieth century. Take a moment to read his 1957 interview with Marlon Brando in *The New Yorker* magazine. He sets the scene of the interview so perfectly that you can almost imagine you're in the room with him. In the following line he looks back to a meeting with Brando ten years earlier, when he discovered 'a brawny young man' asleep on a table on the stage of a New York theatre. 'Because he was wearing a white T-shirt and denim trousers, because of his gymnasium physique – the weightlifter's arms, the Charles Atlas chest (though an opened *Basic Writings of Sigmund Freud* was resting on it) – I took him for a stagehand.'[8]

Direct and indirect speech

Most news stories and features will include both direct and indirect speech. Rather than relying solely on one or the other it's important to balance the two. While direct speech brings a story to life, indirect speech is useful in clarifying points and giving background quickly and easily.

As Ian Reeves and Richard Lance Keeble explained in *The Newspapers Handbook*: 'A report concentrating too heavily on indirect speech will lack immediacy and colour; a report almost exclusively in direct quotations conveys the impression the journalist has surrendered their role of selection and interpretation to the source.'[9]

Using quotes

Journalists use quotes to add life to their copy, to emphasise a point and/or to move a story along. Quotes must earn their place in the piece though; they are not there simply to fill column inches or to show the world that you can use a voice recorder. If your interviewee is articulate and speaks engagingly then use more quotes. If they waffle and say the same thing over and over again use fewer quotes.

While some journalists let their quotes run for several paragraphs, Camilla Long prefers to use short quotes or even single words. She captures the personality and character of her interviewees by using short snippets of quotes and a lot of description. 'I feel it's more natural,' she says. 'Huge reams of quotes are a bit boring and monolithic – and they're unrealistic. Conversations are like tennis matches and you need to get the same energy and pace in your interviews.'

Brian Viner admits that he has 'certain bugbears' about how to write features. He never starts with a quote – 'I just think it's a lazy way in' – and insists on coming up with a good pay-off line. 'A quote is a good way of ending a piece but I would never start with one,' he says.

Editing quotes

How much should you change what interviewees say? This is an issue that journalism students and trainees often raise and the answer is 'as little as possible'. Another frequently asked question is: Should you quote people accurately? The answer? 'Yes, of course.'

The problem is that the majority of us don't speak in sentences and few of us use perfect punctuation and grammar as we talk. Even the most articulate, engaging interviewees have a tendency to repeat themselves and jump erratically from one subject to another. How, then, do we use quotes like this in a news story or feature?

With most interviewees the best advice is to tidy their quotes up minimally and cut out the 'ums' and 'ers'. Never, however, change the sense of what the interviewee said. You can patch a quote very slightly – i.e. take something they said at one point in the interview and follow it with a sentence they used earlier – but you *must* use their words and keep the meaning secure and clear. If the interviewee uses the same word over and over again don't ever be tempted to substitute an alternative word, especially if it's one they wouldn't use in a million years. Either repeat the word in the quote (it shows how much they like the word) or quote it once and explain the rest of the point in indirect speech. As Tony Harcup explained in *Journalism: Principles and Practice*: 'The golden rule when selecting or shortening quotes, and pruning out repetitions and irrelevancies, is to retain not just the interviewee's *voice* but the speaker's *sense*. Otherwise, why bother quoting at all?'[10]

And what if your interviewee says something vivid and quotable – but not in a neat sentence? Actually, this is an easy problem to circumvent. For a start there's no law that insists quotes must have a subject, verb and object. Also, as Camilla Long says, you can use fragments of quotes to great effect.

Attributing quotes

Quotes should be attributed to one (preferably named) individual. This will give your story authenticity and the stronger and more vivid the quote, the more the reader will want to read on and find out more. Avoid attributing a quote to two or more people (press releases sometimes do this, but journalists shouldn't).

There are certain exceptions to naming interviewees. In particular, journalists must never identify victims of sexual assault unless they waive their right to anonymity. As the *Editors' Code of Practice* states: 'The press must not identify victims of sexual assault or publish material likely to contribute to such identification unless there is adequate justification and they are legally free to do so.'[11]

In certain circumstances interviewees can't be named because the consequences of being identified would be dire and/or put them in danger. In instances like these most publications tend to choose a false name, together with a footnote that says something along the lines of 'the names in this article have been changed'. Magazines often do this, particularly when covering sensitive issues.

Uncommunicative interviewees

How do you write your piece when your interviewee barely uttered a single word during the interview? You have to make the best of the material you managed to get. Very occasionally a non-interview works brilliantly. A piece by the late author, broadcaster and film critic William Hall is a case in point. When Hall was commissioned to find and interview the famously elusive Marlon Brando just after he'd filmed *Last Tango in Paris* the journalist tracked him down to his hideaway in Tahiti. Finally, after three weeks, Hall managed to corner him.

Brando was asleep when his wife Tarita let Hall into the house. The moment he awoke he threatened to punch Hall on the nose.

'Gamely I put the questions the world wanted to know as we performed a kind of dance around the room. I was back-pedalling. Brando was leading. "Did you know, Marlon, that *Last Tango in Paris* is banned in several countries?" "I don't care," said Brando, "Get out!"'[12]

Hall didn't despair. He went on to write a famous feature describing how he had discovered Marlon Brando in his South Sea island bolthole. The entire 'interview' consisted of two sentences.

'"I'm going to give you to the count of three and then I'm going to punch you right in the face," was Brando's welcome. His lips were white and his eyes were glazed. He waved hairy knuckles under my nose and bellowed: "I'm warning you, there's going to be great physical personal damage done to you."'[13]

When Camilla Long interviewed the novelist Irvine Welsh of *Trainspotting* fame he was keen to talk about himself and little else. In her entertaining *Sunday Times* profile she made a virtue of this. As she wrote: 'I have never interviewed someone so apparently jolly and friendly and up for it, but so absent, so uncomplicated, so like a cab driver simply fielding the next fare. When I ask him if his mother is still alive, he sighs and absent-mindedly says, "Probably." (She is.)'[14]

Swearing

It's important to quote accurately – but should you quote *exactly* what people say? What if they swear during the interview, for example? Should you still quote them verbatim in print?

In a lads' mag, then yes, you probably should. If you are interviewing a rock star and every other word is a swear word you should try to give a realistic impression of how they talk. Readers are unlikely to be shocked or offended because they'll appreciate that that's how the star speaks. If the interview is for a family publication, the editorial style guide and your editor's preference will be the deciding factors. If the interview is for a sub-teen magazine, you wouldn't use any swear words. It's perfectly possible to remove the swearing and keep the main quotes. What is not acceptable, however, is to substitute a different word.

Correcting grammar

Should you correct grammar? Here the experts differ. If an interviewer says 'less than a thousand people turned up' perfectionists believe you should change the phrase to the grammatically correct 'fewer than a thousand people turned up'.

Others reckon that you should keep the words exactly as the interviewee said them. I take the latter view. Journalists should write what the interviewee said, not what the chief sub wishes that they'd said.

Obscure words

If you're interviewing an academic or technical expert and they drop in an obscure word or phrase, should you quote them exactly?

Well yes, especially if the word is interesting and intriguing, but you should also explain what it means – preferably in the same or next sentence. When I interviewed a head teacher who mentioned that he had introduced 'blended learning' at his school it was clear that some readers would be interested but others wouldn't know what he meant. I therefore wrote: 'The head is a keen advocate of blended learning. This approach involves students learning partly through traditional teaching and partly through digital and online technology.'

So, the bottom line is: don't change quotes, but do clarify them where necessary.

Ridicule

Should you ridicule people by quoting exactly what they say, especially if it's idiotic or wrong?

If you interview someone who spends half the interview boasting about their love of classical music and then goes on to talk about Beethoven's 'Erotica Symphony', should you change that to Beethoven's 'Eroica Symphony' to save them from embarrassment? Only you can decide. If the person has made a genuine mistake then it seems unfair to make fun of them by reporting their mispronunciation. If, on the other hand, they are presenting themselves as an expert on classical music you might express puzzlement at their error.

Sourcing

When it comes to writing up a suspect statement or fact the safest way to deal with it is to attribute it to the speaker and/or put it inside quotation marks. It is a good idea to run it past the lawyers too.

For example, 'there's no truth in the rumour that we're separating' is safer than using the same words in reported (indirect) speech. Similarly, rather than writing that 'the company's sales have risen 60 per cent over the last six months', use the following: 'The marketing manager said: "Sales are 60 per cent up since March"' or 'The marketing manager reported that the company's sales had risen 60 per cent in the last six months.'

Keeping your notes

Journalists must always keep proper notes of their conversations and interviews – and recordings too. This is not only helpful for future reference, when you are writing another piece for example, but it is essential if someone later takes issue with a quote you have used. Get in the habit of keeping your notes and transcriptions from the start of your career.

As Kim Fletcher pointed out in *The Journalist's Handbook*: 'If you are writing a basic, straightforward story you will find it useful to have the material in one place. If you are writing a story that might be challenged, you will find it vital. Always remember the possibility of that court case, with lawyers arguing over every verb in every sentence. If you haven't got notes or tapes of your interviews, made at the time and legible to others, you will be in trouble.'[15]

Placing your interviews

If you're a staff writer your whole output (or certainly most of it) will be for your own newspaper, magazine or online publication. If you're a freelance journalist or a student just starting out, finding an outlet for your work and placing your story can be a challenge.

If you can, contact possible outlets *before* you do the interview. Find out the name of the relevant commissioning editor and pitch your proposed piece to them. Pitching is usually done by email so make sure you spell the commissioning editor's name right and that your email is professional, without any glaring spelling, punctuation or grammar mistakes. My general advice would be to write no more than four succinct paragraphs, explaining the story and why it is important, why it is timely to run the story now, the angle and who you plan to interview and a brief biography of yourself, with a link to your portfolio and details of why you are the best person to write the story.

If, as a journalism trainee or student, you don't find an outlet for your proposed interview then publish it on your own blog (all student journalists should have one). Include text and high-resolution images and, if appropriate, audio and video too. Make sure that you publicise your blog by posting links on social media. You never know, it may get picked up by the mainstream media.

Interviewing task

Think of a person in the news you would like to interview. Choose a publication, research the relevant commissioning editor and write a pitch, explaining what the story is and why you are well-placed to do the interview.

HOW I INTERVIEW: EMMA BROCKES

Emma Brockes is an award-winning journalist. She was named young journalist of the year at the British Press Awards in 2001 and won the feature writer of the year award in 2002. During ten years as a staff writer at the *Guardian*, she interviewed everyone from Liza Minnelli to Madeleine Albright. Now freelance and based in New York, she writes for the *Guardian* and the *New York Times*. She has also written a book about her mother, *She Left Me the Gun: My Mother's Life Before Me*.

For two years Brockes wrote a major weekly interview for the *Guardian's* G2 section. Her copy deadlines were tight but even so, it was important to take time to plan and prepare properly.

'There was never a huge amount of time to prepare but it would take a morning probably, or at the very most a day. If there was a book to read then I would read it the night before. You can over-prepare though. If you read too many interviews with someone it just kills your desire to meet them because you read the same thing a zillion times. The key to preparation isn't reading thousands and thousands of other pieces, it's sitting and trying to think about the best way into the difficult areas of this person's life.'

Rather than preparing a long list of questions, Brockes concentrates on plotting a route through the interview, from the beginning to the end. In particular, she works out 'key turning points' in advance – moments in the interview where she hopes to move 'from the publicity guff that celebrities want me to talk to them about at the beginning to the juicy stuff'.

'I find that there is always a conversion question that changes the atmosphere of the interview,' she says. 'In a way, it's like getting a rocket into re-entry. If you get the angle of entry wrong you just whizz off into Outer Space and there is no getting back.

'The best example I can think of was when I interviewed Charlize Theron just after she won an Oscar for best actress in *Monster* in 2004. She had already been interviewed by about 30 hacks in the morning and I only had 20 minutes with her. She was encased in make-up having done a load of shoots and the whole thing felt ridiculous and contrived. I knew that within those 20 minutes I had to get the conversation round to how her mother had shot her father dead when she was 15. One journalist from a Durban newspaper had said to her: "So, Charlize, in this film you play a serial killer called Aileen Wuornos. Your mum killed your dad – that must have been a good insight." She just said "It's not the same" and shut the interview down.

'I thought for hours about how to approach this with her. After we chatted about the film and the Oscar for a bit I said: "Do you wish your dad was still alive to see you win the Oscar?" She said: "Of course I do. I wouldn't wish something like that on anybody. Nobody deserves that." And then you're in. You know that she doesn't hate him. It's a complicated story but you go from there.'

Choosing the right place

Writers don't usually have a say in where they interview celebrities. But Brockes says that interviews come to life if you can talk to celebrities in a different setting. When she interviewed Liza Minnelli she flew to Florida to watch the singer in concert, spoke to her backstage and then met her for lunch in New York. The interview was interrupted halfway through by a fire alarm and Brockes and Minnelli ended up walking to another restaurant together.

'You feel grateful for anything which puts the person you are interviewing in a context other than a bland hotel room,' says Brockes. 'There's also something to be said for getting people to relax and reveal themselves if you don't have to make eye contact all the time. Liza Minnelli and I went outside and sat on the steps and she started smoking. She didn't have to look me in the eye and she just suddenly started talking like a normal person.

'We often ask PRs to give us travelling time with a celebrity. I interviewed Richard Attenborough at his house and then, to get an extra 20 minutes, went with him in his car to Heathrow Airport. Just seeing the way he interacted with his driver, who'd been with him for 30 years, gave me more of a sense of the real person. He relaxed and was very jolly and funny.'

Brockes's 2003 *Guardian* interview with Lord Attenborough, who died in 2014, is a delight. Here is an extract that features his assistant, Bill, who drove Attenborough and Brockes to Heathrow in the director's Mercedes with personal plates spelling the word 'idyll'.

'"All right Bill?" says Attenborough, as Bill settles him into his seat and starts faffing with the headrest. "Bill," says Attenborough, more testily, and then, "BILL!" – an all-out roar "Darling! we wouldn't want to make ourselves late." Long-suffering Bill disentangles and repairs to the driver's seat.'[16]

Practicalities

Brockes always uses a voice recorder and a notebook for interviews. So far she hasn't had any recording disasters – but admits that most journalist friends she knows have. The only thing to do in those circumstances, she says, is to come clean, ring the interviewee up and ask for a few extra minutes on the phone. When she gets back to the office she immediately uploads her interview on to her computer and then transcribes it herself.

Interviewing techniques

Brockes starts her interviews with 'a really bland, boring question'. If she's interviewing a film star, for instance, she'll begin by asking about their latest movie.

'You have to get the lay of the land and figure what mood they are in, what is going to rankle with them and how to progress,' she explains. 'It is the perfect opportunity for you to ask them about their film and while they are doing that you are trying to work out how to structure the rest of the interview. You both relax a bit after ten minutes and then you can start moving it out. There's a kind of rhythm about it. If you try and move them on too early they will be disgruntled – so you can't make it look too cursory. But often there is a natural progression because there will be something in the film that relates to their life or their experience and you can move it on from there.'

She admits, though, that interviewing involves luck too and often a chance remark can send an interviewee in a direction she might not have thought of.

'The best example I've had is with Gwyneth Paltrow, who is really difficult to interview. I completely ran out of questions and in desperation I asked her if she found that people drink more in Britain than in America. She suddenly started on this weird condemnation of women who drink, which was quite revealing.'

During the interview, Brockes always keeps eye contact with the person she is talking to and doesn't look down at her notes.

'It really helps if they feel they are engaging with a human being who is responding to what they are saying and allowing them to a certain extent to dictate the interview as much as you are,' she says. 'All the stars I talk to about this say the thing that really kills them is when someone comes in with their ten questions and nothing they say can divert them.'

Observing body language is important too, though Brockes reckons that if you do it too much it can become pretentious – 'a parody of the magazine inter-view along the lines of "she scratches her chin and looks wistfully out of the window"'.

At the end of the day, though, Brockes believes that the art of interviewing is all about concentrating on what the person in front of you is saying.

'It comes down to listening properly and being guided by their answers and trying to make it as intense an encounter as you can,' she says. 'All of us who do interviews have those terrible moments when you listen back to the tape and the person you are talking to says something extraordinary. And you hear yourself totally panic and say "And what are you working on next?" It's a question of trying to be alert enough to field the ball when it gets thrown to you.'

Controversial questions

Few experienced interviewers would dream of asking their trickiest question right at the beginning but equally, Brockes believes you shouldn't leave it right till the end either.

'I think there is a slightly moral dimension to it,' she says. 'It's bad to wait till the last five minutes, blurt out "Did you hate your dad?" and then leg it out of the room. Ideally it should come three-quarters of the way through, when you've still got a bit of time.'

Many stars try to deflect interviewers by asking *them* questions. Brockes says Julie Andrews was a particularly 'polished performer in an interview setting' and tried to draw her out by asking how long she had been at the *Guardian*. Brockes's approach to this is to answer briefly and continue with the flow of the interview.

'You have to be really careful about that because before you know it they have knocked 20 minutes off the interview,' she says. 'I remember at the beginning of my career thinking: "Oh, brilliant, they are really interested in me." But when you listen to the tape afterwards you hear yourself wittering on about yourself and realise what a mug you've been. The worst possible fault of an interviewer is to imagine that these people can be your friend. You're dead if you think that – and deluded.'

Best and worst interviews

One of Brockes's most difficult interviews was with the Australian film star Toni Collette, who, she says, was 'totally monosyllabic and didn't honour the transactional nature of these encounters'. Her favourites include the late novelist Muriel Spark, 'because she spoke in complete sentences and was brilliantly funny', actress Jeanne Moreau 'for being very honest and French and scornful of the world', and former US Secretary of State Madeleine Albright, who was 'brilliant and lovely and wanted to talk about how she couldn't get a date'.

Writing the interview

When she first began writing, Brockes let her quotes run a lot longer than she does now. She is strict about quoting accurately but says that 'unless the person speaking has got a very distinctive voice, readers switch off in long stretches of quotes. On the page it often looks like padding or long, dead patches. I always know that an interview I'm writing up didn't go well when I'm letting a quote run to two or three paragraphs.'

She's also careful not to put herself into the interview – unless, as in Liza Minnelli's case, it's part of the story. 'If you've had an argument with someone in an interview you do need to print the transcript of it and in a way you are elevating yourself into being an equal player – but otherwise I don't put myself into it,' she says. 'The worst kind of "me, me, me-ism" is the interviewer who talks about the journey they've had on the way to the interview or what the cab driver said to them. It drives me nuts.'

Extraordinary privilege

During the course of her career Brockes has interviewed hundreds of people all over the world and admits it's possible to get 'interviewed-out' if you do too many in a short space of time. But on the whole, she says interviewing is 'absolutely brilliant'.

'It is the most extraordinary privilege to parachute in, go straight to what you think is the most interesting part of someone's life and be able to ask the most impertinent questions they may ever have been asked.'

Emma Brockes's top tips

Be *present* in the interview; listen intently to what your interviewee is saying and don't be afraid to go off on wild tangents you haven't prepared for. It's useful to have some idea of where an interviewee might give a news-line, but don't be too rigid about this. Never decide what you want to hear in advance.

Notes

1 D. Ross, 'An audience with Dame Judi Dench', *The Times* magazine. Available from: www.thetimes.co.uk/article/au-audience-with-dame-judi-dench-hzx8gglnw (accessed 2 March 2017).

2 E. Day, 'Jilly Cooper: "I'm a reasonable writer but I'm much too colloquial"', *Observer*. Available from: www.theguardian.com/books/2011/apr/24/jilly-cooper-jump-interview-elizabeth-day (accessed 5 August 2016).

3 S. Adams, *Interviewing for Journalists* (2nd edn), Routledge, 2009, p. 94.

4 S. Roberts and S. Pessina, 'Corrections and clarifications', *Guardian*. Available from: www.theguardian.com/news/2016/aug/02/corrections-and-clarifications (accessed 11 January 2017).

5 C. Edwardes, 'Guess who's coming to breakfast', *The Times* magazine, 20 August 2016.

6 H. Davies, *Hunting People: Thirty Years of Interviews with the Famous*, Mainstream Publishing Company, 1994, p. 18.

7 S. Rafanelli, 'I became a parody: Colin Farrell on his return to cinema and sobriety', *Telegraph*. Available from: www.telegraph.co.uk/film/the-lobster/colin-farrell-interview (accessed 5 June 2016).

8 T. Capote, 'The duke in his domain', *The New Yorker*. Available from: www.newyorker.com/magazine/1957/11/09/the-duke-in-his-domain (accessed 8 August 2016).

9   I. Reeves and R. L. Keeble, *The Newspapers Handbook* (5th edn), Routledge, 2015, p. 202.

10 T. Harcup, *Journalism: Principles and Practice* (3rd edn), Sage Publications, 2015, p. 138 (italics in original).

11 Editors' Code of Practice Committee, *The Code in Full*. Available from: www.editorscode.org.uk/the_code.php (accessed 12 August 2016).

12 *The Stage*, 'Obituary: William Hall'. Available from: www.thestage.co.uk/features/obituaries/2008/william-hall (accessed 8 August 2016).

13 S. Adams, *Interviewing for Journalists* (2nd edn), Routledge, 2009, p. 100.

14 C. Long, 'The interview: Camilla Long meets Irvine Welsh', *The Sunday Times*. Available from: www.thetimes.co.uk/article/the-interview-camilla-long-meets-irvine-welsh-wqppz7xbc (accessed 11 August 2016).

15 K. Fletcher, *The Journalist's Handbook*, Macmillan, 2005, p. 78.

16 E. Brockes, 'Richard Attenborough interview: "I'm almost surprised I'm 80!"', *Guardian*. Available from: www.theguardian.com/film/2003/aug/15/features.emmabrockes (accessed 11 August 2016).

13
Law and ethics

Tim Crook

The interview is the fundamental relationship between a journalist and source of information. It is, indeed, the foundation of practically all articles, programmes and publications in all media. This chapter cannot provide you with everything you need to know about relevant media law, but it can certainly cover the necessary professional knowledge that you should have, and offer you a gateway and access for more detailed guidance.

It is often in the area of the interviewing encounter where matters can go wrong. There may be a conflict about what was said between journalist and interviewee. The subject may say things that are libellous of other people, or breach their privacy. The information arising from the interview in publication could undermine somebody's right to a fair trial and amount to the criminal offence of media contempt. The interviewee may provide documents and photographs that if published could be a breach of copyright. The interview could breach legal anonymity for victims of crime, who are complainants of sexual offences, female genital mutilation or people trafficking.

The pitfalls are many and multidimensional. What is not necessarily a breach of statute or case law could be an infringement of Ofcom's *Broadcasting Code* if the interview has been conducted for licensed broadcasting, or the *Editors' Code of Practice* regulated by IPSO if the interview is for one of the publishers subjected to its contractual regulation.

What should you establish at the start of the interview to protect your legal position?

Many problems arise when the journalist and interviewee have not clearly established the purpose of the interview. In most cases the purpose of an interview is for publication. It is courteous and ethical (though not necessarily a legal obligation) to let your interviewees know how the interview will be used, whether the quotations and edited parts will be in a short news package for broadcasting and therefore heavily edited, or whether soundbites and quotations will be taken out and juxtaposed with other people's. You may be interviewing people who want some of what they say published, but other things not reported.

There is a risk that journalist and subject are unclear about what is 'off the record', 'not for publication', 'on the record', 'non-attributable' or 'Chatham House Rules'. There are conventions in journalism that although clear to reporters and editors are not so clear to their subjects. It might be a good practice to be as relaxed and informal as possible to avoid 'spooking' your interviewees, but at the same time it's important to make sure they know whether their comments:

- are for publication and attribution
- are for publication but not attributable and using a conventional description, for example, 'a Whitehall source', 'friends of'
- are not for publication unless confirmed and corroborated by another named source
- are not for publication under any circumstances – the information is background guidance
- are subject to 'Chatham House Rules', which means 'comments can be reported, however neither the identity of the speaker nor their affiliation, i.e. who they work for, must be revealed'. See: www.chathamhouse.org/events/conferences/information-journalists.

In broadcasting, particularly for film and television documentaries, it has become standard practice to ask interviewees to sign consent forms which clearly set out an agreement for the interview to be used by the journalist or programme maker, and with a clear assignment of the rights, copyright included, to the publisher. In most day-to-day news reporting encounters it is usually accepted in law and regulation that where the journalist clearly identifies who they are and the publication they are working for, can be seen taking notes and are openly using cameras and sound recording devices, interviewees are consenting to the process and accept that what they say will be for publication.

Should I record the interview?

There is no doubt that as a professional journalist you need to be skilled in shorthand so that you can keep an accurate record of what is said, and adept at operating recording devices. In the age of the increasingly sophisticated smartphone it has become easier to ensure an electronic record of interviews. Clearly, fast and reliable shorthand is going to be the back-up if your recording device fails. It gives confidence to your interviewees that you are taking great care about your job and it will speed up the production of your piece. Your recording device is going to be convincing proof of what somebody told you if there is any dispute afterwards. It means you cannot be accused of transcribing your shorthand incorrectly or not having been fast enough to take down an accurate note.

Can you give an example of what can go wrong?

There are hundreds of things that can go wrong, but certainly having an electronic record was hugely helpful when *The Times* journalist Rachel Sylvester interviewed Conservative Party leadership candidate Andrea Leadsom in 2016. Sylvester's article caused a political storm with the angle that the politician had suggested that having children made her a better choice to be prime minister. The newspaper's headline was 'Being a mother gives me edge on May – Leadsom'.

After publication Andrea Leadsom said she was 'disgusted about how this had been presented'. In a tweet directed to the journalist and the wider public she declared: 'This is the worst gutter journalism I've ever seen. I am so angry – I can't believe this. How could you?' Rachel Sylvester and *The Times* were able to support their publication because the electronic recording revealed the following:

Sylvester: Do you feel like a mum in politics?
Leadsom: Yes. So . . .
Sylvester: Why and how?
Leadsom: So really carefully because I am sure, I don't really know Theresa very well but I am sure she will be really really sad she doesn't have children so I don't want this to be 'Andrea has children, Theresa hasn't' because I think that would be really horrible.
… But genuinely I feel being a mum means you have a very real stake in the future of our country, a tangible stake … She possibly has nieces, nephews, lots of people, but I have children, who are going to have children, who will directly be a part of what happens next … My children will be starting their lives in that next ten years so I have a real stake in the next year, the next two.

The public were able to judge for themselves about the fairness or not in *The Times*'s headline and the use of the quotations in the published article. In the end Andrea Leadsom withdrew from the leadership election, Theresa May was elected unopposed as leader of the Conservative Party and became Britain's second woman prime minister. She appointed Andrea Leadsom to her cabinet as Secretary of State for the Environment, Food and Rural Affairs.

So should you record all interviews as a journalist?

Now that could be a media law issue. There might be circumstances when people will be happy to talk to you, but simply do not like the idea of being recorded. You should respect that and if you fail to do so, you may not get the interview. You will be fine if everyone consents to electronic recording, and you have asked for prior permission. But if you were on the telephone and recorded somebody without their permission that could be an offence outside the UK. If you went ahead and broadcast the interview on radio or television you are likely to be breaching Ofcom's *Broadcasting Code*. This states: 'Broadcasters can record telephone calls between the broadcaster and the other party if they have, from the outset of the call, identified themselves, explained the purpose of the call and that the call is being recorded for possible broadcast.' We are straying into the question of surreptitious recording and subterfuge, such as pretending to be somebody else in order to obtain information. Such practices could be a civil wrong if the conduct interfered with anybody's reasonable or legitimate expectation of privacy and for which there was no public interest justification.

What are the main areas of media law that I need to know about?

This chapter concentrates on the media law of England and Wales. It is similar in Scotland and Northern Ireland, although there are a number of differences and journalists should take care to find out what they are. UK and US media law is also very similar, although the First Amendment of the US Constitution means there is no print and online regulation and freedom of the media and expression is given much more protection. Broadcasting licensing and content is regulated in the US by the Federal Communications Commission, rather like Ofcom in the UK.

There are six broad areas of media concern. The first is media contempt and protecting the administration of justice, with a growing number of categories of people entitled to anonymity for life. The second is libel – the protection from inaccurate attacks on reputation, and the third is privacy – the protection from misusing private and usually truthful information. It is important to understand the nature of regulation, which can be called secondary media law. There are many areas covered by secondary media law that are not 'policed' by the media law enacted through statute and case law decisions by the judges in the courts.

A fourth key area of media law concern is when you are newsgathering and story finding. It is important to know what kind of crimes you might be committing and whether you have any public interest defence. Copyright and intellectual property is a vital fifth important area of media law obligation. Last but not least is the sixth category of knowledge. You should have a clear idea of how you can protect sources of information that come to you because people have a story to tell but are fearful of being exposed or identified as the whistleblower.

What is media contempt law in the UK and what obligation does it impose upon you?

The 1981 Contempt of Court Act makes it a criminal offence to publish anything that creates a substantial risk of serious prejudice to trials and legal hearings where lay jurors are deciding the facts. It also makes it an offence to 'monster' any criminal suspect to the extent of damaging their defence case. The crime applies when cases are active. This happens after a suspect has been arrested, there has been the issuing of a warrant for the suspect's arrest or when an inquest has been opened into somebody's sudden death.

Can you briefly summarise the criminal justice process?

The criminal justice process consists of there being a suspect, who is first arrested by the police under caution, then charged with the permission of the Crown Prosecution Service, makes a first court appearance at the magistrates' court and is then sent for trial at the crown court if the charge is serious. Lesser charges are usually tried at the magistrates' court where a single district judge or lay justices decide the facts by way of verdict and impose the sentence. The sentences are usually capped at six months and a fine of £5,000. However, the cap on some penalties for summary trials at magistrates' courts can be lifted. In October 2016 the *Daily Telegraph* was fined £80,000 for publishing an image likely to lead to the identification of an under-age sexual offence victim. The breach of the Sexual Offences Act was a summary offence triable at the lower magistrates' court, but parliament had given the courts the go-ahead to increase the penalty in situations of this kind.

At the crown court trial, if the jury finds the defendant guilty the judge will then decide on an appropriate sentence. The maximum penalty for media contempt is an unlimited fine or a maximum of two years' imprisonment. Prosecutions under the Contempt of Court Act can only be made by the government's attorney general at the High Court before a panel of senior judges. Juries do not sit to decide media contempt prosecutions.

What are the kinds of things you could say that would amount to media contempt?

The worst things to do would be to: say an arrested or charged suspect is guilty and reveal seriously prejudicial evidence; associate the suspect with previous trials or convictions; associate the suspect with notorious individuals; publish video/images showing that the suspect might be guilty. The worst time to publish seriously prejudicial information is just before or during a trial or inquest by jury.

In addition to media contempt, there are other criminal offences that apply to publishing anything in breach of court bans or injunctions that can lead to the identity of anonymous witnesses or defendants – for example, sexual offence complainants, blackmail victims, young people aged 17 and under, teachers prior to being charged with offences against children in their care, alleged victims of female genital mutilation and people trafficking.

The anonymity of vulnerable crime victims usually lasts a lifetime as soon as a complaint has been made. Youth defendants can usually be identified once they reach the age of 18, although youth witnesses have anonymity that lasts a lifetime. Anonymity can be waived by anyone aged 16 and over. However, it is very important to make sure that the waiver is committed to writing.

If you are interviewing any crime victim subject to anonymity rights it has now been accepted that it would be unacceptable to present any image, photograph or video from the actual interview, whatever the amount of lighting silhouette, pixelation and voice distortion. The liability has such a high threshold that the risk is too high. The legal term 'likely to lead to identification' means identification by the victim's close friends or family members who are also prepared to do detective work on the internet.

Interviewing jurors about their deliberations after a trial is likely to be a media contempt of court, particularly if they go into the detail of their deliberations. Identifying jurors is a statutory criminal offence in Northern Ireland and likely to be regarded as a contempt of court in England, Wales and Scotland.

Can you define libel and what it means for media publishers?

Libel is doing serious harm to reputation in any media publication and claimants can sue for damages in the civil courts. Libel consists of the following: damaging people in trade, occupation, profession and office; exposing them to hatred, ridicule or contempt; causing people to be shunned or avoided; and lowering the estimation of 'right-thinking' members of society generally. The claimant can be identified by implication, action needs to be taken within a year of first publication, and in England and Wales there only has to be an audience of one for there to be a libellous publication. Group actions are possible – usually up to 25 people. Claimants have to show that the statement caused, or was likely to cause, serious harm to their reputation. Companies have to show that the statement caused, or was likely to cause, serious financial loss.

Can you summarise the defences available?

You have to appreciate that the burden of proof is on media defendants (as with privacy actions). Actions are tried by judges only and defences include absolute and qualified privilege (parliament, courts, government bodies, press conferences), truth (substance and fact), honest opinion (based on true facts or privileged information), public interest, neutral reportage, web operator's defence and innocent dissemination.

Can you summarise the nature of the right to respect for media privacy under Article 8 of the Human Rights Act/European Convention on Human Rights?

Privacy is a civil remedy for misuse of private information where there is a reasonable expectation of privacy that is not cancelled out by public interest justification. This was an extension of the law of confidentiality between a first and second party to third party media publication and distribution. The development of UK media privacy law has stemmed from the Human Rights Act 1998 and Article 8 of the European Convention on Human Rights. Private information includes matters to do with home, family and correspondence, health, education, sexuality, personal relationships and the interests of children. This means that images of children taken in public places or in news coverage usually have to be pixelated, unless permission has been given.

Is privacy a growing area of media law?

It certainly is. Some media lawyers call it the new libel – more actions are being taken every year, whereas there has been a decline in actions for libel. Privacy is also pursued in litigation under the 1998 Data Protection Act, where private information (including photographs) is processed by journalists and media publishers. The 'for the purposes of journalism' defence in this legislation only applies to journalistic activity carried out in the public interest and where the public interest justifies the extent of intrusion into private life.

What is media regulation?

Regulation in the UK usually applies to complaints, investigations and punishment for media transgression not dealt with by the courts in terms of civil litigation or criminal prosecution. As previously indicated it is a form of 'secondary media law'. All transmitted content of licensed broadcasters is 'regulated' by the statutory Office of Communications, known as Ofcom. Ofcom can reprimand, fine and suspend or cancel the licences of radio and television broadcasters.

Print and online regulation is split between non-Royal Charter 'self regulation' by IPSO and IMPRESS, a regulator mainly funded by family funds linked to the media victim campaigner Max Mosley.

What is the difference between IPSO and IMPRESS?

IPSO regulates most of the professional UK media/online publishers – except the *Guardian/Observer, Financial Times, Independent, Evening Standard* and *Private Eye*. It can fine publishers that offend its *Editors' Code of Practice*, runs a low-cost arbitration scheme and can order prominent apologies and corrections.

IMPRESS follows the *Editors' Code of Practice*, but is developing its own code of ethics. It has more than 40 micro-publishers that have agreed to be regulated and will also run an arbitration scheme as an alternative to media law litigation. IMPRESS has been approved by the Press Recognition Panel, set up by parliament through Royal Charter after the Leveson Inquiry. Publishers agreeing to its regulation will be spared penalties arising from the 2013 Crime and Courts Act. Non-IMPRESS publishers will face punitive damages in media law disputes and could be obliged to pay all the legal costs of media legal litigation whether they win or lose.

IPSO and IMPRESS have different approaches in their respective codes. For example, IMPRESS includes 'the discussion or analysis of artistic or cultural works' in its draft definition of public interest – which IPSO's *Editors' Code of Practice* does not. IPSO has clauses regulating financial journalism, which is not covered in the IMPRESS code. IMPRESS proposes the clause that 'publishers must not pay public officials for information, except as permitted by law', which is not in the IPSO code.

What does regulation do that primary media law in the courts does not?

Regulation deals with journalistic ethics not covered by the law, although there is some overlap. It deals with complaints about accuracy, fairness, discrimination and prejudice, payment to witnesses in criminal cases (cheque-book journalism) and conflicts of interest in financial journalism.

For broadcasters, Ofcom polices 'due impartiality, due accuracy, and undue prominence of views and opinions'. Party politically biased journalism is not allowed. The press can be partial but the IPSO *Editors' Code of Practice* expects a distinction to be made between comment, conjecture and fact. Regulation of broadcasting is stricter and different. For example, there is a harm and offence 'watershed' for services likely to have a significant proportion of young people (17 and under) listening or watching. For television services the line is set at 9 pm. The watershed determines what is acceptable by way of language and content that could generate 'harm and offence'.

Why are children seen as such a significant category of people requiring protection by law and regulation?

Protecting children is a significant aim of media law and regulation. It is recognised that they are very vulnerable in an adult and mature world of media publication – and in relation to crime and anti-social behaviour they are young enough to be rehabilitated and become future responsible and law-abiding members of society.

This means that although the minimum age of criminal responsibility in England, Wales and Northern Ireland is 10 and the earliest age at which children can be prosecuted in Scotland is 12, a range of shields and privileges are accorded to children and young people up to the age of 18 in terms of media reporting and publication.

The criminal justice system protects young people aged 17 and under with anonymity restrictions for them and their schools. This has become the same in Scotland. There is no youth court system in Scotland and youth crime is managed in a social-work-oriented system of children's panels. Children are never usually identifiable in any reports of family court proceedings anywhere in the UK.

Ofcom, BBC, independent press regulation and the courts give the protection of children their highest priority. Ofcom's justification for the 9 pm television watershed is that any material that might seriously impair the physical, mental or moral development of people under 18 must not be broadcast. Watershed for radio can be any time when 'children are particularly likely to be listening'.

Through press and broadcasting regulation and privacy law the UK media are legally obliged to protect children so that they are free to complete their school education without unnecessary intrusion. Children under 16 must not be interviewed or photographed without the consent of their guardians or parents and must not be approached or photographed at school without the school's permission.

What are the legal risks in newsgathering and story finding?

There are a number of criminal offences and serious civil wrongs that you could be breaching. If you use an interception device on a phone system that does not belong to you to record conversations that you are not a party to then this is likely to be a criminal offence under the Regulation of Investigatory Powers Act 2000. 'Mobile phone hacking' is also a criminal offence under this act. That involves guessing or obtaining without permission the PIN number of another person's mobile phone and listening to the playing back of messages left for them. Guessing somebody's password to get into their email account – or even using somebody's computer when unattended to get information – is likely to be an offence under the Computer Misuse Act 1990.

Tricking people into giving you private information about another person could be an offence under the Data Protection Act 1998. So is maintaining a database of other people's private information without registering with the Information Commissioner. You could be committing a bribery offence by promising favours or offering money for information, particularly if you are dealing with a public official. Putting pressure on somebody to do an interview that causes them distress on at least two occasions could be criminal or civil harassment. Being abusive and menacing on social media may also be a crime.

Are there are any defences available to journalists in these circumstances?

Most crimes affecting media conduct do not have public interest defences, but they can still be argued in an attempt to persuade the police, Crown Prosecution Service, Director of Public Prosecutions, trial judge and jury that the committing of the offence was venial or pardonable in proportion to the evil and/or crime being investigated.

Where can you find definitions of the public interest?

IPSO has one of the most extensive and most used definitions of public interest. It includes: detecting or exposing crime, or the threat of crime, or serious impropriety; protecting public health or safety; protecting the public from being misled by an action or statement of an individual or organisation; disclosing a person or organisation's failure or likely failure to comply with any obligation to which they are subject; disclosing a miscarriage of justice; raising or contributing to a matter of public debate, including serious cases of impropriety, unethical conduct or incompetence concerning the public; disclosing concealment, or likely concealment, of any of the above, and there is a public interest in freedom of expression itself.

Public interest used to be what interested the readers who bought newspapers, watched television, listened to the radio or went online. Now it is defined by Ofcom, the BBC itself, independent press regulation, politicians in legislation, government law officers such as the Director of Public Prosecutions (DPP) and judges in case law. And the law is what they say, not what the audience says it wants and is interested in. This may be a reason why journalists committing crimes and civil wrongs have public interest defences in a few situations but are denied them in most.

What is copyright?

Copyright is essentially a legal protection for intellectual and creative work. It does not protect ideas, information, slogans, news and facts. It protects the expression of thinking or communication. It is the information you select and the way you arrange that information that makes it unique. In order for material to have copyright protection it has to result from independent intellectual or creative effort. In other words, you must have put some work into it.

Copyright divides between authorial or primary works that are literary, dramatic, musical or artistic and entrepreneurial, derivative or secondary works (which covers sound recordings, films, broadcasts, cable programmes and typographical works). It also applies to designs, computer programs and databases. The protection makes no distinction between printed, analogue and digital online media.

What is the source of copyright law and are there any defences?

In the UK copyright is derived from the last big codifying piece of legislation passed on the subject – The Copyright, Patents and Designs Act 1988, and subsequent amendments arising out of European Union directives.

The best defence is that you obtain the permission of any copyright holder to copy/reproduce their work. The next is something known as 'fair dealing'. This is using a less than substantial extract for the purposes of criticism/review, parody, 'quotation or otherwise' – or use in reporting a current event. You also have a defence for using an extract in teaching.

The fair dealing defence is not available for using images in reporting a current event.

How long does copyright protection last?

For literary, dramatic or musical works copyright lasts for the duration of the author's life plus 70 years. The situation is the same for directors, screenplay authors and musical directors of films, 70 years for sound recordings and 25 years for published typographical editions. Copyright in databases lasts for 70 years in the case of identifiable authors who have made them with intellectual effort and creativity and 15 years for databases of information produced as the result of investment.

Who holds the copyright in an interview?

It sounds like a simple question, but the answer can be quite complicated. If as a journalist you are being employed to conduct the interview, your employer owns the copyright, subject to 'any agreement to the contrary' if you are working as a freelance or have negotiated a special contract of employment. Your record of the interview in terms of an electronic recording or shorthand transcript is your copyright. But technically the speaker you have interviewed is the author of their own words and owns the copyright of their communication.

This is why it is useful to obtain a full assignment of copyright to you as the journalist or publisher through the completion of a signed consent form. Alternatively a recorded exchange that makes it very clear that the interviewee is giving you and your publisher the right to quote and use any parts of the interview for publication should be sufficient.

The signed assignment would be very useful if it is likely that very large passages from the interview are going to be transcribed and included in a feature magazine, journal or book publication.

What does UK law say about the protection of journalist sources?

There are two key pieces of legislation. The Contempt of Court Act 1981 under section 10 states that no court shall require anyone to disclose a source of information unless it is necessary in the interests of justice, national security or the prevention of disorder or crime. Article 10 of the Human Rights Act guaranteeing a qualified freedom of expression would have to be taken into account and in practice disclosure orders should be made only in exceptional circumstances with an overriding public interest.

The Police and Criminal Evidence Act 1984 created shields for journalists in relation to their footage (sound, photograph and video) of public order events. This was defined as 'special material' and police have to obtain a court order to access it. The act also gives protection to 'excluded material', which is information held by a journalist in confidence for journalistic purposes. The act says there should be a court hearing before an independent judge to decide on any application for a production order.

Have these laws proved effective?

Whistleblower Edward Snowden revealed the extent of surreptitious interception of online data by state intelligence agencies. In the UK, the online magazine Press Gazette highlighted police force use of the Regulation of Investigatory Powers Act 2000 to obtain journalists' phone data without any court hearing and scrutiny by an independent judge.

Confidential journalist sources who had been paid for information were revealed to police investigators by the publishers of the Sun, News of the World and Daily Mirror without the permission of their journalists. Most of these confidential sources were prosecuted and some have been jailed. The 2016 Investigatory Powers Act obliges the police and other state investigatory bodies to reference judicial commissioners if the acquisition of communications data or engagement of computer interference is likely to affect the protection of journalist sources.

What is the professional and moral duty to sources?

IPSO states in its *Editors' Code of Practice* that 'Journalists have a moral obligation to protect confidential sources of information'. The Ofcom *Broadcasting Code* says: 'Guarantees given to contributors, for example relating to the content of a programme, confidentiality or anonymity, should normally be honoured.'

What more should I do to be across media law and regulation?

This chapter has only covered the basics. It is strongly advisable that you do a media law course, such as those run and accredited by the National Council for the Training of Journalists (NCTJ), that is recognised and respected in the media profession. If you are unable to do that there is a list of some recommended books below. Ideally, acquire the latest editions as media law and regulation change more rapidly than many areas of the law. It is also advisable to refer to and visit the websites of the regulatory bodies for their respective codes of ethics and adjudications on regulatory disputes.

Tim Crook, *UK Media Law Pocketbook*, Routledge, 2013.
Mike Dodd and Mark Hanna, *Essential Law for Journalists*, Oxford University Press, 2016.
Jonathan Grun, *The Editors' Codebook: The Handbook to the Editors' Code of Practice*, The Regulatory Funding Company, 2016. A free pdf copy is available from: www.editorscode.org.uk/the_code_book.php.
Frances Quinn, *Law for Journalists* (5th edn), Pearson, 2015.
Ursula Smartt, *Media & Entertainment Law* (2nd edn), Routledge, 2014.
Cleland Thom, *Online Law For Journalists*, 2016. Available from: clelandthom. co.uk.

BBC: largest number of journalists of any publishing organisation in the UK. Although subject to full future Ofcom content regulation from 2017 it will still oblige its employees to comply with BBC Editorial Guidelines.
www.bbc.co.uk/editorialguidelines
IMPRESS: 'the first truly independent press regulator in the UK'.
www.impress.press
Information Commissioner's Office: regulates the Data Protection Act 1998 and Freedom of Information Act.
https://ico.org.uk
IPSO: 'the independent regulator for the newspaper and magazine industry in the UK'.
www.ipso.co.uk
Ofcom: the statutory regulator for licenced broadcasters.
www.ofcom.org.uk

Recommended books and films

Interview collections

Lionel Barber (ed.), *Lunch with the FT: 52 Classic Interviews*, Portfolio Penguin, 2013.

Lynn Barber, *Mostly Men*, Viking, 1991.

Lynn Barber, *Demon Barber*, Viking, 1998.

Hunter Davies, *Hunting People: Thirty Years of Interviews with the Famous*, Mainstream Publishing Company, 1994.

Nigel Farndale, *Flirtation, Seduction, Betrayal: Interviews with Heroes and Villains*, Constable, 2002.

Christopher Silvester, *The Penguin Book of Interviews: An Anthology from 1859 to the Present Day*, Penguin, 1994.

General

Lynn Barber, *A Curious Career*, Bloomsbury Publishing, 2014.

John Brady, *The Craft of Interviewing*, Vintage, 1977.

Duncan Campbell, *We'll All be Murdered in Our Beds! The Shocking History of Crime Reporting in Britain*, Elliott & Thompson, 2016.

Peter Chippendale and Chris Horrie, *Stick It Up Your Punter!: The Uncut Story of the Sun Newspaper*, Simon & Schuster, 1999.

Andrew Crofts, *The Freelance Writer's Handbook*, Piatkus, 2007.

John Dale, *24 Hours in Journalism*, John Dale Publishing, 2012.

Nick Davies, *Flat Earth News*, Vintage, 2009.

Vanessa Edwards, *Research Skills for Journalists*, Routledge, 2016.

Harold Evans, *My Paper Chase: True Stories of Vanished Times*, Little Brown, 2009.

Kim Fletcher, *The Journalist's Handbook*, Macmillan, 2005.

Chris Frost, *Reporting for Journalists* (2nd edn), Routledge, 2010.

Tony Harcup, *Journalism: Principles and Practice* (3rd edn), Sage Publications, 2015.

Richard Keeble, *Ethics for Journalists*, Routledge, 2008.

Phillip Knightley, *A Hack's Progress*, Vintage, 1997.

Janet Malcolm, *The Journalist and the Murderer*, Granta, 2012.

Andrew Marr, *My Trade: A Short History of British Journalism*, Macmillan, 2004.

Sharon Marshall, *Tabloid Girl*, Sphere, 2010.

John McEntee, *I'm Not One to Gossip, But . . .*, Biteback Publishing, 2016.

National Union of Journalists' Code of Conduct, www.nuj.org.uk/about/nuj-code

Jeremy Paxman, *A Life in Questions*, William Collins, 2016.

Cedric Pulford, *JournoLISTS: 201 Ways to Improve Your Journalism*, Ituri Publications, 2001.

David Randall, *The Universal Journalist*, Pluto Press, 1996.

Ian Reeves and Richard Lance Keeble, *The Newspapers Handbook* (5th edn), Routledge, 2015.

David Walsh, *Seven Deadly Sins: My Pursuit of Lance Armstrong*, Simon & Schuster, 2012.

Keith Waterhouse, *Waterhouse on Newspaper Style*, Revel Barker, 2010.

Alan Watkins, *A Short Walk Down Fleet Street*, Gerald Duckworth & Co., 2000.

Tom Williamson (ed.), *Investigative Interviewing*, Routledge, 2012.

Tom Wolfe, *The New Journalism*, Harper and Row, 1973.

Body language

Elizabeth Kuhnke, *Body Language for Dummies*, John Wiley & Sons, 2015.

Allan and Barbara Pease, *The Definitive Book of Body Language*, Orion, 2004.

Fiction

Sam Baker, *The Woman Who Ran*, Harper, 2016.

Fiona Barton, *The Widow*, Bantam Press, 2016.

Elizabeth Day, *Paradise City*, Bloomsbury, 2015.

Monica Dickens, *My Turn to Make the Tea*, Penguin, 1969.

Michael Frayn, *Towards the End of Morning*, Faber & Faber, 2015.

Emma Lee-Potter, *Hard Copy*, Piatkus, 1998.

Emma Lee-Potter, *Moving On*, Piatkus, 2000.

Annalena McAfee, *The Spoiler*, Harvill Secker, 2011.

Tom Rachman, *The Imperfectionists*, Quercus, 2010.

Evelyn Waugh, *Scoop*, Penguin, 2012.

Films

All the President's Men (1976): Washington Post reporters Bob Woodward and Carl Bernstein uncover the details of the Watergate scandal that led to President Richard Nixon's resignation.

Defence of the Realm (1986): When a newspaper reporter helps to expose an MP as a possible spy he finds there is far more to the story than that.

Page One: Inside the New York Times (2011): A documentary about the working lives of three writers at the *New York Times*.

Spotlight (2015): This Oscar-winning film is based on the true story of how the Boston *Globe* uncovered the massive scandal of paedophile priests in the local Catholic Church.

State of Play (2009): A journalist investigates the suspicious death of a congressman's mistress. The film was based on a BBC drama of the same name.

The Paper (1994): Chaos reigns during a hectic 24 hours at a New York City tabloid.

The September Issue (2009): A documentary that chronicles the preparations of Anna Wintour, the editor-in-chief of American *Vogue*, for the all important September issue of 2007.

Truth (2015): This newsroom drama follows TV anchor Dan Rather and producer Mary Mapes after they broadcast a controversial report about President George Bush and his military service.

Wag the Dog (1997): Two weeks before the US presidential election a White House adviser enlists the help of a spin doctor to divert voters' attention from the president's scandalous behaviour.

Index